# ADHD

## Non-Medication Treatments & Skills
## For Children And Teens

### 162 Tools, Techniques, Activities & Handouts

## A Workbook for Clinicians and Parents

Diagnosis - Mindfulness - Psychotherapy - Neurofeedback
Nutrition - Sleep - Social Skills - Organizational Skills - Parenting Skills
Emotional Regulation - Movement Techniques

**Debra Burdick**, LCSWR, BCN,
Bestselling author of *Mindfulness Skills for Kids & Teens*

"A brilliant, practical compendium of tools, resources, ideas and techniques to help children who have ADHD without using medication. Well-researched and clearly written, this book is a gem!"

-**Edward Hallowell, MD,** author, psychiatrist
and international expert on ADHD

"Medication which should be a last resort for kids with ADHD, has become the first and often the only offered treatment. This speaks to the crucial importance of Debra Burdick's latest book, *ADHD: Non-Medication Treatments and Skills for Children and Teens.* The book offers 162 techniques, tips, activities and resources that can be used instead of medication to manage and moderate the worst ADHD symptoms. I highly recommend this book for parents, either dealing with a new ADHD diagnosis in a child or for those who wish to try another option other than medication."

-**Dale Archer, MD,** psychiatrist and *NY Times* bestselling
author of *Better Than Normal* and *The ADHD Advantage*

"Debra Burdick did it again! Following the success of her mindfulness book for kids and teens, she offers an array of non-medication treatment skills for ADHD. Anyone working with children and teens will find this a treasure chest of practical, hands-on, effective and engaging tools and activities that are easy for the clinician to use. Tips for identifying and diagnosing ADHD, treatment options, nutrition suggestions, valuable tools for social, organizational and mindfulness skills, along with tips for parents makes this book a one-stop shop for the practitioner's ADHD toolbox. An invaluable go-to resource and a true gold mine!"

-**Judith Belmont, MS,** author of the *T.I.P.S. and
Tools for the Therapeutic Toolbox Series*

"Burdick provides a very accessible reading style and countless well thought-out strategies. This book covers a wide range of approaches to help these children, their teachers and parents, become more successful in managing ADHD. This is a great reference for anyone working with children or teens with ADHD."

-**Roger deBeus, PhD**
Clinical Trial Principal Investigator,
Neurofeedback for ADHD

"An amazingly comprehensive book geared to mental health professionals, parents, teachers and children of ADHD from a holistic approach. Readers who are seeking a non-medication approach to ADHD have come to the best source! With over 162 tools, techniques, tips, activities, resources and worksheets, it is a perfect 'one-stop' book.

As a parent of a child with ADD, now an adult, I wish this book was available years ago! But as a professional working with children and teens, it is invaluable now. *ADHD: Non-medication Treatments & Skills for Children and Teens* is definitely a must-have book for one's professional or personal library."

-**Athena A. Drewes, PsyD, RPT-S**
Director of Clinical Training,
Astor Services for Children and Families
Editor of 9 books on play therapy

Copyright © 2016 by Debra E Burdick

Published by
PESI Publishing and Media
3839 White Ave
Eau Claire, WI 54703

Cover Design: Amy Rubenzer
Layout Design: Bookmasters & Amy Rubenzer
Editing: Marietta Whittlesey & Karsyn Morse
Printed in the United States of America

ISBN: 9781559570336

The information presented in this workbook is not intended to substitute for the advice of your medical doctor or your child's or teen's pediatrician or mental health professional. You are advised to consult with health-care professionals concerning diagnosis, starting or discontinuing medications, and before making any drastic changes in your child's or teen's diet.

This workbook contains information gathered from many sources as well as from the experiences of the author and a number of her clients. It is published for general reference and is not a substitute for medical or psychological counsel. It is sold with the understanding that the author is not engaged in rendering any medical or psychological advice. The author disclaims any liability whatsoever for individuals' use of any advice or information presented with the workbook.

PESI Publishing & Media
www.pesipublishing.com

# Acknowledgements

This book has been almost 30 years in the making and many people have contributed to helping me gain the knowledge about ADHD and the brain that has culminated in this book. My journey into the land of ADHD started when my daughter, Jen, was diagnosed. She has always inspired and delighted me and I thank her from my heart. The book would never have been possible without her. She taught me so much about what it's like to have ADHD and what works and what doesn't work for a parent helping a child with ADHD truly thrive. Thanks, too, to my first business partner, Hank Mann, who prospered with ADHD and helped me begin my journey of helping clients with neurofeedback.

My deepest thanks to Linda Jackson, my publisher at PESI, who has continually guided, supported, and encouraged me along my journey as an author. Many thanks to Karsyn Morse for her invaluable insight and editing suggestions. And thank you to Claire Zelasko, Marnie Sullivan, and Meg Mickelson Graf for supporting my ADHD and Mindfulness workshops, which have allowed me to help so many clinicians help their clients.

Thank you to all my clients with ADHD who have taught me how best to help them and who have continually shown me new ways to succeed with ADHD.

And thanks of course to my love, Al, who always supports, encourages, and cheers for me and so lovingly creates the space I need to write.

# Dedication

Henry Brower Mann, MD
1937-2015
Thank you, Hank,
for helping so many
people thrive with ADHD.
We miss you!

# Table of Contents

## Section V
## Skills to Manage and Improve ADHD Symptoms

## Section VI
## Treatments That Improve Self-Regulation

# Section VII
# Complementary Therapies

# Section VIII
# Environmental Influences

# Section IX
# Nutrition for the ADHD Brain

# Section X
## Sleep and ADHD

# Section XI
## Strategies for Success at School

# Section I
# **Introduction**

# Chapter 1
# Why This Book Is Needed

*ADHD: Non-Medication Treatments and Skills for Children and Teens* is specifically designed to meet the needs of mental health practitioners, teachers, other helping professionals and parents who want non-medication strategies to help children and teens thrive with ADHD. It provides over 162 tools, including techniques, tips, activities, resources and worksheets that can be used with children and teens to help them successfully manage the challenges, as well as reduce the symptoms, unique to ADHD.

The workbook provides specific tools for:

- Making an accurate diagnosis of ADHD
- Teaching the neurobiology of ADHD
- Incorporating non-medication treatments and strategies
- Providing ADHD friendly psychotherapy
- Understanding and incorporating neurofeedback in the treatment plan
- Teaching mindfulness skills that help ADHD
- Understanding complementary therapies
- Creating a positive self-esteem and narrative
- Improving concentration and hyperactivity
- Better behavior and relationships
- Organizational skills
- Social skills
- Parenting skills specific to ADHD
- Improving sleep patterns
- ADHD specific movement and exercise
- Nutrition unique to the ADHD brain
- Creating a toxin-free environment
- School success
- Tracking progress

ADHD affects the lives of a significant number of children and teens. A recent study found that the rates for boys and girls are estimated to be 13.6% and 6.5%, respectively (Ghanizadeh, 2011). Although ADHD is one of the most researched childhood disorders, the exact cause is still uncertain. The symptoms of ADHD can cause difficulty and sometimes failure in school, social settings, and family life as well as cause low self-esteem, anxiety, depression and substance use. ADHD medication has long been the traditional treatment. This can be extremely effective for some, but many factors contribute to the fact that after a year of starting medication, only 33-50% are still taking it (Charach et al, 2013). This workbook provides the information, skills and strategies to help children and teens thrive whether or not they benefit from medication.

## WHAT'S DIFFERENT ABOUT THIS BOOK?

There are many excellent books available about ADHD. I reference many of them throughout this workbook and I recommend you read them at your leisure to gain a better understanding of the disorder. This workbook is different in some unique ways. Although the traditional treatment for ADHD has usually involved medication, this workbook provides evidence-based non-medication strategies that help children and teens with ADHD thrive. It is designed to provide knowledge, skills, worksheets, tips, activities, resources and handouts that you can use to increase the success of children and teens with ADHD in every area of their life.

## HOW TO USE THIS BOOK

The tools provided in this book are organized to provide you with the background behind each tool, instructions for teaching each skill, and guidelines for helping both you and your clients integrate the skills. Step-by-step instructions are provided to help you use the tools with children, teens or parents.

The tools are organized in a logical progression but are designed to be used independently and in any order that makes sense for each particular child or teen.

> **Additional handouts and reproducible worksheets that accompany this book can be found online at go.pesi.com/ADHDworkbook**

For convenience, the tools described in the book will reference their use with "clients." Please translate the word "client" to whatever term you use for the people you work with, such as "patient," "student," or if you are a parent, "your child or teen."

As a licensed clinical social worker, a board certified neurofeedback practitioner, a bestselling author of books on mindfulness, and a parent of an extremely successful daughter with ADHD, I hope my knowledge and experience with what works and what doesn't work for ADHD will help you on your journey of helping a child or teen succeed with ADHD.

Thank-you to all the children and teens with ADHD that have been helped by the strategies contained in this workbook and who continue to show me again and again how much these skills improve their lives.

Please let me know how you use this workbook and how it helps your clients, your child or teen.

# Section II
# Assessment and Diagnosis

# Chapter 2
# Tools for Making an Accurate Diagnosis

Parents often come in asking to have their child or teen 'tested' for ADHD. They are looking for some definitive way to know if the symptoms their child experiences are symptoms of ADHD. They may have heard about ADHD from the media, their friends, other parents or their child's teacher. They expect their child to take a test and know for sure if they have ADHD.

Getting an accurate diagnosis for ADHD is not as simple as taking one test. Although there are some neuropsychological tests, continuous performance tests, and tests that compare brainwave data to normative databases which all aid in the diagnosis of ADHD, these test results must be combined with a thorough clinical assessment to determine if ADHD is present. There are other things that may cause symptoms that look like ADHD and there are a number of things that make ADHD symptoms worse.

This section describes the myriad of factors that need to be considered during the diagnostic process to assure the most accurate diagnosis. It presents a step-by-step process to determine if symptoms of ADHD are present. Additionally, it provides tools for deciding whether the presenting symptoms are truly symptoms of ADHD and not some other issue, such as head injury, allergy, depression, a sleep disorder or other causes often seen in clinical practice.

## Tool 2-1: DSM-5® Diagnostic Criteria

**BACKGROUND:** *The Diagnostic and Statistical Manual of Mental Disorders DSM-5®* (American Psychiatric Association, 2013) contains the specific criteria that must be met for a diagnosis of Attention-Deficit/Hyperactivity Disorder. Clinicians should refer to it often while assessing for ADHD.

In the DSM-5 ADHD was moved from Disorders of Childhood to Neurodevelopmental Disorders. Tool 2-5 Neurobiology and Brain Imaging explains why this move makes perfect sense. If the client's symptoms meet the DSM-5 criteria, a diagnosis of ADHD can be made. This tool provides guidance on using an ADHD checklist to determine if the symptoms of ADHD, as defined by the DSM-5, are present. Tool 2-7, Mimics and Contributors will explore other possible causes of and contributors to these symptoms.

**SKILL BUILDING:**    When symptoms of ADHD are suspected refer to the DSM-5 and use the ADHD Symptom Checklist on Handout 2-1 to determine if there are enough symptoms to meet the criteria of ADHD. Ask each parent, each teacher, and the client (if they are at least eight-years-old and mature enough), care givers, coaches and anyone who spends a lot of time with the child or teen to complete the symptom checklist. Since the symptoms must cause impairment in two or more settings it is important to assess the symptoms in different situations and settings and include school, social, and work functioning. Often, each parent sees their child differently and various teachers may rate the symptoms quite differently due the different demands that may be present in various classes.

To rate the results of these symptom checklists, count any symptom that was given an "OFTEN" or "MOST OF THE TIME" as an indication the symptom is present.

There are three types of ADHD:

- Predominantly Inattentive
- Predominantly Hyperactive/Impulsive
- Combined

Children and teens need to have six or more symptoms of Inattention to meet the criteria of Inattentive Type. They need to have six or more symptoms of Hyperactive/Impulsive to meet the criteria of Hyperactive/Impulsive Type and six or more of both the Inattentive and Hyperactive/Impulsive to meet the criteria for Combined Type (twelve in all). Symptoms must have been present for at least six months at a level that is not appropriate for the client's developmental level. Note that teens (and adults) over 17 only need five symptoms to meet the criteria. DSM-5 includes a new moderator of mild, moderate, severe, or partial remission.

These additional criteria must also be met:

- Some symptoms that cause impairment must have been present before 12 years of age. (This was increased from seven years as previously specified in the *DSM-IV-TR*.)
- The symptoms do not happen only during the course of schizophrenia, or other psychotic disorder and are not better accounted for by another mental disorder such as a mood disorder, anxiety disorder, dissociative disorder, personality disorder or substance use. Note that the Pervasive Developmental Disorder exclusion was removed in DSM-5. You will need to sort out symptoms of these other disorders during your intake assessment. Keep in mind that depression and anxiety are often present with ADHD.

**INTEGRATION:**    Review the results with the client and parents. If criteria are met for any of the three types of ADHD then a diagnosis of ADHD can be made. But, since a child with a learning disability, a hearing problem, a head injury or many other issues may have symptoms that meet these criteria, be careful not to stop here. See Tool 2-7: Mimics and Contributors, to explore other possible causes of and contributors to these symptoms. You will be better able to tailor treatment for this specific client if you gather more information about how his or her brain is functioning.

If each parent rated their child very differently, use this as an opportunity to discuss their expectations and perceptions of their child. If the teachers rated the symptoms differently, look at the demands placed on the client in the various settings. For example, if the gym teacher rated the child better than the reading teacher take their expectations into account. A hyperactive child may be unable to sit still enough in the classroom to read but be fantastic at sports in the gym where his energy is useful, not distracting.

# ADHD SYMPTOM CHECKLIST

Name _____Date _____

Completed by _____Relationship to Client_____

Please circle the number which best describes the person.

| | Never | Sometimes | Often | Most of the Time |
|---|---|---|---|---|
| **INATTENTION** | | | | |
| • Makes careless mistakes or fails to notice details in schoolwork, work or other activities | 0 | 1 | 2 | 3 |
| • Has difficulty maintaining attention | 0 | 1 | 2 | 3 |
| • Easily distracted (by noises, people, talking, sights, things, thoughts) | 0 | 1 | 2 | 3 |
| • Does not follow through on instructions and fails to complete things (gets sidetracked) | 0 | 1 | 2 | 3 |
| • Has trouble organizing stuff, space, time | 0 | 1 | 2 | 3 |
| • Avoids or dislikes tasks requiring sustained concentration (such as homework or projects) | 0 | 1 | 2 | 3 |
| • Loses or misplaces things | 0 | 1 | 2 | 3 |
| • Tuned out, not appearing to listen when spoken to | 0 | 1 | 2 | 3 |
| • Forgetful | 0 | 1 | 2 | 3 |
| **HYPERACTIVITY and IMPULSIVITY** | | | | |
| • Fidgets, moves hands and feet | 0 | 1 | 2 | 3 |
| • Has difficulty remaining seated when expected | 0 | 1 | 2 | 3 |
| • Runs around or climbs when it is not appropriate (in adolescents, may be limited to feeling restless) | 0 | 1 | 2 | 3 |
| • Talks too much | 0 | 1 | 2 | 3 |
| • Physically active as if "driven by a motor" | 0 | 1 | 2 | 3 |
| • Has difficulty playing quietly | 0 | 1 | 2 | 3 |
| • Blurts out answers, responds before question is completed | 0 | 1 | 2 | 3 |
| • Has trouble waiting their turn | 0 | 1 | 2 | 3 |
| • Interrupts. Intrusive (butts into conversations or games, takes over) | 0 | 1 | 2 | 3 |

Must have 6 (5 if older than 17) "Often" or "Most of the Time" from either category, or from both for combined type

## TOOL 2-2: Structured Intake Assessment

**BACKGROUND:**   The goal of the intake assessment is to gather as much information as possible about your client so you can make an accurate diagnosis and create a successful treatment plan. This is similar to any standard mental health intake, but to make an accurate diagnosis of ADHD, there are extra things to look for. It is impossible to make an accurate diagnosis of ADHD without all the facts. Often, clients have been referred after being diagnosed by their pediatrician who simply prescribed medication based on parent report and without examining all the factors that may contribute to symptoms of ADHD. The symptoms of ADHD may resemble and co-occur with other medical or mental health conditions, learning issues, behavior problems and vice versa.

ADHD can be thought of as a result of a dysregulated brain. During the intake process look for anything that might cause the brain to be dysregulated. Children and teens may be hyperactive and distractible for any of a number of reasons. They may be suffering from:

- Food Sensitivities
- Too Much Sugar or Caffeine
- Allergies
- Chemical Sensitivities
- Chronic Illness
- Vision or Hearing Problems
- Head Injury
- Heavy Metal Exposure
- Vitamin or Mineral Deficiencies

- Chronic Stress
- Anxiety
- Fear
- Swollen Tonsils
- A Chaotic Home Life
- A Seizure Disorder
- Trauma
- Sleep Deprivation Including Sleep Apnea

And whether or not the person truly has ADHD, addressing these issues will contribute to overall success. See Tool 2-7 ADHD Mimics and Contributors for more information on things that can contribute to this dysregulation besides ADHD.

**SKILL BUILDING:**   During the intake process, gather information from the referral source, parents, teachers, pediatrician, previous therapists and others involved in this client's life. When working with a child younger than nine or ten years-old, it is wise to do the intake session without them present. Schedule a second session to meet the child and continue the assessment. For teens, it is better to involve the teen immediately, during the first session to allow for a better engagement with you, the clinician.

Use Handout 2-2 as a guideline to gather all the information needed to make an accurate assessment of ADHD and to rule out other causes or contributors to the symptoms.

## STRUCTURED INTAKE SESSION

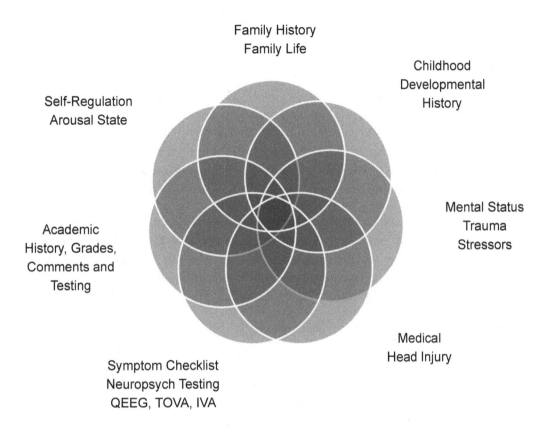

Family History
Family Life

Childhood
Developmental
History

Self-Regulation
Arousal State

Mental Status
Trauma
Stressors

Academic
History, Grades,
Comments and
Testing

Medical
Head Injury

Symptom Checklist
Neuropsych Testing
QEEG, TOVA, IVA

**Psychological Evaluation:** As with any mental health intake, do a complete assessment of mood, concentration, hyperactivity, memory, sleep, energy, appetite, medications, suicidal ideation, mental status, health and substance use. A child or teen that is sleep deprived, anxious, bipolar, learning disabled, obsessive compulsive, drug addicted, or has trouble with sensory processing may have symptoms that look like ADHD that are actually coming from these other disorders. Keep in mind that many of these are comorbid with ADHD. It is very common for the frustration of dealing with symptoms of ADHD to cause anxiety, depression and poor self-esteem. See Tool 2-8 Comorbid Disorders for more detail.

**ADHD Symptom Checklist:** Use the ADHD Symptom Checklist on Handout 2-1 to find out if the child or teen has the symptoms of ADHD. Ask parents (both if possible), the client if mature enough, teachers, and others involved in the client's life to complete the checklist. See Tool 2-1 DSM-5 Diagnostic Criteria for how to use this checklist.

Does the client have trouble paying and sustaining attention? Are they able to organize their time, space, and belongings? Do they lose their homework, books, or jacket? Are they able to sit still? Are they revved up and wired? Do they interrupt others, talk all the time, say or do things without thinking? Are they tuned out, not paying attention, missing what people are saying to them? Do they try really hard but still take too long or make careless mistakes?

I often say to my client "imagine that you are sitting in class, the teacher is speaking, the student next to you is tapping their pencil, the window is open and the lawn mower is going, the door to the hall is open and the janitor walks by. What are you paying attention to?" If they have ADHD they often say "everything," "not the teacher," "the lawn mower."

***Observe Self-regulation and Arousal State:***   Observe the child or teen as they interact with you and/or their parents in session. Watch their body. Is it constantly moving? How long can they sit still? Are they fidgeting? Do they appear to be listening when you talk to them? Do they understand what you say? What's their response time? If they are playing, how long do they stay with one toy before moving to another? Are they getting bored? Are they getting into everything?

Do they seem revved up, wired, over activated? Are they slowed, have a flat affect, not engaged, distracted? Are they complying with requests to put things away or to the rules of the session? Are they touching things that are off limits despite cues from you or parents? How long do they stay on topic? Are they telling you about one thing after another with no apparent connection between topics? How often do you have to bring them back to the topic you are discussing? Are they zoned out, not paying attention nor responding? Are they interrupting when you or their parents are talking? Are they demanding attention? What is their level of self-awareness, if any?

Phew! You will learn a lot about the child's ability to regulate their arousal state just by watching them. If they are over- aroused they may have the hyperactive/impulsive type of ADHD. If they are under-activated they may have the inattentive type. Additionally, you will discover how they comply with adult requests, who is in charge in this family (often not the parents), what their frustration tolerance is, whether they are comfortable in their own skin or anxious, depressed, or oppositional.

This is just one important piece of the diagnostic puzzle.

***Family History:***   There is a genetic link for ADHD which makes it more likely to have ADHD if a family member has it. During the intake process ask about family history of symptoms similar to those the client experiences (Wolraich, 2006). Keep in mind that a grandparent or parent might not have been diagnosed with ADHD, but the family may be well aware if they exhibited symptoms of ADHD. ADHD is not 100% inheritable. Therefore, having a family member with ADHD *does not* necessarily mean your client has it, but makes it much more likely. Also, not having a family history of ADHD does not rule it out for your client.

***Developmental History:***   Ask about any issues with the mother's pregnancy, the birth, and early medical issues. Did the child meet normal developmental milestones such as crawling, walking, talking and toilet training? Were there any particular problems the parent can remember? Was there an event that occurred that seemed to derail development or reverse it? A developing brain can be impacted by many things that often go unnoticed. Is there any history of neglect or abuse? Is there any evidence of reactive attachment disorder?

***Medical History, Mimics and Contributors:***   Were there any medical issues during the pregnancy, at birth, and/or up until now? Ask about illnesses, ear infections, injuries, accidents, sleep, medications, allergies, food sensitivities and genetic issues. See Tool 2-7 for things that can mimic and contribute to ADHD, Chapter 21 Assess and Improve Sleep for more information about sleep and ADHD and Chapter 19 Common Sensitivities for help with identifying food sensitivities.

***Head Injury:***   Head injury is often overlooked or minimized. A person does not have to have a traumatic brain injury (TBI) to experience symptoms that look like ADHD symptoms but that are really caused by a head injury sometimes sustained years ago. The brain can sustain damage even from a 'bump' on the head. The brain floats in fluid and when the head is hit the brain bounces up against the skull on the opposite side of the head and then back again. There is evidence that brain injury can be cumulative. This is showing up in teenagers who hit their head while playing football.

Children and teens often hit their heads and seem to be okay afterward. Even if a CT scan or an MRI indicates no problem, the functioning of the brain can be impacted for years afterward. The symptoms of a head injury can be similar to ADHD symptoms, but the treatment may differ.

When talking with your client or their caregiver, be sure to ask about any history of hitting their head no matter how insignificant it may have seemed at the time. Did they get a bump or a bruise, lose consciousness, need stitches or receive a concussion diagnosis? See Tool 2-3 QEEG for a case example of a seven-year-old girl initially diagnosed with ADHD, who had a concussion at age two, and its impact showed up on a quantitative EEG (QEEG) five years later.

**Sensory Integration:** If a client has a sensory processing or modulation disorder they have difficulty regulating and organizing responses to sensory input from the environment and their body. This can impact their motor function, emotional state, arousal and attention. The overlap of symptoms of Sensory Modulation Disorder (SMD) and ADHD makes it difficult to differentiate between the two. A client who appears wired or distracted may look like they have ADHD but may actually be having trouble processing sensory input (Miller, 2012), (Mangeot et al, 2001). See Tool 14-1 Sensory Integration Therapy for more detail.

**Trauma:** A child or teen that has experienced trauma may exhibit symptoms that look like ADHD as the trauma can dysregulate the brain in specific ways. Trauma can be a result of verbal, emotional or physical abuse, injury, illness, neglect, or witnessing or experiencing something that felt traumatic to the child. Look for any history of trauma and rule out Posttraumatic Stress Disorder (PTSD).

**Academic:** How is this child performing in school? Children with ADHD often do very well in the first few grades but then start to struggle as the work gets harder and more demanding, usually by third grade. Learning disabilities may mimic the symptoms of ADHD and may be present in addition to ADHD. It is important to make sure the child receives all the necessary testing in school to assess this. Look at the comments on their report card. If a child or teen has ADHD the comments will likely contain statements such as: trouble sitting still; difficulty staying on task; not working up to potential; talks out of turn; fails to raise his hand to speak; annoys other students who are trying to work; easily distracted; loses his homework, books, pencils; very social; needs constant attention and cueing; daydreams a lot. The comments usually give a more accurate picture of the symptoms of ADHD than the grades.

**Family Life:** Explore the dynamics of this client's family life. How is the family functioning? Is there a lot of conflict, anger, lack of structure, or chaos? Where does this child or teen fit into the family? How are they treated by parents and siblings? What words do the parents and siblings use to describe them? What is the birth order of this child? How do they get along with their parents and siblings? What expectations do the parents have of this child or teen? Are the client's symptoms stemming from family issues and not truly ADHD? Is there appropriate structure in place throughout the day? Family life can have a significant impact on the child or teen's functioning and ADHD symptoms can have also have a significant impact on the functioning of the family.

**Social:** ADHD symptoms can interfere with a client's ability to have good relationships with parents, peers, teachers and others. Some clients become alienated from peers due to their impulsivity, hyperactivity, less developed social skills, and behaviors that annoy potential friends. Even when children with ADHD have friends in elementary school, these friends may fall away as they get older and more mature. Some friends may no longer have the patience to deal with the annoying behaviors. On the other hand, some children and teens with ADHD are very successful socially and have lots of friends.

Find out how the client is doing socially. Do they have friends? Ask them to name a few. Do they ever connect with them outside of school? Who do they sit with at lunch? How do they get along with the neighborhood kids? Are they wishing for more friends? Do they struggle socially and not understand why? Do they have self-awareness about how their behaviors may push others away?

***Nutrition:***   Find out what this client is eating. What does their daily diet consist of? Nutrition can have a significant impact on the brain of a child or teen with ADHD. Look for excessive sugar and caffeine consumption. How often do they eat? What proteins, fruits, vegetables and whole grains do they include in their diet? Do any foods bother them or make their symptoms worse? See Section IX Nutrition for the ADHD Brain for specific nutritional information and guidance for ADHD.

***Stressors:***   What types of stressors are present for this client? Are they under a lot of pressure at school? Are they behind in their work? Are they failing courses? What pressures exist at home? Are parents angry with them? Is anxiety about performance or fear of failure a factor? Look at how this client is functioning in his environment. Do their symptoms cause stress for them? Perhaps there are accommodations that might remove some of the stress at school. See Chapter 22 School and ADHD for common accommodations that might be helpful.

***Previous Testing:***   Get copies of all previous testing that has been done in school and elsewhere. This may include psychological testing, IQ testing, testing for learning disabilities, and assessments for ADHD. Review the results to see if they indicate that ADHD may be present. Also look for indications of anxiety, depression, low self-esteem, bipolar disorder and oppositional defiant disorder.

***Records from Previous Treatment:***   If possible, get a "Release of Information" form signed to talk with the referral source and gather as much information verbally and via treatment records as possible. Get discharge records from previous therapists or communicate with other therapists that are still involved.

***Neuropsychological and Academic Testing:***   There are a number of excellent tests that measure concentration, intelligence, short term and long term memory, response time, impulse control and more. Neuropsychological testing can isolate the area of the brain that is underperforming and can aid in the diagnosis of ADHD. Neuropsychologists and school psychologists are the professionals who typically administer these tests. Each neuropsychologist or school tends to use their favorite set of tests.

**INTEGRATION:**   Now that you have gathered information about all the pieces of the diagnostic puzzle, review everything. Does the client have symptoms of ADHD and meet the DSM-5 diagnostic criteria? Are the symptoms truly coming from ADHD or something else? Does the client have comorbid diagnoses such as anxiety, depression, bipolar disorder, PTSD or sensory processing disorder? Do they have food sensitivities, hearing or vision issues, allergies, a chaotic home life, or a head injury that mimics or contributes to their symptoms?

# STRUCTURED INTERVIEW CHECKLIST

☐ Psychological Evaluation, Comorbid Diagnosis

☐ ADHD Symptom Checklist

☐ Observe Self-regulation and Arousal State

☐ Family History

☐ Developmental History

☐ Medical History, Mimics and Contributors

☐ Head Injury

☐ Sensory Processing

☐ Trauma

☐ Academic

☐ Family Life

☐ Social

☐ Nutrition and Food Sensitivities

☐ Stressors

☐ Obtain and Review Results of Previous Testing

☐ Records from Previous Treatment

☐ Refer for Neuropsychological and Academic Testing

☐ Refer for QEEG, Test of Variables of Attention (TOVA®), Integrated Visual and Auditory Test (IVA)

## Tool 2-3: QEEG

**BACKGROUND:**    The quantitative electro-encephalograph (QEEG) is a brain imaging and mapping technology that provides us with an electrical picture of how a brain is functioning compared to normal brains. This technology is being used extensively in assessment when using neurofeedback and is proving to be an invaluable tool to truly understand what is going on inside the brain. The QEEG can identify the brainwave patterns typically found in ADHD. Besides showing ADHD patterns, it can distinguish brain injury, learning disabilities, mood disorders, autism, sensory, language problems and more. This tool provides an explanation of what a QEEG is and how it is being used to diagnose ADHD.

**SKILL BUILDING:**    Use Handout 2-3 to explain to parents and teens what a QEEG is and how it can help them understand exactly how their child or teen's brain is functioning compared to norms.  This will help them to get a more accurate diagnosis and treatment tailored to their specific needs.

QEEGs are most commonly done by neurofeedback practitioners who use QEEGs to guide their treatment protocol selection. A list of board certified neurofeedback providers (BCN credentials) can be found at the Biofeedback Certification International Alliance www.bcia.org or search online for "neurofeedback providers" or "QEEG providers."

> *Case Example:*    *I worked with a second grader who was previously diagnosed with and treated (unsuccessfully) for ADHD. Her symptoms met the criteria for ADHD Combined Type. She was in the 20th percentile on standardized academic tests and was consumed with rage. Her social skills were very poor and she had no friends. A round of stimulant medication had sent her through the roof with rage and hyperactivity.*
>
> *A QEEG revealed an area on top of her head where the brainwaves in the higher frequencies were huge. Her brainwave patterns did not indicate ADHD. After seeing the QEEG her parents finally remembered that their daughter had fallen out of her crib when she was two, landed on top of her head, and had been diagnosed with a concussion. The doctors who treated her after the fall told them that based on a CT scan and an MRI there was no brain damage. The parents didn't even remember this event when I asked them about it during the initial intake session.*
>
> *Although this child demonstrated many symptoms of ADHD, these symptoms were in fact caused by head injury. I used neurofeedback to improve her brain's ability to regulate itself. Eight months later she was in the 80th percentile on the standardized tests, symptoms of ADHD significantly decreased, her rage dissipated and she was invited to a classmate's birthday party, a good indicator of improved social skills.*

**INTEGRATION:**    The QEEG can be a definitive diagnostic tool when combined with clinical assessment information. When possible, refer your client to get a QEEG. This will give you all a much clearer understanding of what is actually going on in their brain. It will help you rule in or out ADHD as well as brain injury, learning disabilities, autism, sensory processing and integration issues, depression, anxiety, and much more. It will also provide the information needed if the client decides to proceed with neurofeedback treatment.

# WHAT IS A QEEG?

**The QEEG is a quantitative electroencephalograph (EEG).** As with a regular EEG brainwave, data is recorded and can be read by a neurologist to rule out seizure disorders and other disorders that will show up by observing the EEG. Then the brain wave data are compared to a database of normal brainwaves. A statistical analysis is done which provides specific information about how the brain is functioning at any given site and brainwave frequency compared to norms. The QEEG is used in computational neuroscience research centers and neurofeedback centers all over the world to study and treat ADHD, autism spectrum disorder, depression, bipolar disorder, PTSD, and other anxiety disorders, learning disabilities, traumatic brain injury and memory disorders such as Alzheimer's disease and other forms of dementia.

**When you get a QEEG your brain's electrical activity is recorded at 19 sites on your head while you sit quietly with your eyes open for about 10 minutes and then with your eyes closed.** Your EEG tracings are then converted to numbers and compared to the EEG of individuals with no known brain- based difficulties. This allows you to see patterns of brain dysfunction that may be related to your difficulties in life: you can see the basis in your brain for your problems.

**There are a number of patterns commonly seen in ADHD.** ADHD can be thought of as a dysregulated brain. The QEEG can help you understand what the source of your symptoms is and give you a better understanding of how your brain is regulating itself. It will help you know if you have ADHD or perhaps some other disorder such as a learning disorder, sensory integration issues, mood dysregulation and more. This will help you get a more accurate diagnosis and treatment better tailored to your needs. Then those areas of the brain can be targeted for change with neurofeedback.

## Tool 2-4: TOVA® and IVA

**BACKGROUND:**   Continuous performance tests (CPTs) measure the client's ability to pay attention and control impulses and can be very useful in assessing ADHD symptoms.  The Test of Variables of Attention (TOVA®) and the Integrated Visual and Auditory (IVA) Continuous Performance Test are two CPTs commonly used in the ADHD diagnostic process.  This tool discusses the use of a CPT when diagnosing ADHD.

**SKILL BUILDING:**  Explain to clients and parents that a continuous performance test can help measure their child's or teen's ability to pay attention and regulate impulsivity, both typically problematic in ADHD.  Two popular CPTs are the TOVA and the IVA.  Discuss the benefit of using a CPT to determine if their symptoms are out of normal ranges for age and if they have more difficulty visually or auditorially.  This will provide a more accurate diagnosis and aid in providing the most effective treatment.

Both of these tests are available online:
TOVA –  www.tovatest.com
IVA – www.braintrain.com

**INTEGRATION:** Consider using one of these CPTs to assess your client's ADHD symptoms. They are a great way to actually measure attention and impulsivity which can then be combined with symptom rating checklists (based on observation) to get a more complete picture of how the client's brain is regulating itself and increase the likelihood of an accurate diagnosis of ADHD.

Use both the visual and auditory tests as many clients perform better visually than auditorily and vice versa. A visual test might be normal and the auditory out of norm. If we only administer the visual test we would not pick up on the auditory problem. The IVA-2 integrates both visual and auditory. The TOVA has two separate tests each about 22 minutes long.

## Tool 2-5: ADHD Neurobiology and Brain Imaging

**BACKGROUND:**   There are a number of brain differences that have been found in children with ADHD as compared to those without ADHD. These include differences in dopamine production, the size of certain brain waves, the electrical communication within the brain, gene variations, maturation rate and basal ganglia volumes and shapes (in boys). These delays and abnormalities may underlie the hallmark symptoms of ADHD and help to explain how the disorder may develop.

**SKILL BUILDING:**   Use Handout 2-5 to explain the neurobiology of ADHD and how the brains of those with ADHD differ from those without. This will help clients and parents understand that ADHD is a brain-based disorder, especially those who are skeptical that ADHD really exists. This may reassure some, but scare others. Be sure to reassure them that despite the delay in maturation, the brain does eventually mature to normal or near normal levels. Approximately 60% of children with ADHD will become adults with ADHD. Neurofeedback is a particularly effective treatment for creating more normal brainwave patterns. See Chapter 10 Neurofeedback. Explain that the treatments and skills provided in this workbook all work towards normalizing brain function.

**INTEGRATION:**   Help clients and parents identify and explore their feelings after reviewing Handout 2-5. Find out if this information scares them or reassures them. Help them understand the neurobiology and relate it to symptoms of ADHD. Let them know there are many treatments that actually change the brain in positive ways. Encourage them to learn about the treatments and skills included in this workbook which help the brain with ADHD become more normal.

# NEUROBIOLOGY OF ADHD

**Brain Differences Found in Children with ADHD:**

**Smaller Brain Structures (Basal Ganglia):** A positron emission tomography (PET) study shows that boys with ADHD have significantly smaller basal ganglia volumes compared with typically developing boys, and remarkably different basal ganglia shapes. No volume or shape differences were revealed in girls with ADHD.

**Neurotransmitter Dopamine:** Studies found differences in dopamine production although a recent study found that dopamine dysregulation per se is unlikely to be the primary cause underlying ADHD pathology in adults.

**Brainwave Patterns:** The QEEG brain imaging technology has found differences in the size of certain brain waves as well as the electrical communication (coherence) within the brain. Some subsets of these patterns are being studied as well.

Three typical brainwave patterns seen in children with ADHD:
- **Increased Focal Theta** (daydreaming brainwaves) localized within frontal and/or midline regions on the brain 92% of the time.
- **Abnormally Large Alpha Brainwaves** (spacey, internally focused) localized within posterior and/or midline regions 84.1% of the time
- **Increased Beta** brainwaves (fast, revved up) in 13.1% of the study population with ADHD that was localized in frontal and/or posterior regions of the brain – basically all over the brain.

**Coherence:** Abnormal communication among different areas of the brain.
- **Hypocoherent:** Not communicating well enough
- **Hypercoherent:** Not differentiated enough

**Delayed Brain Maturation:** Brain imaging studies show in youth with ADHD.
- The brain matures in a normal pattern but is delayed, on average, by about 3 years (Shaw, et al, 2007). The delay is most pronounced in frontal brain regions involved in thinking, paying attention and planning.
- The outermost layer of the brain, the cortex, shows delayed maturation overall (Shaw, et al, 2012).
- A brain structure important for proper communications between the two halves of the brain shows an abnormal growth pattern.
- The motor cortex matures faster, which may be related to hyperactivity.

**Gene Variations**
- Hundreds of gene variations were found in children with ADHD not found in controls without it.

## Tool 2-6: ADHD: Executive Function Dysregulation

**BACKGROUND:**　　Russell Barkley states that ADHD can be thought of as a dysregulation of executive function. Various theoretical explanations of symptoms and cognitive problems in ADHD nearly all address aspects of self-regulation in some form. Self-regulation, or cognitive control, is the ability to suppress inappropriate actions in favor of appropriate ones. The executive functions are neuropsychological processes needed to sustain problem-solving toward a goal which is exactly what self–regulation involves. Self-regulation and the ten executive functions take place in the front of the brain, the prefrontal cortex (PFC).

Use this framework as a way for young clients and parents to understand and explain their symptoms.

**SKILL BUILDING:**　　Explain to clients older than about age nine and to every parent that ADHD can be thought of as a dysregulation of executive function. Talk to clients about what an executive at a business does. An executive has the job of managing or directing the work of others. Ask them if they know anyone who is an executive. Discuss how people with ADHD have an executive who isn't doing their job very well.

Another way to present this concept is to explain that the role of executive function is similar to an orchestra conductor, only instead of directing an orchestra, it directs the activities of the brain. It is involved in paying attention, planning, organizing, personality expression, decision making and moderating social behavior. Use Handout 2-6-1 to help clients understand this concept.

Use Handout 2-6-2 Executive Functions to explain the ten executive functions and help your clients identify some examples of when their executive (function) or conductor wasn't doing a good job and then when it did a great job. Discuss the terms used on the handout and give them some examples to make sure they understand before they fill it out.

**INTEGRATION:**　　Was the client able to understand what an executive or conductor does? Were they able to identify examples of when theirs didn't doing a good job and then when it did a great job? Help them increase their self-awareness of self-regulation by asking them to pay attention to when it is and isn't doing a good job this coming week and discuss what they noticed at your next session.

# EXECUTIVE/CONDUCTOR IN THE PFC

**Girl touching PFC**

**Conductor**

### Activity

Let's pretend we are conducting an orchestra. (Do it with them.) Use your imagination and your conductor baton to bring in the violins, quiet the flutes, make the trumpets louder, and now speed up the drums.

Now pretend we are the conductor or Prefrontal Cortex (PFC) in our brain. Use your imaginary conductor baton to tell your brain to concentrate a little more over there, calm down your body a bit over here, speed up, slow down, turn down that worry, spiff up how it plans and organizes, and turn up happiness.

### Exercise

What does a conductor do in an orchestra?

_____

_____

Imagine that your PFC is the conductor of your brain. List the ways it "conducts" the activities of your brain, particularly the executive functions such as paying attention, planning, organizing, making decisions, mood regulation, motivation and time management.

_____

_____

List things you have trouble doing that are controlled by the PFC.

_____

_____

List things you do well that are controlled by the PFC.

_____

_____

Is there anything your PFC has trouble doing? (For example, concentrating?)

_____

_____

What might happen if the PFC is offline and not working well?

_____

_____

# EXECUTIVE FUNCTIONS

**List an example of when your Executive or Conductor didn't do his job well.**
**List an example of when your Executive or Conductor did a great job.**

1. Impulse Control

_____

_____

2. Sustaining Attention

_____

_____

3. Shifting Attention

_____

_____

4. Controlling Emotions

_____

_____

5. Initiating or Starting Activity

_____

_____

6. Working Memory

_____

_____

7. Planning

_____

_____

8. Organizing of Material

_____

_____

9. Self-Monitoring

_____

_____

10. Managing Time

_____

_____

## Tool 2-7: ADHD Mimics and Contributors

**BACKGROUND:**  Both the inattentive and hyperactive/impulsive symptoms seen in ADHD may be caused by or mimicked by things other than true ADHD. There are also a number of factors that can make the symptoms of ADHD much worse. This tool explores these factors and helps the clinician and the parent be more aware of how these may be impacting the client. Use this tool during the assessment phase to be sure that the symptoms are not better accounted for by one or more of these factors.

**SKILL BUILDING:**  Use Handout 2-7 ADHD: Mimics and Contributors as a guideline to find out whether the client's symptoms are being caused by or worsened by other factors. While performing the psychiatric evaluation, look for symptoms of depression, anxiety, mania, oppositional/defiant behavior, stress, psychosis, dissociative symptoms, reactive attachment disorder and trauma. Although many of these can co-exist with ADHD, find out which symptoms are primary and which are secondary.

As discussed in Tool 2-2 Structured Intake Assessment, **anxiety and depression are commonly seen in addition to ADHD**. But a client who is highly anxious or very depressed may have difficulty concentrating and/or experience psychomotor agitation that may look like ADHD when in fact they do not have ADHD. When the anxiety or depression is treated the concentration and psychomotor agitation improve.

On the other hand, it is very common for someone who is dealing with the challenges of ADHD to become anxious (performance anxiety, "Can I get it done on time?") and/or depressed ("I am stupid," "I can never do anything right"). Children and teens may often exhibit behavior that looks like oppositional defiant behavior that is simply how their poor concentration impacts their life. They often become depressed and oppositional when they are dealing with being yelled at or criticized for not completing tasks, losing things, etc.

**ADHD can interfere with sleep**. If a client with ADHD doesn't sleep well their symptoms may be magnified. But a client who routinely gets poor sleep may look like they have ADHD when in fact they are suffering from sleep deprivation. Large tonsils contribute to sleep apnea which in turn impacts concentration during the day.

Develop a professional relationship with your local naturopathic physicians, pediatricians and allergists with a more holistic practice. Refer clients to them and consult with them when there is a suspicion of food sensitivities, chemical sensitivities, hearing or vision problems, sleep apnea, swollen tonsils, heavy metal exposure, vitamin/mineral deficiencies or a sleep disorder. Chapter 19 Common Food Sensitivities May Mimic or Increase ADHD Symptoms contains guidance on how to help clients determine if they have a food sensitivity. Utilize Chapter 21 Assess and Improve Sleep to help them improve sleep.

Some studies suggest that middle ear disease in school-age children may be associated with hyperactivity and/or inattention, independently of learning disability (Adesman, 1990). Deficits in the inner ear due to allergy and infection may result in increased fluid which can cause motor coordination issues and difficulties regulating behavior (Ramsey, 2010). Find out if there is a history of ear infection, allergy, or inner ear fluid and see if this correlates with their symptoms of ADHD. Encourage them to consult with an ear professional to discuss the potential need for treatment. Some physical therapists use an Epley maneuver (a sequence of specific body and head movements) to help correct ear related issues.

If the school has not yet done testing for learning disabilities, sensory processing issues, or if warranted, central auditory processing, talk with the parent and assist them in requesting these tests. See Tool 22-1 Getting the School Involved for guidance on working with the school.

***Case Example:*** *One of my colleagues found that by simply asking her client's parents to follow a specific diet regimen for a week, the ADHD symptoms of more than half of her clients decreased to the point that they no longer met the criteria for ADHD.*

*One client discovered that her son was so allergic to milk that it was interfering with his eyesight, learning and behavior. When she removed milk from his diet his concentration improved and his hostile behavior disappeared. Another discovered that her son's swollen tonsils were causing sleep apnea. Once his tonsils were removed his ADHD symptoms decreased.*

**INTEGRATION:**    Once you have completed this step you will have a much more complete picture of your client and what may or may not be contributing to or mimicking their ADHD symptoms. Although as a clinician, you are probably not trained to do all of the medical assessments, you can certainly be involved in recommending options to the parents of your clients about what tests might give you valuable information.

# ADHD: MIMICS AND CONTRIBUTORS

- Diet: Sugar, Caffeine[N]

- Allergies[M,N]

- Vision Problems[M]

- Hx Of Heavy Metal Exposure[N]

- Vitamin/Mineral Deficiencies[N]

- Anxiety, Depression

- Learning Disabilities[S]

- Sensory Processing[S]

- Manic Episodes

- Sleep Disorder[M]

- History of Inner Ear Problems[M]

- Food Sensitivities[N]

- Chemical Sensitivities[N]

- Hearing Problems[M]

- Sleep Apnea[M]

- Swollen Tonsils[M]

- Stress

- Head Injury[M]

- Childhood Trauma

- Oppositional Behavior

- Family Chaos

- Reactive Attachment Disorder

- Psychosis, Dissociative Disorders

N - These can typically be assessed by a naturopathic physician
M - These can be assessed by a medical doctor
S - These can be assessed by the school

## Tool 2-8: ADHD Comorbid Disorders

**BACKGROUND:**    As discussed in Tool 2-7 ADHD Mimics and Contributors there are a number of disorders that may co-occur with ADHD. When doing your intake assessment, and as you work with your client, keep these in mind as they will also need to be addressed and treated. Russell Barkley states that 80% of clients with ADHD have one comorbid diagnosis and 50% of them have two comorbid diagnoses.

**SKILL BUILDING:**    When doing your assessment look for symptoms of the following disorders that co-occur most commonly with ADHD. It is likely that your client will have at least one of these diagnoses in addition to their ADHD. Use the graph below to explain the prevalence of these commonly co-existing disorders and to explore the possibility that these are present for the child or teen.

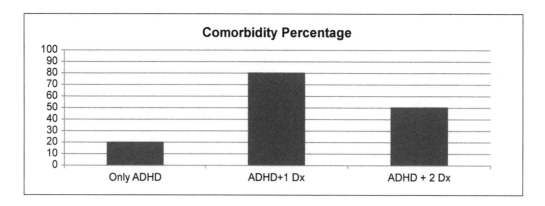

- Depression
- Anxiety
- Learning Disabilities
- Tics and OCD
- Sleep Disorder
- Bipolar Disorder

- Conduct Disorder
- Addiction
- Sensory Processing Disorder
- Allergies
- Oppositional Defiant Disorder
- Middle Ear Issues

**INTEGRATION:**    Children and teens with ADHD often feel depressed and/or anxious. They might exhibit oppositional behaviors which actually stem from their difficulty managing life with ADHD. As their ADHD symptoms are addressed, and hopefully decreased, and as they learn skills to better manage their symptoms, these secondary issues may resolve on their own. But, they may persist as these patterns of depression, negativity and anxiety might have become wired into their brain. Thus, it is important to assess and address any symptoms of comorbid disorders.

# Section III
# **Tools for Tracking Progress**

# Chapter 3
# Track Treatment Progress:
# Set the Stage for Success

Tool 3-1: Define Treatment Goals
Tool 3-2: Symptom Tracking

## Tool 3-1: Define Treatment Goals

**BACKGROUND:**   Defining treatment goals is important for several reasons. First, by defining treatment goals, the client is setting an intention to focus on meeting these goals. Second, the treatment goals clarify and provide structure for the work to be done with the client. Third, best practice methods and most managed-care insurance companies require them.

It is important to involve the parents as well as the children or teen clients in defining treatment goals. This process will ensure that the child or teen client understands why their parents brought them in for treatment. It will also provide a way to monitor progress during the treatment episode. This tool discusses the process of defining treatment goals related to ADHD.

**SKILL BUILDING:**   Ask the client how they will know if working with you has helped them. This directly addresses what their treatment goals are. Some kids and teens are extremely tuned in to what they need help with while others will need help with this task. Ask them for five to ten goals that they would like to achieve or symptoms they would like to improve. Involve the client as well as the parents in this step whenever possible. Refer to Handout 3-1 Sample Treatment Goals for ADHD for examples of treatment goals.

While you are doing this step, it is a great opportunity to discuss parental expectations. See Tool 7-1 Parenting Skills for more information about this. Find out if they expect more from their child than is reasonable for the child or teen to achieve given they have ADHD. Help them identify and adjust any unrealistic expectations to take into account the ADHD specific challenges that their child or teen faces. For example, to expect a child with ADHD to complete three chores in a row on their own is probably not realistic. But it may become more realistic if the parent provides cues, reminders, site of performance aids (See Tool 9-2 Site of Performance Skills and Systems), and uses the scaffolding technique (See Tool 7-1 Parenting Skills) to help the child learn and practice. A starting goal might be to feed the cat with the parent. Then, when they can do that regularly, the goal could be changed to feeding the cat with a parental reminder. A more advanced goal might be to feed the cat on their own using an alarm as a reminder.

**INTEGRATION:**   Assist the client and their parent in mindfully defining their treatment goals. Ask them to reflect on what the process was like for them. How was it helpful to clarify what they hope to improve/achieve? Was the child or teen aware of what the parent wanted them to be able to do or was it a surprise to them? Did the client and parent agree on the goals? Were their expectations realistic? Encourage them to update these goals periodically.

# SAMPLE TREATMENT GOALS FOR ADHD

## Symptoms

- Improve concentration
- Increase task completion
- Reduce hyperactivity
- Develop coping skills for managing ADHD symptoms

## Treatment Options

- Explore treatment options such as psychotherapy, play therapy, neurofeedback, chiropractic, naturopathic medicine, nutrition
- Explore options for getting an ADHD coach
- Explore joining an ADHD support group
- Examine feelings about taking medication for ADHD

## Emotion Regulation

- Increase emotion regulation
- Improve mood
- Decrease anxiety
- Increase ability to repair negative mood states
- Improve self-esteem
- Identify and explore feelings about having ADHD
- Increase sense of well-being
- Decrease anger
- Improve self-awareness
- Improve stress management skills
- Decrease negative self-talk

## Strengths and Challenges

- List everything you did right this week
- Explore what is working well for you
- Identify strengths
- Identify what gets in the way of success

## Social Skills

- Improve social skills
- Use role play to learn social and communication skills
- Improve relationships
- Improve compassion for self and others
- Improve memory
- Increase knowledge about ADHD and how it impacts you

## Organizational/Study Skills

- Learn and use organizational skills
- Organize briefcase or backpack
- Set up distraction free homework area
- Use headphones with boring music to block out distractions
- Learn and use mindfulness techniques
- Design method for organizing homework
- Use an electronic calendar with alarm to remind you of assignments and activities

## Sleep, Diet, TV

- Learn effective habits for managing an ADHD healthy diet
- Exercise at least 3 times per week
- Design bedtime routine to get to sleep on time
- Improve sleep
- Limit TV
- Quit smoking (teens)
- Stop alcohol or drug use (teens)

## Tool 3-2: Symptom Tracking

**BACKGROUND:** Tracking client progress is helpful for several reasons. First, it keeps the treatment focused on meeting treatment goals. Second, it provides a way for therapist and client to track improvement and monitor symptoms/goals as work progresses. Third, it provides a way to assess the effectiveness of treatment. Children and teens are typically more invested in the treatment when they can see their progress. And they often enjoy watching their ratings improve. This tool provides a technique for tracking symptoms or monitoring treatment goals.

**SKILL BUILDING:** After defining treatment goals using Tool 3-1 Define Treatment Goals, ask parents and older children and teens to rate each symptom/goal on a scale of 0 to 10 where 10 is worst and 0 is no problem. Depending on developmental level and maturity kids as young as six or seven may be able to attach a valid number to their symptom. Some kids and teens with poor self-awareness will need their parents to rate the symptoms. Occasionally, it may prove useful to ask older kids and teens to rate their symptoms and then ask the parents to do so on a separate sheet.

List the goals/symptoms in the left-hand column of Handout 3-2-2 Client Symptom/Goal Rating Chart. Then place the date at the top of the next column and fill in their rating of each goal/symptom. Tally the total at the bottom. The goal will be to lower the rating on each symptom and the overall total as treatment progresses. Ask clients to rate their symptoms/goals periodically as treatment progress. Show them how their ratings are improving. See Handout 3-2-1 for an example of a partially completed symptom rating form.

Some clients and their parents may have trouble rating a symptom with a number. They may find it easier to describe changes they are noticing. That's okay. If possible, use this information to rate symptoms yourself. Or, skip the numeric rating and keep a log of changes they report.

**INTEGRATION:** Most clients and their parents find this process easy while a few do not. The goal of this tool is to provide a way to notice change and document symptom improvement. Encourage clients to rate symptoms. Most will provide a consistently accurate rating over time. Showing them their progress inspires hope and motivation for continuing the changes they are making. Did the parent rate the symptoms better or worse than the client?

# SAMPLE CLIENT SYMPTOM/GOAL RATING CHART

| SYMPTOM | DATE | | | | | | | | | | |
|---|---|---|---|---|---|---|---|---|---|---|---|
| | 11/7/13 | 11/14/13 | 11/21/13 | 12/2/13 | | | | | | | |
| Concentration | 10 | 9.5 | 9 | 8 | | | | | | | 0 |
| Hyperactivity | 8 | 8 | 7.5 | 7 | | | | | | | 0 |
| Anxiety | 5 | 4 | 4 | 3 | | | | | | | 0 |
| Sleep | 6 | 5 | 4 | 4 | | | | | | | 0 |
| Self-esteem | 8 | 7 | 6 | 5 | | | | | | | 0 |
| Homework | 9 | 8 | 7 | 3 | | | | | | | 0 |
| | | | | | | | | | | | 0 |
| | | | | | | | | | | | 0 |
| | | | | | | | | | | | 0 |
| TOTAL Score | 46 | 41.5 | 37.5 | 30 | | | | | | | 0 |

# CLIENT SYMPTOM/GOAL RATING CHART

| SYMPTOM | DATE | | | | | | | | | | | |
|---|---|---|---|---|---|---|---|---|---|---|---|---|
| | | | | | | | | | | | | |
| | | | | | | | | | | | | |
| | | | | | | | | | | | | |
| | | | | | | | | | | | | |
| | | | | | | | | | | | | |
| | | | | | | | | | | | | |
| | | | | | | | | | | | | |
| | | | | | | | | | | | | |
| | | | | | | | | | | | | |
| | | | | | | | | | | | | |
| TOTAL Score | | | | | | | | | | | | |

# Section IV
# Psychotherapy for ADHD

# Chapter 4
# Tailoring Psychotherapy for ADHD

Tool 4-1: Confidentiality, Engagement and Buy-In
Tool 4-2: Guidelines for Sessions with Children and Teens with ADHD
Tool 4-3: What Works and What Doesn't For ADHD
Tool 4-4: Ingredients of Effected Psychotherapy Sessions

## Tool 4-1: Confidentiality, Engagement and Buy-In

**BACKGROUND:** As in any psychotherapy session for any issue it is important to be mindful of following guidelines to maintain confidentiality for those with ADHD. This is particularly important for children and teens who may feel ashamed or embarrassed by their ADHD symptoms and the negative feedback they receive from their world. Often children and teens have already been to a variety of therapists that they feel haven't helped much and they may be skeptical that this will be different. Therefore, it is extra important to connect with them, get them to help you understand how ADHD impacts their life, and help them "buy-into" working with yet another therapist.

**SKILL BUILDING:** In order for the child, and especially the teen client, to successfully engage with you, the therapist, they must know that what they tell you is confidential. The exceptions to confidentially include disclosing abuse, neglect, at-risk of injury or suicidal thoughts. If they feel that you will tell their parent everything they tell you, they won't tell you much. Be sure to explain the limits of confidentiality to the client and their parent.

You, the clinician, are not the extension of the parent. Avoid the pattern of the parent telling you about all the bad things the child or teen did before the session and expecting you to "take care of it." Although you need input from the parents, you are the therapist, not the disciplinarian or "police."

On the other hand, you will need input from the parent. Without parental input you won't know what happened during the week, get accurate information or know what progress is being achieved. Make sure that parents understand they are an important part of the therapeutic process and insist on regular parent guidance sessions.

In order for the client to engage in treatment and "buy into" the therapeutic process they must feel safe and understood, and believe that you will be able to help them with issues that are important to them. Use the standard skills of therapeutic engagement, but tailor them to the issues specific to ADHD. Many children and teens with ADHD feel ashamed and guilty about their symptoms and often feel totally misunderstood. They will engage more quickly when they realize that you "get it" and really understand how ADHD impacts their life.

Ask them what is working well and what isn't. Repeat back to them what you hear about how ADHD is impacting their life until they let you know you understand. Help them connect their challenges with their symptoms of ADHD to help them increase their self-awareness. Ask for children and teens to "buy into" working with you by asking them if they are willing to come to session every week and try new things. Establish treatment goals and have a discussion about "what's in it for me" with older children and teens to help them understand how you can help them. This will also give them hope.

**INTEGRATION:** Have you established treatment goals and do the child, teen and parent understand them? Did you review the limits of confidentiality with them? Is the child or teen willing to work with you? Are you able to show them you "get it" and to give them hope that you can help them feel better and function more successfully?

## Tool 4-2: Guidelines for Sessions with Children and Teens with ADHD

**BACKGROUND:**    Children with the hyperactive/impulsive type of ADHD can often have trouble regulating their behavior and emotions in session and in their daily life. They may be extremely busy with a very short attention span going from one toy to another. They may have little regard for your belongings and poor boundaries with what they touch or try to get into. Without your planning and preparation they can leave your office space (and your energy) in a shambles. The inattentive type may seem tuned out, not engaged, not listening and easily bored. This tool provides some things to think about in setting up your space and sessions to provide a safe, structured environment in which the child with ADHD can thrive and learn skills. Parents can use the same techniques in setting up their home.

**SKILL BUILDING:**

*Office Environment:*    Set up your office space to be child friendly. Make sure it's safe. Remove objects that can be swallowed by young clients. Cover the electrical outlets. Put your favorite, breakable knickknacks up high, out of reach or take them home. Create an environment where you don't have to say "no, don't touch that!" Provide toys and games that can be used effectively in therapy. Arrange the toys and games so that your client knows where they are and gradually gets comfortable and in control of themselves in your office.

*Provide Structure:*    Provide structure during the session. Tell them what options they have for play or activity in the session. Let the child know how long they have with you and when the session will end, tell them when they have 10 minutes left, 5 minutes left, 1 minute left. This is especially helpful for clients with ADHD who have trouble with transitions. Teach their parents to do the same thing.

*Tell Them the Rules:*    Children with ADHD do best when they know what to expect. Tell them the rules at the beginning of treatment and remind them at the start of each session. Some rules I have found helpful are:

- Don't leave the room without permission
- Put one toy away before taking out another toy
- Treat toys and games with kindness
- Stop playing when time is up
- Clean up at the end of the session

*Set Limits:*    Let children know what they are allowed to do and touch in the room and what they are not. This will vary depending on the particular client's behavior and your style. When one of my clients tried to break my computer with his shoe, I set a very firm limit that he was not allowed to hurt my computer and that we could not play that neurofeedback computer game if he ever tried to hurt it again. He never did it again.

*Hovering Presence:*    Be a positive non-judgmental presence in the room so the client can learn to trust you. Help them learn to feel good about themselves while they are working with you. Connect with the client. Have fun. Use humor. Find out what they enjoy doing. Learn about their life. Encourage them to show you what's going on inside of them through their play. Talk with them while you are playing with them. Ask them questions. If you don't understand something, ask them to explain it again, and again, if necessary until you do. Allow them to be in control of the play within reasonable and safe limits.

***Avoid being Critical or Judgmental:***   Children and teens with ADHD get lots of criticism in their life about their behavior, their school performance, their hyperactivity, their poor attention span, forgetfulness etc. Be the hovering presence that understands their frustration with how the symptoms of ADHD impact their life. Use statements like "Wow, it seems like it is hard for you to sit still. Is it?" Instead of "sit still." Or "why can't you just sit still?" Or, "It sounds like you are upset (or angry or embarrassed) that the teacher made you stay in for recess to finish that test. How did you manage that?" Teach their parents to do the same.

***Avoid Power Struggles:***   Some children and teens with ADHD are masters at sucking the adults in their lives into power struggles. Give clients choices or ask them how to solve a problem. For example, if they have trouble putting one toy away before getting out another, give them a choice. Say, "Would you like to put this away and play with a different toy or keep playing with this one?" "It is time to clean up. Would you like to help me put this away or not be able to play with it next time?"; "It seems like you are having trouble stopping and cleaning up"; "What can you do to be ready to leave on time?"

***Behavior Management:***   Learn and use the behavior management techniques discussed in the behavior management/regulation section of Tool 7-1 Parenting Skills. Remember you are not their parent and avoid setting up the session where you become an extension of their parent. Be proactive in gently and positively helping them manage and regulate their behavior.

**INTEGRATION:**   What have you noticed about how psychotherapy for clients with ADHD differs from psychotherapy for clients without ADHD?  Have you set up your office so you feel comfortable with hyperactive and impulsive clients touching your stuff?  Are you able to help clients mange their behavior in your space? Are you succeeding at providing a positive environment where the client feels safe, accepted and understood? Are the parents learning these skills from you?

## Tool 4-3: What Works and What Doesn't for ADHD

**BACKGROUND:**   Having worked with clients of all ages for the past 30 years I discovered that psychotherapy for a client with ADHD needs to include a wider approach than generally used for clients without ADHD. First, it must include the typical techniques to improve emotional and behavioral regulation, self-esteem, depression and anxiety which are so challenging for those with ADHD. The second component of psychotherapy needs to include an emphasis on skill building. Clients with ADHD need to feel better about themselves, decrease their negative self-image and narrative, as well as learn specific skills that help them manage and decrease the symptoms unique to ADHD.

This tool presents a review of the styles of psychotherapy that do and do not work well with ADHD.

**SKILL BUILDING:**

**What styles don't work as well for ADHD?**

***Traditional Psychotherapy:***   This focuses on emotions and examines the past to find causes of current problems. Clients with ADHD do need help managing their emotions and their symptoms but the focus needs to be on right now in the present moment. They need tools, skills, techniques for emotional and impulse regulation, social skills, time management, and organizational skills. Poor concentration often results in not picking up on many of the skills other children and teens do automatically.

***Psychodynamic:***   This is not the first choice for those with ADHD as they need help right now, in the present to get their symptoms and their life under control. Once that is done, psychodynamic therapy may help them understand how their current feelings and beliefs are coming from their past challenges with ADHD. This type of therapy is best reserved for adults.

***Blank Screen:***   If you present a blank screen to children and teens with ADHD they will have trouble focusing, self-regulating and learning skills. Psychotherapy for clients with ADHD needs to be more active with a lot of feedback and skill development.

***Blaming:***   Clients with ADHD get blamed a lot for the manifestation of their symptoms. They will respond better in therapy with a non-judgmental, supportive and encouraging approach that helps them recognize and development their many strengths.

***Disciplinarian:***   Children and teens with ADHD respond best when you provide structure and let them know the rules and what to expect. You will need to set firm limits in session, but be sure to give them choices and options to learn and practice self-regulation. Use an educational rather than a disciplinarian approach. Teach this to their parents as well.

***Dream Analysis:***   As helpful as dream analysis can be to many clients this is not the best approach for children and teens with ADHD. Maybe when they are adults and have mastered the challenges of ADHD, but not now.

## What Styles Work Best for ADHD?

***Cognitive Behavioral Therapy (CBT):***   CBT is a good option for helping children and teens succeed with ADHD. CBT uses options for making thoughts, feelings and behavior contribute to success. It contains a focus on skill building, including managing emotions, interpersonal skills, behavior and whatever that particular child or teen may need. It's a tool for getting organized, staying focused, and improving one's ability to control anger and get along with others.

CBT works to reduce irrational thoughts and expectations that affect behavior and stop clients from doing what they need to do. Many clients with ADHD develop a pattern of negative thinking and negative self-talk. Use Tool 5-2 Replace Those ANTs (Automatic Negative Thoughts) to help them identify and replace their automatic negative thoughts. Mindfulness-based cognitive therapy is also helpful in increasing self-awareness and self-regulation.

***Play Therapy:***   Play therapy recognizes that young children are not usually capable of talking about their feelings. Play therapy provides a way for the therapist to interact with a young child within the child's fantasy metaphor. Often, the child will display their feelings through their play with a dollhouse, through drawings or other creative play media such as sand play or make believe.

A skilled play therapist can help the child via the vehicle of play without ever having to leave the child's theme of symbolic play. Some parents are dismayed when their child tells them they just 'played.' Discuss this with your client's parents. Research has proven the positive results gained from play therapy.

See Handout 4-3 for common play therapy techniques.

***Parent Guidance:***   Parents need to be involved in treatment. They need specific skills for helping their child or teen with ADHD succeed. A dramatic change usually occurs when the parents change how they interact with their children. Often, it seems that parents think that if they just drop their kids off at counseling some magic will happen and their child won't have ADHD anymore. How parents treat their child, how they react, the tone of voice they use, the words they say, and how they nurture, support and love their child will have a huge impact on success. See Chapter 7 for Parenting Skills Tailored to ADHD.

**Family Therapy:**    When one or more members of a family have ADHD the whole family system will be affected. In family therapy the family dynamics will typically play out in the session right in front of the therapist's eyes. Then you can help the family establish more effective patterns that better support the child with ADHD and create a healthy family environment.

**INTEGRATION:**    You as the clinician will already have your own style of therapy when working with children and teens. Keep in mind that clients with ADHD need an emphasis on **skills**. This is the ingredient I have found missing most often when I see clients who have already seen other therapists.

# PLAY THERAPY TECHNIQUES FOR CHILDREN WITH ADHD

**Dollhouse:** A simple dollhouse with rooms in which the client can place furniture and dolls. Watch how they set up the house, where they put things, and where they place the dolls. Listen to what they say as they work/play. Ask them open questions like "who is that doll"; "what are they doing?"; "why is the baby in the basement?" Look for themes about how they are feeling about themselves, how they see themselves or how they think others see them. Fears and beliefs may become evident as well.

**Sand Play:** A sand box with a rake to smooth the sand and lots of small characters, cars, trucks and other objects clients can use to tell a story in the sand. Ask questions about what's going on in the story. Watch for their play to become more organized as treatment progresses.

**Draw a Picture:** Ask the client to draw you a picture. Let them choose between colored pencils, erasable markers, regular pencils, crayons or even watercolors. The picture could be of their family and once that is done, anything they would like to draw. You might ask them to draw something that happened to them this week in school, at home, with friends, in sports. Ask them to explain what they drew. Ask them who the people are and what they are doing. See if they used a particular color for any reason. Notice any unusual features of the drawing. Look for symbolic representations of how they feel about what may be going on in their life.

**Fantasy Characters:** Collect a variety of fantasy characters and then ask the client to tell you a story with them. Look for themes that indicate self-esteem, power and control and their feelings. You may choose to enter into the play. Stay in the child's fantasy metaphor. For example say, "Wow, it looks like that dragon sure is angry. What's he angry about?" as opposed to, "were you angry this week?"

**Puppets:** Provide a variety of hand puppets using animals or characters. Ask the client to put on a play for you with the puppets. Look for themes, feelings and beliefs. Ask lots of questions. Reflect understanding. Perhaps ask the child which puppet they would like you to use and enter the play with them. Stay in their metaphor. When appropriate, use this opportunity to provide a healthy, appropriate emotionally corrective response to the child's play.

**Crafts:** Provide materials such as paint, clay, beads, plastic canvas, bracelet parts, etc. While the client works on the craft, ask questions about what they are doing. You can carry on a casual conversation with them about something they bring up for example, about something that happened during the week. Give them feedback if you see they are off task. You might say, "Gee, it looks like you are getting distracted. What can you do to get back on task?"

**Play "What's Different?":** An effective technique to help children express themselves and to help the therapist understand what the child is feeling is a game that engages the child's imagination. Tell the child to pretend they are sleeping, and now it's morning and something has changed overnight. What is different? You would be amazed at what the child may tell you. I have heard many responses from 'I have a new bike' to 'Daddy is nicer to Mommy and doesn't yell so much' to 'I can concentrate better and get good grades.' This gives you information about what is going on for the child and opens the door for you to understand and help the child. This is effective for teens as well.

**Mindfulness Skills:** Teach the client a variety of mindfulness skills to help increase their self-awareness, mood, impulse control, hyperactivity and concentration. See Chapter 11 for mindfulness skills specifically for ADHD.

**Role Play:** Use role play to help a client rehearse what to say or how to act in a difficult situation. This can help a client try out an interaction by pretending the therapist is someone in their life. Let them practice what to say so they will be better prepared for the possible reactions they might get. This can be very helpful for children and teens who do not have good social skills. It can also help them practice how to talk with their parent, teacher, peers, etc.

Reverse roles and pretend to be your client and they pretend to be you. When they experience you acting like them they will gain a better understanding of how their behavior impacts others and improve their self-awareness.

**Play Games:** Use games that help children and teens that:

- Identify and express feelings such as: Faceland; The Talking, Feeling and Doing Game; The Feelings Game
- Encourage self-control such as: Pick-up-sticks, Jenga, Operation, Don't Break the Ice, Slow Motion, Wait and Win, various Wii games
- Increase focus and concentration such as: Memory, Focus, Beat the Clock, various Wii games
- Practice organizational skills such as: Connect 4, Othello, Game of Life

**Resources:** For the details of 15 play therapy games and techniques that can be used and adapted for clients with ADHD see: Fifteen Effective Play Therapy Techniques Professional Psychology: Research and Practice Copyright 2002 by the American Psychological Association, Inc. 2002, Vol. 33, No. 6, 515–522 (Hall et al, 2002)

Websites that sell popular games for play therapy specifically helpful for ADHD:
www.childtherapytoys.com
www.playtherapysupply.com

## Tool 4-4: Ingredients of Effective Psychotherapy Sessions

**BACKGROUND:**    Due to the challenges that ADHD presents to children and teens they often feel depressed and anxious, experience negative thinking, have low self-esteem and feel out of control. Be sure to include and emphasize the following skills.

**SKILL BUILDING:**

*Understanding:*    Children and teens with ADHD really need to know and feel that you truly understand what they are going through and what it is like to have ADHD. Learn as much as you can about how ADHD is impacting this particular client and let them know you really "get it" and "get them."

*Validation:*    Clients with ADHD are dealing with significant challenges and frustrations that make it hard for them to succeed and feel normal. Validate their feelings. They feel the way they feel for good reason. Keep in mind that you will be gradually helping them to feel better and improve negative feelings. But start right where they are. Acknowledge and validate their feelings without trying to change them or telling them they shouldn't feel that way. They will begin the process of feeling better right away when you do this important step.

*Identify Strengths:*    Despite the challenges presented by ADHD, clients with ADHD have many important strengths. Identifying them and discussing them helps shift clients out of their negative self-talk and poor self-esteem. Use Handout 4-4-4 I Am Good at These Things to help clients identify their strengths. Include parents by asking them to complete this for the strengths they see in their child.

*Identify Feelings:*    Help clients identify how they feel about themselves and about having ADHD. Use the feelings chart on Handout 4-4-1 How I Feel to help children express how they feel. Use Handout 4-4-2 How Having ADHD Makes Me Feel for teens and older children who are able to verbalize their feelings. Use Handout 4-4-3 What I Like About ADHD to help them identify some of the benefits of ADHD and how it may help them in some ways. Play some of the many therapy games on the market to help clients identify when they felt a certain way.

*Increase Awareness:*    Help clients improve their self-awareness. Use Handout 4-4-5 ADHD In My Life to help clients pay attention to how their symptoms of ADHD show up for them and impact their life. Use this Handout at the start of treatment and periodically as treatment progresses to see how this is changing.

*ADHD Education:*    Teach clients about ADHD. Talk about the symptoms of ADHD. Show older kids and teens a SPECT scan (amenclinics.com) or a QEEG that show what a brain with ADHD looks like. Explore what can be done to help them thrive with ADHD. Give them hope that they can succeed with ADHD. Show them how to find famous people who have been unofficially and officially diagnosed with ADHD on Handout 4-4-7 Famous People with ADHD.

*Finding What Has Worked:*    Ask clients and their parents what they have already tried and what helped and what didn't. Be sure to incorporate what has worked into their treatment. Use Handout 4-4-6 What We Already Tried.

***Building Skills:***    Psychotherapy for ADHD must include more skill building than for most other diagnoses. Plan to incorporate the following:

- Tools for Teaching Social skills: See Chapter 8

- Tools for Improving Organizational Skills: See Chapter 9

- Time Management: See Tool 9-1

- Parenting Skills: See Chapter 7

- Nutrition for the ADHD Brain: See Section IX

- Sleep and ADHD: See Section X

- Movement to Optimize Brain Function: See Chapter 15

- Strategies Tailored to Their Needs: Be a detective to help clients and parents figure out solutions and strategies tailored to their particular needs.

***Case Example:***    *I worked with a teen with ADHD who was failing school because he never turned his homework in. He felt really bad about himself and started describing himself as stupid. I helped him devise a way to organize his homework with colored folders and he started doing his homework. But he still wasn't turning it in.*

*When I explored this further with him, he told me he put his binder containing his folders under his desk in each classroom and then would forget to take it with him to the next class. Often it was gone when he went back to find it. We solved this by having him put his binder under his feet instead of under the desk when he sat down at his desk. When he stood up to go to the next class he would feel the binder under his feet and remember to take it with him. This simple detective work turned him into an A student! He was very bright, but his ADHD symptoms were interfering with his ability to organize, complete homework, and remember to take his binder with him. He needed help to find a solution to his specific problem with homework. When his grades improved his self-image and self-talk became much more positive.*

**INTEGRATION:**    Which skills discussed here have you been able to incorporate. How did using them help the client? Which have you found to be most effective for your client? How did the handouts help clients improve self-awareness? Did the handouts give you information that helped you understand and help the client? What have you noticed about this process that is different for clients with ADHD than those without it?

# HOW I FEEL

playful

ill

angry

joyful

resentful

satisfied

sad

surprised

calm

Worried

happy

proud

natural

frightened

thoughtful

silly

# HOW HAVING ADHD MAKES ME FEEL

**Check off all that apply. Give an example of a time when you felt this way.**

☐ Frustrated: _____

☐ Anxious: _____

☐ Depressed: _____

☐ Happy: _____

☐ Stressed: _____

☐ Calm: _____

☐ Angry: _____

☐ Discouraged: _____

☐ Proud: _____

☐ Resentful: _____

☐ Joyful: _____

☐ Surprised: _____

☐ Scared: _____

☐ Helpless: _____

☐ Hopeless: _____

# WHAT I LIKE ABOUT HAVING ADHD

**Check off all that apply. Give an example.**

☐ Fun: _____

☐ Quick Thinking: _____

☐ Lots of Energy: _____

☐ Enthusiasm: _____

☐ Smart: _____

☐ Lots of Ideas: _____

☐ Creative: _____

☐ Spontaneous: _____

☐ Think Outside the Box: _____

☐ Hyperfocus: _____

☐ Leadership: _____

☐ Other: _____

☐ Other: _____

☐ Other: _____

☐ Other: _____

# I AM GOOD AT THESE THINGS

**Make a list of things that you are good at:**

1. _____

2. _____

3. _____

4. _____

5. _____

6. _____

7. _____

8. _____

9. _____

10. _____

11. _____

12. _____

13. _____

14. _____

15. _____

# ADHD IN MY LIFE

**Fill in the bubbles. How does ADHD show up in your life?**

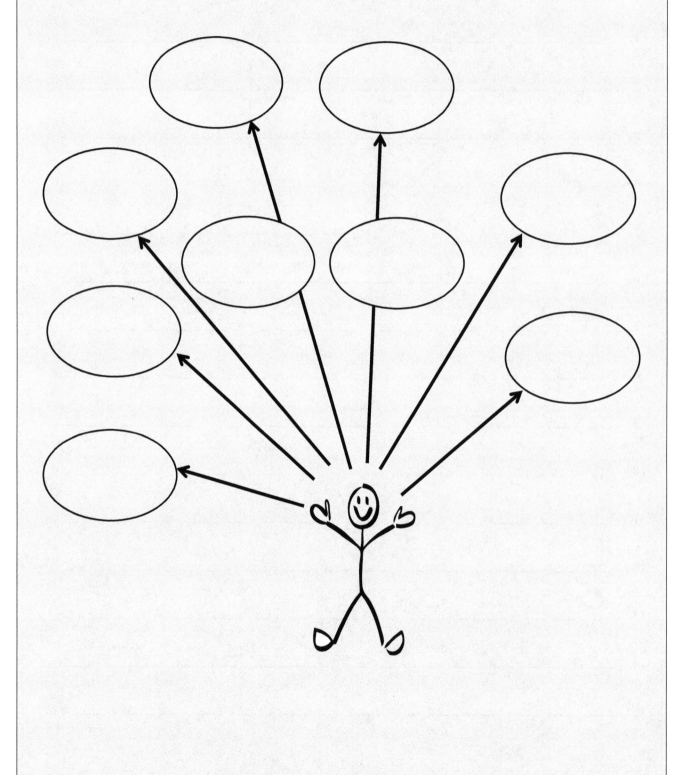

# WHAT WE ALREADY TRIED

**List things that worked. Include what happened.**

_____

_____

_____

_____

_____

_____

**List things that didn't work. Include what happened.**

_____

_____

_____

_____

_____

_____

# FAMOUS PEOPLE WITH ADHD

Many very successful people both living and from history have either been formally diagnosed with ADHD or have symptoms of ADHD. This exercise will help you find people online who have the symptoms of ADHD and are very successful.

**Search online for people with ADHD**
- Use keywords such as:
  Famous People with ADHD
  Does Adam Levine have ADHD?
  Walt Disney and ADHD
  10 most successful people with ADHD
  Presidents with ADHD
  Justin Timberlake and ADHD

**Make a list of actors who have ADHD symptoms**

_____

_____

**Make a list of presidents who have ADHD symptoms**

_____

_____

**Make a list of musicians who have ADHD symptoms**

_____

_____

**Make a list of inventors who have ADHD symptoms**

_____

_____

**How does it feel to know you can be very successful with ADHD?**

_____

_____

**What do you want to be when you are an adult?**

_____

_____

**How will ADHD help you succeed?**

_____

_____

# Section V
# Skills to Manage and Improve ADHD Symptoms

# Chapter 5
# Tools for Emotional Regulation

Tool 5-1: Improve Self-esteem, Depression, Anxiety
Tool 5-2: Replace Those ANTs (Automatic Negative Thoughts)

## Tool 5-1: Improve Self-Esteem, Depression, and Anxiety

**BACKGROUND:** Clients with ADHD often experience low self-esteem, depression, anxiety, guilt and shame. This may be the result of the symptoms of ADHD that cause repeated failures to succeed, getting yelled at in school or by parents, hearing negative comments such as "you are lazy," "your brother can do this, why can't you?" and being rejected by peers due to inappropriate social skills or behavior. This tool provides guidance on helping children and teens improve self-esteem and decrease anxiety and depression.

**SKILL BUILDING:**

*Understanding Gives Hope:*   When children and teens come in for treatment it is common for them to start to feel better as soon as they realize that you understand ADHD, you "get them,", and they learn that they are dealing with a brain-based disorder. They give a sigh of relief when they discover that they are not lazy, stupid, or "retarded" as one client described himself to me. When you teach them about ADHD and how it is treated and help them find famous and successful people with it they begin to feel hopeful. This is the first step in helping them improve their self-esteem, anxiety and depression.

*Improve Their Narrative:*   Many clients with ADHD have a negative narrative. They see themselves in a negative way and their inner dialogue consists of a continual pattern of negative self-talk. Explore what they tell themselves. If you discover they feel and tell themselves they are stupid, lazy, not good enough, or a failure, use Tool 5-2 Replace Those Ants (Automatic Negative Thoughts) to help them find a positive self-statement. This must be a true statement that they can believe and that is more positive. Teach them to notice when they say "I'm stupid" and replace it with something like "even though I feel stupid sometimes, I am learning to stick with my homework until I understand it." Or, "even though I feel stupid, I did get a good grade on my spelling test." With practice, this shifts their energy and self-image and gradually rewrites their narrative.

*Identify Their Strengths:*   Unfortunately, many clients with ADHD get so focused on their deficits (or differences) that they overlook their strengths. Use Handout 4-4-4 I Am Good At These Things to help clients notice and identify their many strengths. Although ADHD is called an "attention deficit" it is much kinder, as well as accurate, to call it an "attention difference." **A brain with ADHD works differently than a brain without ADHD but not necessarily in a negative way.** Explain that many people thrive and succeed in spite of, and probably because of, their ADHD. Give them Handout 4-4-7 Famous People with ADHD to show them many people who focus on their strengths to be highly successful.

***Change the Channel:***   Help clients replace their chronic anxious or depressed thoughts with thoughts that feel better. Use Tool 11-13 Changing the Channel which is a mindfulness skill that can be used to interrupt the pattern of negative or anxious thoughts by imagining they are "changing the channel" from their worry or sad channel to their happy or calm channel.

***Stress Management:***   Dealing with the challenges of ADHD can be very stressful for clients. Teach them stress management techniques. Use the mindfulness skills to help them calm their stress response.

***Anger Management:***   Clients with ADHD can be volatile and sometimes explosive one moment, then be calm the next moment, while we, their therapist (or parent), are feeling shell-shocked. Explore the client's triggers for anger and the resultant behaviors. Use Handout 4-4-1 How I Feel to help them identify and express their feelings. Validate their feelings. Teach them anger management skills to help them reduce both the anger and the angry behavior. Use play therapy games that teach anger management. Teach them the relaxation breath (Tool 11-4) to calm down their anger. Make a mindfulness glitter bottle (Tool 11-12) with them and practice using it to calm the angry thoughts and feelings whirring around in their head. Teach them to do a quick Body Scan (Tool 11-7) or Mindfulness of Surroundings (Tool 11-5) as soon as they feel angry.

***Mindfulness Skills:***   Use the following mindfulness skills provided in Chapter 11 to help clients calm their worry, bring themselves into the present moment, and reduce negative and anxious thoughts.

- Basic Relaxation Breath: See Tool 11-4

- Mindfulness of Surroundings: See Tool 11-5

- Body Scan for Children and Teens: See Tool 11-7

- Mindful Movement: See Tool 11-9

- Core Practice: See Tool 11-11

***Neurofeedback:***   Neurofeedback improves anxiety and depression. See Chapter 10 for information about using neurofeedback as a treatment for all aspects of ADHD.

**INTEGRATION:**   Guide the client to incorporate these skills into their daily life one at a time. Ask them how they feel now that they know that having ADHD does not mean they are stupid or lazy. Was the client able to identify their strengths? Did they become more aware of their negative self-talk? What channel are they choosing to watch instead of their worry of sad channel?

## Tool 5-2: Replace Those ANTs (Automatic Negative Thoughts)

**BACKGROUND:**    Many kids and teens are already experts at generating a steady stream of automatic negative thoughts. This is particularly true in depression, anxiety, ADHD and trauma. Many of these negative thoughts originate from false core beliefs that get programmed into the brain very early in childhood, ostensibly for survival.

Often, children and teens internalize the negative messages that they receive from their world. A six-year-old boy told me he knew his new ADHD medicine was working because "no one yelled at me all day." Already, at six, he felt bad about himself and experienced negative self-talk. Cognitive behavioral therapy works to identify and change these automatic negative thoughts. Daniel Amen calls these automatic negative thoughts "ANTs" and categorizes them into "species of ANTs" (Amen, 1998). This tool uses Amen's framework to identify automatic negative thoughts (ANTs) and to change the ANTs by replacing them with realistic thoughts that feel better.

**SKILL BUILDING:**    Explain to children and teens that have developed the pattern of automatic negative thinking that in order to get rid of an automatic negative thought (ANT), we must first identify the ANT and then change it to a butterfly by replacing it with a more positive reality-based thought. Review Handout 5-2-1 Species of Automatic Thoughts with clients and help them identify some of their automatic negative thoughts. Help them label their various thoughts by identifying the ANT species. Then help them change the ANT into a butterfly by replacing it with a positive thought that feels better. Read the example from Handout 5-2-2 Change the ANT To A Butterfly and ask them what species that thought is. Then ask them to change the ANT by coming up with a thought that feels better. Encourage them to post the ANT/butterfly graphic on Handout 5-2-3 where they can see it every day to remind them to be mindful of their ANTs and to change them to positive thoughts, butterflies.

**INTEGRATION:**    Ask clients what ANTs they have become mindful of. Help them discover if they have a pattern of negative thinking. What species of ANTs have they identified? Help them identify the species if they cannot. Explore how they have begun to replace the ANTs with thoughts that feel better (butterflies). What have they noticed about how they feel after they change the ANT to a butterfly by replacing the negative thought with a thought that feels better? Where did they post the ANT/butterfly graphic?

# SPECIES OF AUTOMATIC NEGATIVE THOUGHTS (ANTS)

- **All-or-Nothing Thinking:** You see everything as entirely good or entirely bad. For example if you don't do something perfectly, you've failed.

- **Always/Never Thinking:** You see a single negative event as part of a pattern. For example, you *always* lose your homework.

- **Mind-reading:** You think you know what people think about you or something you've done without asking them—and it's usually bad.

- **Fortune-telling:** You are certain that things will turn out badly.

- **Magnification and Minimization:** You exaggerate the significance of minor problems while trivializing your accomplishments.

- **Guilt-beating with "Should" Statements:** You focus on how things *should* be, leading to severe self-criticism as well as feelings of resentment toward others.

- **Personalizing:** You take everything personally.

- **Focusing on the Negative:** You see only the negative aspects of any experience.

- **Emotional Reasoning:** You assume that your negative feelings reflect reality. Feeling bad about your grades means "I'm doing badly and will probably fail this class."

- **Comparative Thinking:** You measure yourself against others and feel inferior, even though the comparison may be unrealistic.

- **Labeling:** You attach a negative label to yourself or to someone else.

- **Blaming:** You blame someone else for your own problems. It's always someone else's fault.

# CHANGE THE ANT TO A BUTTERFLY EXAMPLES
## REPLACE AUTOMATIC NEGATIVE THOUGHTS

| Species | Example | Change ANT to Butterfly |
|---|---|---|
| Always/Never Thinking | *Nobody ever likes me.* | *Jan talked to me today.* |
| Blaming | *It's all your fault I lost my homework.* | *Homework is my own responsibility so next time I will put it in my folder.* |
| Personalizing | *She ignored me.* | *Maybe she ignored me because she was in a hurry.* |
| Labeling | *I'm stupid.* | *I didn't do well on this test, but I got an A in Spelling.* |
| Guilt-beating | *I forgot to feed the cat.* | *I will set an app on my phone to remind me next time.* |
| Mind-reading | *My teacher hates me.* | *Maybe my teacher doesn't know me very well.* |
| Fortune-telling | *I won't finish on time.* | *I am learning to pace myself so maybe I will be done on time today.* |
| Focusing on the Negative | *I got 2 wrong on the test.* | *Yes, but I got 98 of them right.* |

# CHANGE THE ANT TO A BUTTERFLY

Copy the ANT/Butterfly and hang it up where you will see it to remind yourself to be mindful to change negative thoughts (ANTs) to positive thoughts (butterflies).

# Chapter 6
# Tools for Improving Core Symptoms of ADHD

Tool 6-1: Improve Concentration
Tool 6-2: Tame Hyperactivity and Impulsivity

## Tool 6-1: Improve Concentration

**BACKGROUND:**   Poor concentration is the hallmark of the inattentive and combined types of ADHD. Not being able to pay attention is a significant factor in poor academic success, poor task completion, failure to learn, as well as low self-esteem, anxiety and depression. This tool provides strategies to help children and teens improve their concentration and help them be more successful in all areas of their life.

**SKILL BUILDING:**   Explain and teach the following techniques to your clients and/or their parents to help them focus and reduce distractibility.

*Environment:*   Guide clients and parents to set up a distraction- free homework space. Encourage them to simplify the stuff in the client's bedroom and to limit distraction from the TV, computers, tablets, phones and traffic from other family members. See Chapter 22 School and ADHD for information on how to request a distraction-free environment at school.

*Headphones or Earbuds:*   Wearing headphones while doing a task can reduce distractibility. They can be used with or without music to block out sound. Make sure the music is not grabbing their attention but rather providing a sound screen to filter out ambient noise. Avoid listening to a radio station with commercials designed to get your attention. See Tool 9-3 Headphones for a case example where headphones helped a client get her homework done.

*Determine Attention Span:*   Teach older children and teens to recognize the length of time they can hold their attention to tasks. They can set a timer when they start a project or homework and notice how much time has passed as soon as they realize they are distracted. Then encourage them to divide tasks into chunks that do not exceed this time and use an alarm to alert them to take a short break.

*Alarms and Timers:*   Encourage clients to use tools such as alarms and timers to help stay on task. Set an alarm to sound every 15 minutes while doing homework to remind them to re-focus on their homework if their attention has wandered. Set a timer for a few minutes ahead of when they need to have something done or to leave for an appointment. Set an alarm to remind them to do something such as start homework, feed the dog or get ready for bed. Here's a great resource: http://www.timetimer.com

*Distractibility Delay:*   Teach clients to write down distractions when they emerge as opposed to impulsively acting on them.

***Mindfulness Skills:***   Teach clients mindfulness skills that teach their brain to stay focused such as:

- Mindfulness of Intention for ADHD: See Tool 11-3
- Mindfulness of Tasks: See Tool 11-6
- Meditation for Concentration: See Tool 11-10
- Core Practice: See Tool 11-11
- Mindfulness Glitter Bottle Core Practice: See Tool 11-12

***Neurofeedback:***   Teach parents about the benefits of using neurofeedback to improve concentration. See Chapter 10 Neurofeedback.

***Complementary Therapies:***   Explain the benefits of therapies discussed in Section VII.

***Sleep:***   Poor sleep can negatively impact concentration. Use Chapter 21 Assess and Improve Sleep to help clients improve their sleep.

***Zinc and Ferritin:***   Zinc and ferritin are sometimes deficient in clients with ADHD (Brown, Gerbarg, 2012) and (ADDA, 2011). If these are low, supplements may improve attention and cognitive deficits. Encourage clients to have their levels tested. See Section IX Nutrition for the ADHD Brain for more details.

**RESOURCES:**   Visit go.pesi.com/ADHDworkbook for Handout 6A on How to Improve Concentration.

**INTEGRATION:**   Encourage clients and their parents to incorporate these techniques one by one and see which ones make a difference in the client's ability to concentrate and stay on task. Explain that thriving with ADHD requires a multi-faceted solution and the long term inclusion of skills and techniques. How are they staying organized and addressing the various options for improving concentration?

## Tool 6-2: Tame Hyperactivity and Impulsivity

**BACKGROUND:**   Hyperactivity and impulsivity are the hallmark symptoms of the hyperactive/impulsive type of ADHD. Children and teens with hyperactivity move constantly and often have trouble sitting still. They may annoy their classmates or their family with their fidgeting, constant motion and unconscious noises. They interrupt others, have trouble waiting for their turn and do things without thinking. This tool provides techniques and strategies to calm down and reduce the hyperactivity and impulsivity and to help the child or teen gain some control over it.

**SKILL BUILDING:**   Tools for reducing hyperactivity and impulsivity aim first to increase self-awareness and body awareness, then to practice self-control and physical calming. Review the following options for reducing hyperactivity with clients and parents.

***Mindfulness Skills:***   Use these mindfulness skills to improve body awareness, self-regulation and calming.
- Mindful Movement: See Tool 11-9
- Body Scan for Children and Teens: See Tool 11-7
- Balancing Chips: See Tool 11-8
- Mindfulness Glitter Bottle: See Tool 11-12
- Bring Attention To The Present Moment: See Tool 11-14
- Core Practice: See Tool 11-11

**Neurofeedback:**   Use neurofeedback to decrease hyperactivity and improve impulse control. See Chapter 10.

**Sensory Integration:**   Clients with sensory processing issues often look like they have hyperactivity. Use Tool 14-1 Sensory Integration Therapy to explore this further with the client and their parent.

**Food:**   Although the research on the effects of food on hyperactivity is not consistent, food sensitivities can be a significant contributor for some clients. When my own daughter was young she became out of control with hyperactivity when she had certain food dyes, sugar or milk. (I guess she didn't read those studies.) Refer to Chapter 19 and use the Food/Symptom Diary on Handout 19-1-2 to help clients find out if food is a factor for them.

**Mineral Deficiency:**   Several studies have shown a reduction in hyperactivity and impulsivity with zinc supplementation (Bilici et al., 2004). Others show a correlation between hyperactivity and magnesium deficiency (Starobrat-Hermelin, 1997). See Tool 20-1 Common Mineral and Fatty Acid Deficiencies for more information on this and encourage the client's parents to have levels tested.

**Movement:**   Make sure the client is getting lots of exercise and opportunities for movement. Movement has been shown to have a positive effect on the brain (Hillman, 2014) and (Hoza, 2014). Make sure the teacher is not keeping the client in from recess to finish work. They will concentrate better if they get outside and play. See Chapter 15 Movement to Optimize Brain Function.

**Impulse control:**   Children with ADHD often do things without thinking about the consequences. I teach my clients to close their eyes and picture a traffic light with red, yellow and green lights. I tell them that when they first think of doing something or saying something, to stop long enough to picture the traffic light with the red light on. Then while they cautiously consider the consequences of what they are about the say or do, picture the light turning yellow. Then when they make a good choice, they can turn the light green and go ahead and do or say it – or not—whichever was the better choice. This gives them time to stop, think and make a good choice. It only takes a few seconds. There is power in this process.

Another option is to teach your client to consider how they would feel if someone said or did to them what they are about to do or say to someone else. Helping them imagine what others might feel helps them learn empathy. It will help them manage their impulse control and improve their social skills.

Use role play to help clients increase their awareness of how their impulsive behavior impacts others and to practice less impulsive behaviors.

**Complementary Therapies:**   Explain the complementary therapies discussed in Section VII to help parents with other options for decreasing hyperactivity.

**Games:**   Play games that encourage self-control and patience. See Handout 4-3 on Play Therapy.

**RESOURCES:**   Visit go.pesi.com/ADHDworkbook for Handout 6B on How to Reduce Hyperactivity.

**INTEGRATION:**   Explore each of these strategies with the client and their parent. Be prepared to employ a structured process for addressing all of these things. Avoid depending on the parent to do this unless they are obviously very organized. Keep in mind, there is a 75% chance that the client inherited their ADHD from one of their parents.

# Chapter 7

# Parenting Skills Tailored To ADHD

Tool 7-1: Parenting Skills

## Tool 7-1: Parenting Skills

**BACKGROUND:**    Parents need to be involved for ADHD treatment to be successful. The reality is that a child with ADHD is typically more challenging to parents than one without ADHD. This does not mean they are any less sensitive, caring and loveable. It does mean that their parents need to learn how to interact with them in ways that preserve their self-esteem, while helping them accomplish everyday tasks. Children and teens with ADHD often feel like they are not good enough and cannot please their parents. When a therapist works with a child to improve their self-esteem and the child returns to a household where their parents yell at them and their siblings are angry with them, their self-esteem cannot improve. Negative patterns typically evolve over time in families who are dealing with a child with ADHD. Parents often feel angry and overwhelmed with the role of parenting.

Parents need to learn about ADHD to develop and use skills that will help their child succeed. This chapter provides a collection of tools to help parents engage in the process of helping their child with ADHD. Keep in mind that this is not an in depth discussion of all parenting skills but rather, it focuses on those tailored specifically for ADHD.

Remember that ADHD is highly heritable. Some studies suggest that there is a 75% chance that at least one parent of a child with ADHD will also have ADHD (Reitveld et al, 2004). This means that a significant percentage of your client's parents will also have ADHD. Parents often get diagnosed with ADHD when their children are diagnosed. Keep this in mind as you educate them about ADHD and teach them skills. They may have difficulty being consistent, providing structure and following through. They may benefit from receiving their own treatment for ADHD.

Remind parents that their child or teen cannot change in their family system if they keep doing everything the way they have always done it.

**SKILL BUILDING:**

**Expectations:**    Explore what the parent's expectations are for their child or teen. Are these realistic? Help them see the strengths and gifts their child has. Make sure their demands are attainable by their child given their symptoms of ADHD. What do they think success looks like for their child: getting into a good college; having friends; being loving and loveable?

Remind parents that with ADHD their child or teen will most likely:

• Not respond to your first request

• Rarely complete three tasks in a row without getting distracted

• Lose things and forget to do what they are supposed to do

• Interrupt you

• Fidget, make annoying noises and have trouble sitting still

- Be able to watch TV or play video games for hours, but not be able to stay on task for a few minutes when you ask them to do something.
- Have trouble listening
- Have a messy room
- Do things without thinking
- Hate school
- Talk, talk, talk
- Get really angry

Help them understand that these are all symptoms of ADHD and not symptoms of a bad or defiant child. Emphasize that their child or teen can improve these symptoms but will need reminders, site of performance systems and lots of practice.

***Parent Self-Care:*** Although parenting can be incredibly rewarding, it can also be one of the most demanding, frustrating and overwhelming jobs in the world. It can be really hard. Parenting a child who has ADHD can be especially difficult as many of the common parenting methods don't work as well for the child with ADHD. I often see parents who have "tried everything" and feel that nothing works with their child. No matter what suggestions I make, they have already tried it to no avail. They feel powerless, frustrated and guilty. They feel like they are failing. They feel ready to give up, when there is no option to give up.

It is extremely important for all parents, but particularly those with children with ADHD, to learn to take exceptionally good care of themselves. If you have ever flown, you have heard the flight attendant demonstrate how to use the oxygen masks. Remember how they always say "if you are traveling with a child, place the mask over you own nose first and then put your child's mask over your child's nose." The theory here is that if you don't have oxygen soon enough you may pass out and you won't be able to help your children get their masks on. If you take care of yourself first then you will be able to help your children.

The same theory applies to parenting. If you are exhausted, worn out, angry, or at your wits end you will not be in good enough shape to take care of your child effectively. Your child will suffer. But if you take good care of yourself, you will have the energy, emotional stability, consistency, enthusiasm, and love to be a much more effective parent.

Review Handout 7-1 Self-Care for Parents with parents to explore some ways they can take better care of themselves.

***Communication:*** Teach parents how to communicate effectively with a child or teen who is distractible, daydreaming and maybe tuned out. Use Handout 7-2 Better Communication for ADHD to help parents learn and use communication techniques. Demonstrate the techniques for parents and clients. Ask them to practice these techniques in session and help them find what works best for their child or teen.

***Behavior Management/Regulation:*** Help parents learn and practice techniques to teach their child or teen to be responsible for their own behavior. Provide options for dealing with their child's forgetfulness, impulsivity, lack of task completion, lack of motivation and hyperactivity. Use an approach that educates the child rather than punishes them. Reasonable consequences for negative behaviors can be effective, such as Time Out (See Handout 7-3 Time Out – Step By Step) or losing privileges for a short time, such as an hour for young children or the rest of the day for older kids (See Handout 7-4 Sample Consequences/Privileges).

Remember clients with ADHD typically do things impulsively, not deliberately. Help parents teach their children to become aware of their impulsivity and lessen it with gentle reminders and consequences that fit the severity of the behavior. Avoid punishments that are so long clients forget why they are being punished.

Teach parents to "be a robot" when helping their child stop negative behaviors such as talking back, disrespect, angry outbursts, body language (ex. rolling their eyes) or ignoring adult requests. Children and teens with ADHD can be really good at pushing their parent's buttons. If the child sees that the parent is responding emotionally, they now have the edge.

Use Handout 7-5 Be A Robot to help parents practice this technique. Tell them their goal is to stay calm, avoid getting rattled and repeat this over and over until the child stops.

Children with ADHD love to succeed. Most are motivated to earn points, privileges or rewards for positive behavior. Teach parents to choose a few things they would like their child or teen to do such as get ready on time in the morning, do their homework, get their chores done or be kind to their sibling. Then help them create a system of rewards for when their child does any of these things. Make sure they give the reward immediately and avoid telling the child they earned it but not giving it to them. This will defeat their investment in doing well. A simple reward system that is very tangible is to place marbles, cotton balls, or small pom-poms in a jar on the back of the toilet every time the child brushes their teeth or gets ready on time. When the marbles or cotton balls reach a line on the jar, the child earns a reward. Explain to parents that they will need to be prepared with a variety of reward systems as their child becomes either more successful or bored with the current system.

Reward systems can be useful to get children started on creating healthy habits. But eventually they need to be able to sustain the positive behavior without needing the reward. This happens automatically for some children but others slack off as soon as the rewards stop. Some parents have difficulty organizing and following through with a reward system, especially if they also have ADHD. If this is the case for your client, other options may be needed.

Help parents avoid breaking Grandma's Rule. Grandma's Rule states: "Never let the child or teen have the privilege before the desired task is done" (Clark, 2005). Their child will be much more motivated to get something done when they can't do what they want to do until the desired task is done. Saying "You can go to your friend's house as soon as you clean your room" will work way better than "you can go to your friend's house if you promise to clean your room when you get home."

Teach parents to avoid the five reinforcements of ADHD behavior. Their child's behavior may serve (1) to get attention, (2) get accommodations made for them, (3) acquire something they want, (4) avoid doing something or (5) be antagonistic when they are angry. Craig Wiener covers this in detail in his book *Parenting Your Child with ADHD* (Wiener, 2012). Help parents to see what their child gets for behaving the way they do and help them stop reinforcing the negative behavior.

Teach parents to create rituals that make living in their household fun, while still helping their children do what they need to do. For example, when their child whines about going to bed and refuses to go, encourage parents to say something like "Come on, I'll race you to the bedroom and see who gets their first." Or tap into their imagination when they don't want to eat and ask them to pretend they are a rabbit stealing the vegetables from the garden. Tell them "whatever you do rabbit, don't eat that spinach. That's my garden. No, no, no!" Watch them laugh as they delight in eating (ravaging) your garden.

**Use Positive Language:**    Help parents become more aware of the language they use with their child. Encourage them to develop a cooperative rather than coercive relationship with their child (Wiener, 2012).

For example, rather than saying, "You have to do xyz" say "You could do xyz" or "it would help if you do xyz." Or instead of saying, "you can't do xyz" say "it would be better if you do abc." This can be a subtle shift but children with ADHD typically respond well to feeling more in control of what they do. Give them choices. Help them see how doing something helps them or the family. Ask them for their input and suggestions on what they, or perhaps the family, can do differently to solve a problem they are experiencing.

Help parents replace negative statements with more positive statements. Encourage them to tell their child what they can do rather than what they can't, or what they want them to do instead of what they don't want them to do. For example, instead of saying "don't jump on the bed" say "please get off the bed now." Then they will hear "get off the bed" instead of "jump on the bed" as they will tend to ignore the word "don't."

**Avoid Power Struggles:**    Children and teens with ADHD can be masterful at pulling parents into power struggles. No one wins a power struggle. Explain what a power struggle is and help parents recognize when their child is trying to engage them in one. Give them some examples. Teach parents to avoid power struggles by simply refusing to engage in them. Encourage them to give their child choices. In some cases they may need to walk away from the child and go in another room. Show them how they get sucked into the power struggle.

Power struggles typically occur when the child wants something or to do something that the parent doesn't want to allow. For example a teen may want to attend a party. When the parent discovers there will be no chaperone they say "no." Then the teen continues to tell them all their friends are going, no other parent is refusing to let them go, etc. They get angry, they nag. You get the idea. The parent may find themselves defending their position, explaining why they can't go while the teen continues to hound them.

Thus a power struggle ensues. Help the parent recognize when this happens. Encourage them to leave the conversation after stating their decision and to avoid continuing to reply to the teens nagging. Guide them to use the Be A Robot technique (See Handout 7-5) to block the continued nagging by saying "Please stop asking me to go to the party. It is not safe for you to go without a chaperone present." Parents may offer to call the parents of the party host to get more details but chances are the teen will not want this.

**Anger Management:**    Clients with ADHD often have trouble regulating their emotions. They can be intensely angry one minute and fine the next. Help parents manage their own anger so it is not easily triggered by their child's behavior. Then help parents help their child regulate and manage their anger.

Suggest that parents use humor instead of anger to help their child get things done. Humor often works more effectively than anger with children and teens with ADHD. Laughter is a great tool to get them to complete a task, which will reduce their oppositional behavior and help them engage in doing what they are supposed to do. Making things fun helps them know the parent is on their team and lessens their resistance. This will avoid confrontation and power struggles and will teach the child that life can be fun. It will also bring a level of acceptance to the table that children with ADHD so desperately need. Encourage parents to be mindful not to laugh at their child or teen.

**Scaffolding to Build Competence:**    Clients with ADHD often miss important clues and information that they could use to learn skills. Therefore, they may have skill gaps in academics as well as organization, self-regulation and social skills. Teach parents that these skills will need to be taught to their child.

Children learn skills in a progression. For example, a hyperactive child may first need to learn what it means to be hyperactive. Then they may learn to be more aware of when they are being hyperactive. Next they may learn some skills to calm themselves and get their body to be still. Then they may learn how to periodically bring their attention to their hyperactivity to notice it and calm it. In addition they may learn how to exercise regularly to manage their hyperactivity. Review Handout 7-6-1 to help explain the concept.

This is an example of the concept of scaffolding. Beginning skills are built upon to eventually gain mastery. Help parents understand this concept and support their children in gaining necessary skills without expecting perfection when they are just starting.

Another example of scaffolding is: clean the child's bedroom; then clean it with the child for a while; then help the child clean it a number of times, and then ask the child to clean it by themselves using site of performance aids such as a list of tasks and a timer to help them stay focused. They may eventually be able to clean it themselves without the aids but many will continue to need them. Use Handout 7-6-2 to explain.

**Provide Cues:**   Explain to parents that children and teens with ADHD need extra help staying on task and getting things done. Caution them against expecting their child to be able to do more than one chore without needing some cueing to remind them to stay on task and what needs to be done next. Providing cues can be done in the moment by the parent. It can also be accomplished by using a checklist that the client refers to when they are done with each task.

For example, when getting ready in the morning, the parent can post a checklist in their child's bedroom with a list, in order, of everything that needs to be done before coming down for breakfast. This might include: get out of bed by 6:15 AM, wash face, brush teeth, comb hair, get dressed, make bed, bring backpack downstairs, and be ready to eat by 6:45. Or perhaps after school: take Scruffy out for a walk, do homework, set the table for dinner, relax. Sticky notes can also be posted at the site of performance to provide a visible cue for the child. Color-coded index cards on a ring can be used with each card listing the things to be done at a particular time of day. This removes the parent from the interaction and decreases power struggles.

Most children and teens with ADHD will need monitoring and regular cuing. Help parents understand that this is normal and that by giving the child or teen cues and gradually moving to using checklists, the child will gain more autonomy. Remind them of the concept of scaffolding.

**Structure and Planning:**   Children with ADHD like to know what to expect and will do best when their parents provide daily structure. Help the parent incorporate structure into the life of their child to help them thrive with ADHD. This may involve designing a predictable schedule for the child (and family) and helping the child to organize their stuff, their space and their time. See Tool 9-1 Systems for Organizing Time, Space and Activity Use Handouts 7-7-1 and 7-7-2 Activity Planner (or an app) to help parents think about their daily schedule and create a way to organize and keep track of their daily routine, activities and appointments.

Clients with ADHD rarely like surprises and can be discombobulated by unexpected appointments, activities or demands. Keep a family calendar or an app, and talk about what's happening for the day each morning. They might use a white board and write down the schedule for the day with the time and activity. This can be particularly helpful for a day when the kids are home from school with "nothing to do." Then they can remind the kids by saying "now it's time to do xyz." If they are tech savvy they might use an electronic calendar that can sync with every family member's phone.

Explain to parents that doing this will keep their family organized, help their child with transitions, and help their child or teen learn how to organize their own life.

**Avoid Overload:**   In an attempt to prepare children and teens for college, parents often sign their kids up for so many things that they all end up exhausted and on overload. Help parents look at their child's schedule and discuss their motivation in having them participate in each of the activities. Help them work with their child or teen to set priorities and cut down commitments when possible. Make sure there is plenty of time to get homework done every day and lots of totally stress-free, supervised down time for the client to play, make believe, create and rest.

***Supervise:***   Stress to parents the importance of supervising their children as well as teens. Children and teens with ADHD tend to be impulsive and easily distracted which can lead them to get into trouble and to not do what they are supposed to be doing. Parents need to remind kids what they should be doing and avoid leaving them on their own for longer than about a half hour before checking up on them, even if they are doing their homework or playing in their own room. Encourage working parents to hire a babysitter for their children after school, or enroll them in a sport, activity, job or volunteer position.

***Mindful Parenting:***   Explain to parents that mindful parenting is the process of being totally present and in the moment with your child. It is being able to see and accept your child for who they are even if their behavior is making it hard to like them right now.

Explain to parents how being a mindful parent is good for their child or teen with ADHD. Their child will benefit greatly from their mindful, undivided attention. Having a mindful parent will prepare their child for a more successful adulthood. They will feel more secure, have more self-confidence and like themselves more. They will also learn to be mindful in their own relationships.

Explore how being a mindful parent is good for the parent as well. When they are more mindful in their parenting they will enjoy parenting much more. They will notice the beauty and wonder of their child as they grow and develop their personality. They will be more present to the feelings of the moment and experience a much deeper relationship with their child. They will feel less distracted, less overwhelmed and more peaceful.

Explore how they are already being mindful and what they might do to be more mindful. Help them identify how their child or teen benefits from having their parent's undivided attention. Use Handout 7-8 10 Ways To Be A Mindful Parent to help them practice being a more mindful parent.

**INTEGRATION:**   Are the parents involved in their child's or teen's treatment? Are they open to learning skills and making changes that will benefit their child? Which skills do they need the most help with? What positive changes have they made? How is their child or teen responding to these changes? Would they benefit from a parenting class? Are their expectations of their child or teen realistic? How are they managing their anger? Are they able to use positive cooperative language? How good are they at being a robot? How do they feel now that they understand the challenges their child or teen faces? In what ways has their parenting style changed? Are they able to love and accept their child or teen without judgment despite challenging behaviors? Are they taking good enough care of themselves?

# SELF-CARE FOR PARENTS

- Find resources so you can take a break periodically
  - Babysitters, family, trade babysitting with other parents
- Take a break without the kids on a regular basis
  - Daily
  - Weekly date night
- Ditch the guilt
- Share the parenting chores
- Trade sleep-in mornings with other parent
- Build a support system
  - Other parents of ADHD children, family, friends, ADHD parent support group, professionals
- Find someone to talk to
  - Family, other parents, therapist
- Get some help
  - Cleaning, grocery home delivery
- Get regular exercise
- Get enough sleep
- Eat a nutritious and healthy diet
- Develop a meditation practice
- Have some FUN!
  - With children, with partner, by yourself
- Make a list of ways to rejuvenate with and without the kids. Examples:

  - Go for a nature walk
  - Take a warm bath
  - Read a book with a positive story
  - Have lunch with a friend
  - Cook your favorite food
  - Meditate
  - Play tennis or golf
  - Go for a swim
  - Go sailing
  - Go for a bike ride

  - Play a game with your child
  - Spend an hour with your child with nothing planned and see what comes up
  - Go to dinner with your significant other
  - Watch a really funny movie
  - Go to the beach
  - Go float in the ocean
  - Do absolutely nothing
  - Go away for the weekend
  - Write in your journal

# BETTER COMMUNICATION FOR ADHD

- Be sure you have your child's or teen's attention before speaking to them

- Make eye contact before speaking

- Lightly touch the child's or teen's shoulder to get their attention before speaking or asking them to do something

- Ask the child or teen to repeat back what they heard you say to make sure they understood what was being said

- Avoid interrupting them when they have permission to watch a TV show, play a video game or talk on the phone. If they are still watching, playing or talking after the time allotted is up, ask them to stop. If they refuse, simply turn it off or take it away.

- Smile and let them know you love them

# TIME OUT – STEP-BY-STEP

**If your child is between the ages of 2 and 12, time out works great to stop negative behaviors!**

### Find a good location for time out
- BORING – nothing to do but wait for timer
- Bottom step of stairs, on a chair or couch
- No interaction with others

### Define target behaviors – 2 at first, then up to 4
- Time out works to STOP behaviors
    - Whining, talking back, hitting, bad language

### Get a timer
- Put it in child's view so they can see how much time they have left

### When target behavior occurs
- Put child in time out by saying 10 words and speaking for 10 seconds or less
- Name the target behavior
- Example: "You talked back to me. That's a time out"
    - Expect them to stay put but if they don't, place them on your lap facing away from you and hug them
    - Protect your legs and head from getting kicked
    - They typically would rather sit in time out than be restrained

### Set timer
- 1 minute per year of age – example: 6 minutes for a 6-year-old

### Ignore
- DO NOT TALK to them during time out
- Do not make eye contact in time out
- Do not answer their questions
- Let them cry
- Look at their feet. If their feet are safe, you know they are okay

### Ask why they are in time out
- When timer rings ask them why they were in time out
- If they don't tell you, tell them. "You were in time out for talking back to me"
- Move on – do not get stuck here. They served their time out so let it go

# SAMPLE CONSEQUENCES

- Loss of TV for a few hours, a day, or up to a week depending on age and behavior severity. Make the punishment fit the "crime"
- Loss of video or computer games for a day or up to a week
- Loss of cell phone use
- Loss of use of article/toy left outside in the rain
- Loss of an article they lost – natural consequences
- Being grounded – not allowed to leave the house except for school
- Being grounded to their room except for meals and bathroom after school for one day - severe
- Life on hold until child does what is supposed to be done
- Apologize

# SAMPLE PRIVILEGES

- Computer time
- TV time
- Cell phone
- Electronic game time
- Have a friend over
- Go to friend's house
- Stay up later for one weekend night (1/2 hour)

- Schedule one on one time with parent
- Allowance
- Money for fast food or snack
- Money toward a video or computer game
- Money toward a toy
- Points towards a reward (token economy)

# SAMPLE NEGATIVE BEHAVIORS

- Lying
- Stealing
- Talking back
- Disobeying
- Disrespectful language
- Hitting or throwing
- Deliberately mean to sibling
- Inappropriately noisy

- Ignoring parents
- Yelling
- Whining
- Overstepping boundaries
- Forgetting to do something
- Losing items
- Breaking things
- Annoyingly hyperactive

# BE A ROBOT

**Use the "Be a Robot" technique to stop negative behaviors.**

**Make a list of negative behaviors your child or teen has that you want them to stop.**
Examples: Disrespect, hitting their sister, talking back, tantrums, begging, whining, jumping on the bed…

**Think of your favorite robot such as R2D2 or Wally.**

**Get a picture of the robot and post it where you can see it every day.**

**When your child engages in the negative behavior:**

1. Stay calm

2. Talk like a robot: no emotion, monotone voice

3. Name the behavior

4. Ask them to stop the behavior

5. Wait and see if the child stops the behavior

6. If they don't stop repeat from step 1

**Examples: Using a flat affect, monotone voice, no emotion, say:**

"Please don't speak to me that way, it's disrespectful."

"Please keep your hands to yourself. You are hurting your sister."

"Please don't ask me that again."

"Please get off the bed."

"Please take a breath and calm yourself down."

Adapted from Epstein, S. (2012) Over 60 Techniques, Activities, & Worksheets for Challenging Children & Adolescents.

# BUILDING COMPETENCE WITH SCAFFOLDING

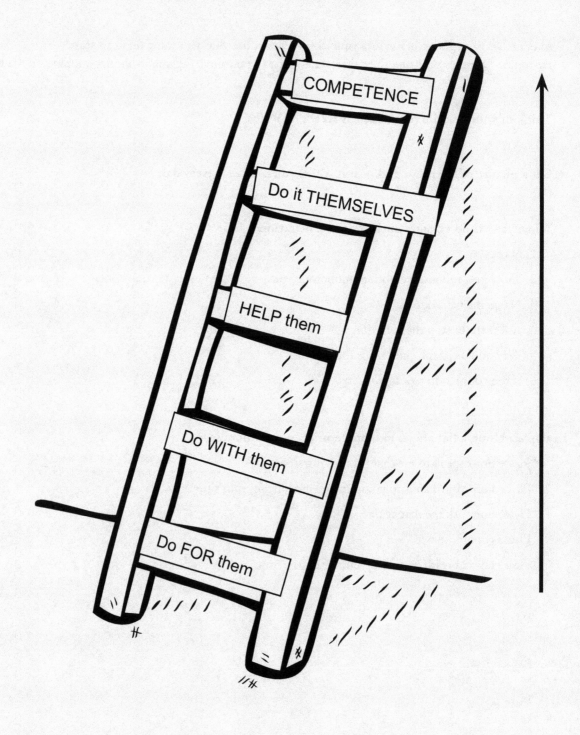

# EXAMPLE OF BUILDING COMPETENCE WITH SCAFFOLDING

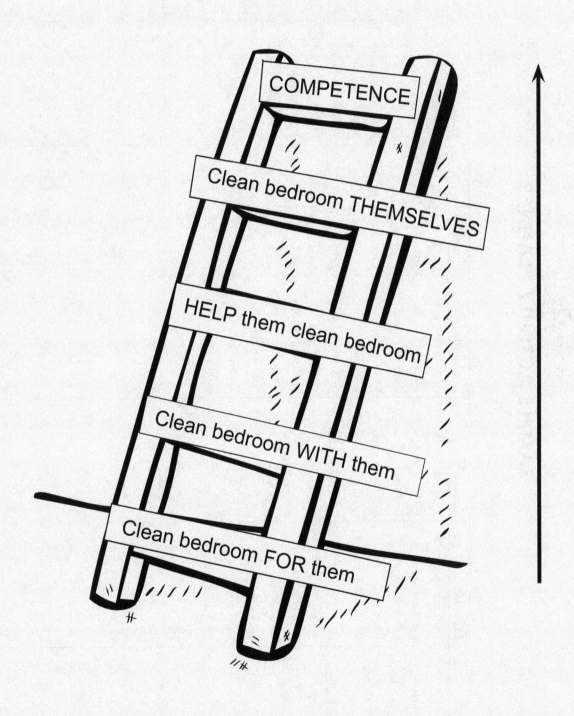

# SAMPLE ACTIVITY PLANNER

| Sunday | Monday | Tuesday | Wednesday | Thursday | Friday | Saturday |
|--------|--------|---------|-----------|----------|--------|----------|
| 9:30 Church | 7:00 get up | 7:00 eat, brush, dress | 6:30 Go for run with Dad | 7:00 eat, brush, dress | 6:30 run with Dad | 9:00 eat, brush, dress |
| 12:00 Lunch | Get breakfast, brush teeth, get dressed | 8:00 bus | 7:00 eat, brush, dress | 8:00 bus | 7:00 eat, brush, dress | 10:00 chores |
| 1:00 Soccer - Jess | | 3:30 swim class | 8:00 bus | 3:30 Snack and free time | 3:30 go to friend house | 11:00 soccer |
| 4:00 Homework | 8:00 Catch bus | 4:15 shower | 3:30 snack and homework | 4:30 Homework | 7:00 arrive home | 12:30 lunch |
| 6:00 Dinner | 3:30 arrive home Snack, homework | 5:00 homework | 5:00 healthy fast food | 6:00 Dinner | Free time until bed | 1:00 free time |
| 7:00 Pack backpack | 4:30 Dance class | 6:00 dinner | 6:00 soccer | 7:00–8:00 TV | 8:30 bedtime | Work on project with mom. |
| | 6:00 Dinner | 6:45 homework | 7:15 shower | 8:00 bedtime | 9:00 lights out | Have friend over. |
| | 6:45 shower | 7:30 TV | 8:00 in bed | 8:30 lights out | | Finish homework |
| | 8:00 read in bed | 8:00 to bed | | | | Go sledding |
| | 8:30 lights out | | | | | Build a fort out of the couch cushions |

# ACTIVITY PLANNER

| Sunday | Monday | Tuesday | Wednesday | Thursday | Friday | Saturday |
|--------|--------|---------|-----------|----------|--------|----------|
|        |        |         |           |          |        |          |

# 10 WAYS TO BE A MINDFUL PARENT

1. **Stop what you are doing and be totally present with you child.** Listen to them. Look them in the eye. Smile at them. Give them your undivided attention. Let them know you think they are terrific. Show them your unconditional love and acceptance. Tune in to what you are feeling.

2. **Ask "What does my child or teen need from me right now?"** At each stage of your child's life and in every moment-to-moment situation it is important to understand what they need from you. Ask yourself: What are the life lessons my child needs to learn? How can I best support my child's growth, self-confidence and ability to have healthy relationships?

3. **Try to see the world from your child's or teen's point of view.** Remember how you felt when you were their age. What stressors do they have that you never had to deal with? How would you feel if you were them?

4. **Write down your expectations for your child or teen.** Are your expectations realistic? Are they in your child's or teen's best interest?

5. **Learn to accept your child or teen exactly the way they are.** Love them unconditionally. Let them know you love them no matter what. Look past their difficult behavior to the beautiful being underneath. They were born good enough.

6. **Understand what your child or teen is feeling.** Validate their feelings.

7. **Avoid the trap of constantly telling your child or teen what to do or how to do it.** Let them learn by doing. Children and teens usually feel criticized and not good enough when even the best intentioned parent tells them to do it a different way.

8. **When correction is required, do it out of love and awareness of what your child or teen needs from you right now.** Be clear, firm, and kind.

9. **Practice mindfulness regularly.** Allow yourself to be still. Be silent.

10. **Take care of yourself so you can be in the best condition to be a mindful parent.** Take a break from parenting periodically even if only to take a walk or a warm bath. Recharge your own batteries so you can be more mindful with your child or teen.

# Chapter 8

# Tools for Teaching Social Skills

## Tool 8-1: Why Teach Social Skills?

**BACKGROUND:**   Children and teens with ADHD may have difficulty with social skills (de Boo and Prins, 2007). In children with ADHD, the social problems are not merely a result of lack of social and problem-solving skills, but rather from a failure to perform those social skills when needed (Wheeler & Carlson, 1994). This may depend on whether the child or teen solely has the inattentive type of ADHD versus impulsive/hyperactive or combined. Therefore, it is important to make sure the child or teen has adequate social skills, knows how to use them and uses them when appropriate. This tool provides guidance on social skills training specific to ADHD.

**SKILL BUILDING:**   Social skills form the backbone of personal and professional success. They help us navigate such everyday interactions such as (a) exchanging greetings and holding conversations, (b) starting friendships and maintaining them, and (c) asking for help and instructing others. They help children and teens with ADHD get along better with peers, avoid being rejected due to their inappropriate and often annoying behaviors, and give them self-confidence that is so often lacking.

Review Handout 8-1 for social skills that often need improvement in children and teens with ADHD.

Techniques for providing social skills training include:

- Teaching specific skills
- Coaching
- Role-playing
- Social skills groups
- Practicing normal social interactions
- Watching videotapes of good social skills and discussing
- Videotaping the client and watching it together and discussing
- Giving immediate corrective feedback about social interactions
- Using behavior management techniques to reward positive social skills
- Practicing ways to settle conflicts

See Tool 8-2 Mindful Greeting, Tool 8-3 Let's Listen Game, Tool 8-4 Role Play Game for Social Skills and Tool 8-5 Play Dates for Social Skills for some specific social skills.

If poor social skills are a major issue for the client, consider referring them to a social skills group. These may be found in the school, community centers or in local child guidance clinics and private psychotherapy practices. The Resource Directory at Children and Adults with ADD (CHADD.org) may contain some local providers.

**RESOURCES:**    Shapiro, L., (2004). *101 Ways To Teach Children Social Skills. A Ready-To-Use, Reproducible Activity Book*

**INTEGRATION:**    Which social skills does the client need to learn? Which ones will make the biggest impact on their social success? What social behaviors do you observe that need improvement? How aware is the client of these behaviors? What techniques have you incorporated to teach them skills? Do they learn the skills but forget to use them? What can you do to help them remember to use the skills they know or are learning?

# SOCIAL SKILLS NEEDED FOR ADHD

**Relating to Others**

Greeting Others

Listening

Joining In

Having Conversations

Making Eye Contact

Sharing

Waiting Your Turn

Offering Assistance

Complimenting

Showing a Sense of Humor

Making and Keeping Friends

Interacting with the Opposite Sex

Maintaining Personal Space

Communicating

Interpreting Social Cues

Reading Non-verbal Communication

Negotiating

Being Left Out

Controlling Impulsivity

Controlling Hyperactivity

Handling Group Pressures

Expressing and Managing Anger

Coping with Aggression

Expressing Feelings

**Social Skill Areas**

Survival Skills

Listening

Following Directions

Ignoring Distractions

Using Appropriate Talk

**Interpersonal Skills**

Communicating

Joining an Activity

Sharing

Asking for Permission

Waiting Your Turn

**Problem-solving Skills**

Asking for Help

Apologizing

Accepting Consequences

Deciding What To Do

**Conflict- Resolution Skills**

Teasing

Losing

Accusations

Being Left Out

Peer Pressure

Adapted from: (Walker, 1988) and (National Association of School Psychologists, 2002)

## Tool 8-2: Mindful Greeting

**BACKGROUND:**   The first step in good social skills for children and teens is to greet one another. This can be done at the beginning of each session or one-on-one as a method to teach social skills, self-confidence and mindfulness of others.

**SKILL BUILDING:**   Use Handout 8-2 Mindful Greeting to teach and practice how to greet another person.

Use the same process with the following modifications to increase social comfort, interaction and getting to know another person.

- Encourage the child or teen to make eye contact when doing the greeting.
- After the greeting ask them to:

  - Name their eye color. Say "I see you have (blue) eyes."

  - Notice something about them. "I see you are wearing a red shirt."

  - Compliment them. "I like your red hair."

  - Tell each other about something you did today while maintaining eye contact.

  - Tell each other what you like to do until you find something in common.

**INTEGRATION:**   Help clients reflect on what this exercise was like for them. Were they shy, embarrassed or comfortable doing this? Did they make eye contact? What did it feel like to tell someone their name? What did it feel like to have someone's undivided attention if only for a moment? Did they learn anyone's name they didn't know? Did they find something in common and if so, how did they feel when they did? Did they speak loud enough for everyone to hear? When might they practice this in their life?

# MINDFUL GREETING

In a group, sit in a circle and ask one of the children and teens to look at the person to their right and say, "Hello, my name is _____. What's your name?"

Then after the person they greeted says their name, the first person will say "Hello, I hear that your name is _____. My name is _____. Nice to meet you."

Then the second person says back "Hello, I hear your name is _____. Nice to meet you, too."

Then the next person in the circle does the same until everyone in the circle has had a turn. Encourage them to look at each other while speaking and listening.

Ask all the kids and teens to listen and raise their hand if they cannot hear the two who are speaking. If a hand is raised, ask them to repeat louder. This will keep everyone engaged while they practice mindful listening.

For an individual client, do the same process between them and you.

## Tool 8-3: Let's Listen Game

**BACKGROUND:**   The ability to communicate is a core social skill and necessary for success in life. Children and teens are often too hyper, impulsive, distracted or tuned out to pick up normal communication skills on their own. This tool provides guidance on teaching an active listening skill.

**SKILL BUILDING:**   Teach active listening skills by explaining that only one person should talk at a time and that it is important to:

- Wait for others to finish speaking before speaking
- Maintain appropriate eye contact while listening or talking
- Learn to stay on topic

Use the exercise on Handout 8-3 Let's Listen Game to practice good listening skills and to listen without interrupting or getting distracted.

**INTEGRATION:**   Does the client have trouble waiting their turn to talk? Do they interrupt others? How has their self-awareness about listening changed since practicing these exercises? How did their listening skills change? Did they have fun with the "talking stick" exercise?

# LET'S LISTEN GAME

**Ask the children or teens what it means to listen. Encourage some discussion.**

**Ask them to describe a time they listened to someone. Or, ask them to listen while you tell them about something you did over the weekend.**

**Ask them to explain what it is like for them to listen to someone.**

- Is it easy?
- Do they get distracted?
- Do they look at the person?
- Do they butt in?
- How do they let the talker know they are listening? (Eye contact, "Um-hmm", "Then what?")
- Do they change the topic?

**Ask them to tell about a time when someone listened to them. Or listen to them and have them answer these questions afterward.**

- Was the person looking at them?
- Did they seem interested? How could they tell?
- Did they butt in?
- Did they ask questions?
- Did they change the subject?

**Let's Listen**

- Tell them that you are going to play a game called "Let's Listen."
- Give one person a "talking stick." This can be anything they can hold in one hand and easily pass to another person such as a pencil, a small toy or stick.
- Explain that in order to talk, they must be holding the "talking stick" and if they want to talk they have to wait for the person holding the "talking stick" to finish talking and hand the stick to them.
- Ask them to repeat back what they heard the person before them say before they talk and see if they were listening and understood what was said.
- Let them pick something to talk about or suggest a topic.
- Keep a tally on a paper or a white board of the number of times a person talked when they weren't holding the "talking stick." With repeated practice, see if the tally decreases.
- Encourage them to look at the person who is talking, make eye contact and notice their body language.
- Discuss what body language they observed and ask what they think the person was saying with their body.

## Tool 8-4: Role Play Game for Social Skills

**BACKGROUND:**   Often children and teens with ADHD have little to no self-awareness about how they behave socially. Role play can be a fun and effective way to increase their self-awareness as well as teach appropriate social skills. This tool provides several approaches to using role play.

**SKILL BUILDING:**   Explain to children and teens that you would like to play a game called "Role Play."

Use the suggestions on Handout 8-4 Role Play Game to help them practice social skills needed in different situations and in different roles.

Tailor the scenarios to situations the child or teen is having difficulty with in their own life plus add in some fun ones.

Help them practice healthy social skills in each of their roles. Play a role that will model good social skills for them when they are in their different roles and when you are pretending to be them.

Make it fun!

> **Case Example:**   *A fifth grader with ADHD would play with LEGOs for 10 minutes chattering away, and never once look at me to see if I was even listening. We made a game out of reversing roles. While he pretended to be me, I pretended I was him and talked on and on while playing with the LEGOs without ever looking at him.*
>
> *He finally said, "how come you're not looking at me?" That was the first time he noticed anything to do with non-verbal communication. After that I asked him to try to figure out how I was feeling about what he was telling me. I asked him to look at my eyes, mouth, face and body posture while he was speaking as well as when he was listening to me. I would look bored and tap my fingers, look out the window, look at my nails, yawn, or act interested and make eye contact with him. By showing him different reactions I let him practice noticing and interpreting my facial expressions and my body language.*
>
> *With practice he got much better at looking at me during conversation and correctly interpreting my reaction. This helped him pick up social cues with his family and at school with his peers and teachers.*

**INTEGRATION:**   What social skills difficulty does the client have that the Role Play Game can help with? Were you able to tailor the scenario to fit their needs? How did you use your role to teach socially appropriate skills? Was the client able to increase their self-awareness by role playing? What social skills did they improve? Was it fun?

# ROLE PLAY GAME

- **Explain to children and teens that you would like to play a game called "Role Play."**

- **Ask them to pretend they are someone in their life such as a teacher, parent, or friend.**

- **Ask them to pretend they are you and you are them.**

- **Ask them to pretend they are in a social situation such as:**

  - Finding a place to sit in the lunchroom at school
  - Trying to join a group playing on the playground
  - Introducing themselves to someone they would like to be friends with
  - Asking the teacher for help
  - Dealing with a peer who just said something mean
  - Sitting with a group of peers
  - Playing with a peer or a sibling
  - Being rejected by a peer or a group at school
  - Sitting in the classroom
  - Doing their homework
  - Reading a book in the library
  - Inviting a friend (or potential friend) over
  - Finding out what they have in common with a peer
  - Feeling frustrated or angry
  - At sports practice
  - In a play
  - At the dentist
  - Meeting the President
  - Having lunch with their favorite movie or TV character

  Note: Tailor the scenarios above to situations the child or teen is having difficulty with in their own life plus add in some fun ones.

- **Help them practice healthy social skills in each of their roles.** Play a role that models good social skills for them when they are in their different roles and when you are pretending to be them.

## Tool 8-5: Play Dates for Social Skills

**BACKGROUND:**    Children and teens with ADHD often have difficulty with social skills and can have trouble making friends. They are often rejected by their peers because they act differently (hyper, impulsive, annoying, tuned out.) This is not always the case, but even so, they need help with social skills. Inviting one peer from school over for a play date can help them in several ways. It can improve their social skills. They can practice getting along with a peer in a safe, friendly, and familiar environment. And when the play date goes well, they will now know a peer who knows them and is likely to be friendly at school. This tool provides a way to make sure the play date goes well and doesn't backfire.

**SKILL BUILDING:**    Encourage parents to help their child develop some friendships by asking one of their classmates to come over for a play date. Use Handout 8-5 Successful Play Dates as a guide for helping them set up a play date that helps their child or teen learn social skills and develop some friendships. Help them find time on a weekly basis to have a play date. A one-on-one playdate will be more likely to succeed than having several children or teens at a time as it prevents triangulation where two children leave the third child out.

> **Case Example:**    *When my daughter was young, we made a list of kids with their phone numbers that she could invite over for a play date. Then we would keep calling until we found someone who could come over to play.*
>
> *The play dates improved her social skills, gave her something fun to do, and helped her create friendships, some of which have become life-long. The kids would have a great time playing. I just kept my eye on them, gave them a snack, and made suggestions if they ran out of ideas for playing. I would also moderate conflict or tension and make sure it went well.*
>
> *She developed a large network of friends and now in adulthood has an amazing social life with healthy connections with many great friends. Sometimes neighbors were surprised when I told them my daughter was an only child because they said there were always two kids in the yard playing whenever they saw her outside.*

**INTEGRATION:**    Was the parent able to identify some peers to invite over? Were they resistant due to time constraints? Were they able to find a time that would work? If they have trouble finding a peer from school to invite, help them brainstorm about peers they know from the neighborhood, church, sports, scouts, social skills groups or support groups. Process what happened after a play date. Was it a success? Did both of the children or teens enjoy it? How has the play date changed social skills? Has it helped create friendships?

# SUCCESSFUL PLAY DATES

**Many children and teens with ADHD have trouble making friends due to poor social skills as well as their symptoms of ADHD. A successful play date can help them develop some friendships.**

- Ask one classmate at a time to come over for a play date.

- If you need help with who to ask, talk to the teacher about who would be appropriate for your child to play with.

- Phone and meet the child's parent if appropriate.

- Include an activity that most every child would love to do to ensure they will come even if they don't know your child or teen well.

- Limit the play date to two hours for young children.

- Supervise closely and provide snacks (check with their parent about food allergies) as well as suggestions for things to do.

- Make it successful so the other child wants to come back again. Help your child (and their guest) share, cooperate and avoid being bossy.

- Hopefully the guest child will then invite your child over but invite them again even if they don't.

- Having a classmate over helps your child at school because then they have someone they know better in their class and that knows them.

- Keep doing it.

- Find someone to invite over at least once a week and keep calling until you find someone who can come.

- Gradually focus on those peers that your child has succeeded in making a good connection with and limit those who create conflict or bad feelings when visiting.

- If no classmates are available or appropriate, look for peers from the neighborhood, church, sports, activities, or other groups they are involved in.

# Chapter 9
# Tools for Improving Organizational Skills

## Tool 9-1: Systems for Organizing Time, Space and Activity

**BACKGROUND:**    Children and teens with ADHD are often particularly challenged by poor organizational skills. They do not seem to assimilate these skills by observing how their parents or teachers organize their stuff or their schedule. This tool provides the framework for providing systems that help children and teens organize their stuff, space, time and after school or weekend activities.

**SKILL BUILDING:**    Find out if the child or teen has trouble with organization and planning and if so, help them identify the areas that challenge them the most. Find out what they have tried before and why it did or didn't work for them. Be prepared to continue to encourage them to use the various tools presented below until their new organizational skills become a habit.

*Time:*    Use Handout 9-1-1 Plan and Organize Time to help children and teens with ADHD organize their time. Avoid overwhelming them with too many things at once. Start with one or two items on the list and help them get that in place before adding others.

Encourage them to get a planner and homework assignment book to keep track of their homework. There are a number of excellent homework and calendar apps available for smartphones that can be found online by searching for "homework app" or "time management for students app." See Tool 22-2 Organizational Strategies for Homework for more information.

*Space:*    Encourage children and teens with ADHD to be mindful of how much stuff they have and encourage parents to help them sort through it and get rid of anything they no longer need or use. Less is more for those with ADHD. Too much stuff is simply overwhelming. Help them pay attention to their backpack, their locker, their desk and their bedroom. Encourage them to find a place for each thing and to put it back their when they are not using it. Help them make this a habit.

Use Handout 9-1-2 Organize Space to help them organize their space. Encourage parents to consider hiring a professional organizer who specializes in working with ADHD to help them set up systems to organize space and stuff and to keep them organized. Search online for "professional organizer ADHD" to find one.

***Activity:*** Encourage children and teens and their parents not to "bite off more than they can chew." Many are overscheduled with after school and weekend activities and sports. Help them prioritize activities and pare them down to a minimum to help them feel less stressed and more successful.

Use Handout 9-1-3 Organize Activity to help them increase their mindfulness of how many activities they have scheduled and what this does to their stress level. Then they can choose the most important things to keep doing. Encourage them to put the family schedule on a family calendar (Handout 7-7-1).

**INTEGRATION:** What areas of organization and planning does the client struggle with the most? Were they able and willing to incorporate new systems to help them organize more successfully? How long is it taking for them to develop new organizational habits?

# PLAN AND ORGANIZE TIME

- Create a daily schedule

- Use a notebook (or app) with a task list (small enough to fit in pocket makes it harder to lose)

- Use a family calendar/planner system to improve organization for school assignments and daily activities. Use Handout 7-7-2 Activity Planner for Household or use an app.

- Use a homework planner app

- Set alarms on smartphone as reminders

- Use a timer to stay on track

- Break large tasks into smaller and more manageable steps

- Create an action plan for overwhelming tasks

- Identify areas that are the most challenging

- Devise and use systems that remove the guesswork

- Use a clock on your desktop that uses a diminishing red disc to graphically indicate time passing (timetimer.com)

- Wear a waterproof programmable watch (don't take it off so you won't lose it)

- Eliminate paper by using tablet to take notes

- Use stylus instead of finger to write on tablet

- Set up backpack before going to bed

- Design a morning routine

- Design an after-school routine

- Design a bed-time routine

- Schedule mealtime

- Minimize and prioritize activities to keep life manageable

# ORGANIZE SPACE

- Get rid of stuff (stuff is overwhelming)

- Make a place for everything to live and put it there when not in use

- Use labels on shelves

- Organize and regularly clean out backpack

- Set up locker and clear it out every Friday

- Keys: find a place to put them and to carry them

- Put a hamper or laundry chute for dirty clothes where you undress and put clothes there as you get undressed

- Store things in cubbies

- Get in the habit of putting things back where they belong as soon as you are done with them

- Grandma's Rule: Let child or teen do an activity they want to do AFTER they clean their room or organize their backpack

# ORGANIZE ACTIVITY

List current activities (include afterschool and weekend). Include the day and time of the activity. After completing the list, go back and rank them in order of priority starting with #1 as the highest priority. Also, rate how much the child or teen enjoys the activity on a scale of 1-10. Do this for each child in the family. Use this process to increase awareness of how much activity is scheduled and to determine which things are the most important for the child or teen and which might be postponed to another time or discontinued.

| Activity | Day/Time | Priority | Enjoys |
|---|---|---|---|
| | | | |
| | | | |
| | | | |
| | | | |
| | | | |
| | | | |
| | | | |
| | | | |
| | | | |
| | | | |
| | | | |
| | | | |
| | | | |
| | | | |
| | | | |
| | | | |
| | | | |
| | | | |
| | | | |
| | | | |
| | | | |
| | | | |
| | | | |
| | | | |

## Tool 9-2: Site of Performance Skills and Systems

**BACKGROUND:**　　The site of performance is the place and time in their natural settings where children and teens with ADHD should use the skills they know, but may not. It can be extremely helpful to place key information and systems at the site of performance that remind them. This tool discusses using systems that can help those with ADHD stay on track.

**SKILL BUILDING:**　　Children and teens with ADHD often need reminders and systems placed where they are doing a task to help them stay on task. This can be accomplished through a variety of ways including setting up their environment to minimize distractions, using rewards to motivate them to stay on track and using any of a multitude of systems to substitute for working memory deficits.

Use Handout 9-2 Site of Performance Systems to help clients (and parents) implement systems at the place of performance that will help them stay on task. Help them identify when and where they are most distracted and help them choose one or two techniques from the list on the handout to help them get started. Then when those are in place, add more from the list. Avoid trying to do them all at once as this will likely overwhelm them. Be prepared to do some problem solving with them to find a system that works for their specific needs.

**INTEGRATION:**　　Does the child or teen with ADHD have trouble with staying on task? What distracts them the most? What has worked for them in the past? Were they able to incorporate some of the ideas from the handout? Which ones helped the most? Were you able to fine tune and tailor the techniques to meet their individual needs?

# SITE OF PERFORMANCE SYSTEMS

**Set up the environment to minimize distractions**
- Remove TV, social media, games, phone, sounds
- Use space with minimum activity or people traffic
- Use study carrel to block out visual distractions
- Use headphones with music to block out noise distractions

**Provide external rewards/motivation**
- Earn a privilege when task is done
- Earn a chip, token and/or praise when each subtask is completed
- Set a timer and try to "beat the clock" while doing a good job on a task

**Put clock on student's desk or on their computer desk top**
- Set a time the task needs to be complete
- Break projects in short tasks (10 minutes or less depending on age)
- Set a timer with an alarm

**Display rules at point of performance**
- List what needs to be done
- List what is allowed and what behavior is expected

**Take frequent breaks**
- Find out how long focus lasts for you
- Set an alarm as a reminder to take a short break periodically within your optimal focus time
- Do some movement to keep the mind alert

**Use systems to stay on track and to substitute for working memory deficits**
- Sticky notes, signs, lists, cards, charts, posters, personal journals, digital recording devices, day planners, personal organizers, computer organizers, Watch-Minder watches, timers, counters, alarms, phone apps: calendar, schedule, organization, to do lists, homework assignments
- Find apps and systems by searching online for "organization apps," "timers," "apps for ADHD," etc.

## Tool 9-3: Headphones

**BACKGROUND:**   Children and teens with ADHD are often easily distracted by sounds and activity in their environment. This tool explains how to use headphones to reduce distraction.

**SKILL BUILDING:**   Encourage children and teens with ADHD to use headphones when they need to concentrate on a task such as a homework assignment. Explore what music would best block out external noise while not grabbing their attention. This will vary from person to person. Often, their favorite music will distract them as they pay attention to it and perhaps sing along with it so this might not be the best choice. Music they are unfamiliar with, instrumental music without words that draw attention, classical music (try Mozart to activate the brain's ability to concentrate), and even sitar music can work. Avoid radio stations with advertisements designed to get their attention. Suggest they try a variety of types of music to discover which ones help them focus the best.

If music is too distracting encourage them to try headphones with no sound playing which may be enough to block out external distracting noise.

Ideally, they might try noise cancelling headphones which do a great job of eliminating external noise. Earbuds may also be helpful but might not filter out as much background noise as headphones. See which work the best for each individual.

Also, they may be able to concentrate better when listening to instructions or schoolwork that is presented on headphones.

> ***Case Example:***   *One of my clients lived in a group home where all eight residents did their homework at the same time at the dining room table. She was severely distracted by the other girls until she started using headphones. Wearing headphones helped her get her homework done and her grades improved.*

**INTEGRATION:**   Was the client able to use headphones and find music that improved concentration on the task at hand? Explore what happened when they used headphones? Were they able to concentrate better and stay on task? What situations are they able to use headphones? Is the school open to allowing them to use headphones in the classroom?

# Section VI
# Treatments That Improve Self-Regulation

# Chapter 10
# Neurofeedback

Tool 10-1: Neurofeedback and the Treatment Process
Tool 10-2: How to Become a Neurofeedback Practitioner

## Tool 10-1: Neurofeedback and the Treatment Process

**BACKGROUND:** Neurofeedback is an effective, medication-free treatment for many brain-based disorders including ADHD that can improve and gradually reduce the symptoms of ADHD. As the research continues to prove the effectiveness of neurofeedback, it is becoming more well-known and parents are searching for it for their children and teens. Neurofeedback is a form of biofeedback that teaches a person to change their brain waves into more normal and functional patterns. Whenever possible, neurofeedback should be included in the treatment plan for anyone with ADHD. This tool provides an explanation of what neurofeedback is and how to find a neurofeedback provider.

**SKILL BUILDING:** Use the following handouts to explore neurofeedback with your clients.

- Use Handout 10-1-1 What Is Neurofeedback to explain what neurofeedback is.
- Use Handout 10-1-2 Typical Neurofeedback Treatment Process to explain what neurofeedback treatment involves.
- Help parents explore the benefits of neurofeedback for their child or teen. Give them resources about the research and how to find a neurofeedback provider.

*Case Example:* *One of my clients was nine when he started neurofeedback treatment with me. He had been kicked out of regular school for violent and aggressive behavior and was attending a psychiatric clinical day school. He couldn't concentrate, his impulse control was poor, he was manipulative, he lied, he was irritable, uncooperative, impatient and couldn't control his anger. All this was true despite taking three psychotropic medications plus two stimulant medications! After 46 neurofeedback sessions over the course of one year he was back in regular school and earned an A+ on his science exam. His neighbors were complimenting him on his behavior, AND he was off all the medications. Then, at age ten, he told me, "Miss Debbie, I have a new life." Two years after treatment ended all his improvements remained intact.*

*Case Example:* *A 15-year-old client struggled with concentration so much that he missed 24 days of school, because he was too anxious to go to school fearing he wouldn't do well. After completing neurofeedback treatment he was attending school every day, organizing and getting caught up on his homework and getting better grades. He was also able to learn and remember dance steps in a play. Additionally, his friends told him he wasn't as annoying to be around anymore since he wasn't so hyperactive and impulsive.*

**Case Example:**    *When my daughter was in elementary school we put her on stimulant medication for her ADHD and her grades improved. When she was 13, we did neurofeedback training. Then we discontinued her medication and her grades continued to improve. In college she was on the dean's list for three years straight!*

## RESOURCES:

- Visit go.pesi/ADHDworkbook for the following online Handouts:
    - Handout 10A Types of Neurofeedback.
    - Handout 10B How to Find a Neurofeedback Provider.
    - Handout 10C Research Summary.
- Thompson, L, & Thompson, M. (2003). *The Neurofeedback Book*, Wheat Ridge, CO: The Association for Applied Psychophysiology and Biofeedback.
- Hirshberg, PhD, L, Chiu, MD, PhD, S, & Frazier, MD, J (2005). Emerging Interventions. Child and Adolescent Psychiatric Clinics of North America. 14, 1-176.
- Demos, J (2005). *Getting Started with Neurofeedback*, New York, NY: W. W. Norton & Company, Inc.
- ISNR (International Society for Neurofeedback and Research) http://www.isnr.net/

**INTEGRATION:**    Does it make sense to add neurofeedback to the treatment plan? What symptoms can be improved? Is the client/parent open to this type of treatment? Do they know anyone who has done neurofeedback treatment? Have they tried neurofeedback previously? In what ways was it helpful? Is there a local neurofeedback provider you can work with? If not, have you found someone who provides home training? Have you considered becoming a neurofeedback provider yourself?

# WHAT IS NEUROFEEDBACK?

**Neurofeedback is an effective, medication-free treatment for many brain-based disorders including ADHD.** It is a form of biofeedback that teaches a person to change their brain waves into more normal patterns. The American Academy of Pediatrics placed biofeedback on its best support treatment strategies list for ADHD based on several neurofeedback studies (American Academy of Pediatrics, 2012).

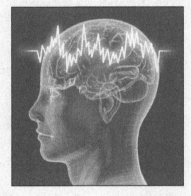

**Neurofeedback is a learning strategy that directly addresses the underlying brain dysregulation present in people with ADHD.** It teaches the brain to regulate itself better. Information about a person's brain wave characteristics is made available to the person in real time via a computer. The person controls a video game without using their hands, just by learning to control their brainwaves.

**Neurofeedback works via the principle of operant conditioning and neuroplasticity.** When the neurofeedback client is successfully changing their brainwaves to be more normal, they get a "reward" which typically consists of beeps, points, game motion or movie being displayed. Within a few moments of beginning to train they are changing their brainwaves. Neuroplasticity is the ability of the brain to change. With repeated practice the brainwave patterns change and remain closer to normal ranges.

**Because neurofeedback training is a learning process, results are seen gradually over time.** For most conditions, initial progress can be seen within about ten sessions with some changes as early as the first few sessions. Initial training goals may be met by twenty sessions. For others, training is expected to take about forty sessions and sometimes more for more complicated brain dysregulation. The total number of sessions needed has been decreasing steadily as more is learned about the brain and the neurofeedback technology has expanded.

**Neurofeedback can help with many conditions.** These include: ADHD, learning disabilities, depression, anxiety, sleep disorders, chronic pain, migraines, sleep disorders, memory, behavioral problems, addictions, traumatic brain injury, seizures, autism, anger, cooperation and much more. It is a great treatment option for ADHD as it improves concentration, calms hyperactivity and impulsivity, and addresses anxiety, depression, sleep and most of the other conditions that are often comorbid with ADHD.

**Studies show that when enough neurofeedback has been completed, the improvements gained will persist after the treatment ends.** A meta study on the efficacy of neurofeedback treatment in ADHD stated that "it can be concluded that the clinical effects of neurofeedback are stable and might even improve further with time." (Arns et al, 2009)

**Resources:** Robbins, J (2008). *A Symphony in the Brain: The Evolution of the New Brain Wave Biofeedback.* New York, NY: Grove Press.

Larsen, S (2012). *The Neurofeedback Solution: How to Treat Autism, ADHD, Anxiety, Brain Injury, Stroke, PTSD, and More.* Healing Arts Press, Rochester, VT.

Swingle, P. (2010). *Biofeedback for the Brain: How Neurotherapy Effectively Treats Depression, ADHD, Autism, and More.* Rutgers University Press, Piscataway, NJ.

# TYPICAL NEUROFEEDBACK TREATMENT PROCESS

**Before neurofeedback training begins, an initial intake interview is done to obtain a description of symptoms, health history, and family history.** Often a QEEG (brain map) is recorded. A QEEG is a classic EEG, often reviewed by a neurologist, and then compared to a data base of 'normal' brainwaves. (See Tool 2-3 QEEG) A statistical analysis is done that shows exactly what parts of the brain are and are not working properly. Research has identified typical patterns that occur in ADHD, learning disabilities, depression, and anxiety (and more).

**A computerized continuous performance test (CPT) might also be administered which provides information about how the brain is regulating itself.** The TOVA and the IVA are two popular tests. See Tool 2-4 TOVA and IVA.

**The QEEG and CPT results combined with the clinical assessment are combined to select neurofeedback training protocols that indicate where to place sensors and what brainwaves to increase or decrease.** Neurofeedback training is then done to make these specific areas of the brain more normal which in turn normalizes symptoms.

**Traditional neurofeedback training is a painless, non-invasive procedure.** One or more sensors are placed on the scalp and one on each ear. The brain waves are then displayed on a computer in an EEG video display as well as by means of a video game. The person operates the video game with his brain. No hands! As desirable brainwave activity increases the person is rewarded by the video game moving faster, scoring points, and hearing beeps. Some systems use a movie as feedback.

**Gradually, the brain responds to the feedback that it is given and a "learning" of new brain wave patterns takes place.** The new pattern is one which is closer to what is normally observed in individuals without such conditions or disabilities. Symptoms gradually improve as the brainwaves become more normal.

**Ideally neurofeedback sessions are scheduled at least twice per week.** Since neurofeedback is a learning strategy the brainwaves change during each session but then the change needs to be reinforced until it persists. Some practitioners schedule sessions every day. The more often neurofeedback is done, the fewer total sessions are generally required.

**Neurofeedback targets the specific areas of the brain that are not working properly and teaches the brain to normalize brain-wave activity.** Studies show that it has the ability to teach the brain to self-regulate to the point that symptoms of ADHD are decreased and sometimes eliminated and may continue to improve even long after treatment has ended.

## Tool 10-2: How to Become a Neurofeedback Practitioner

**BACKGROUND:**    Many clinicians wonder about what is involved in becoming a neurofeedback practitioner. This tool provides information on what training is typically involved as well as requirements to become certified.

**SKILL BUILDING:**    There are a number of training programs available, often offered by the vendors of the neurofeedback hardware and software systems. Although the programs vary, in order to purchase a system most require that the provider already be (or be supervised by) a licensed health care practitioner in psychiatry, psychology, social work, counseling, nursing, physical therapy, occupational therapy, rehabilitation, chiropractic, recreational therapy, physician's assistant (with certification or license), exercise physiology, speech pathology, music therapy, or sports medicine.

Before choosing a training program it is wise to think about certification and make sure the program will meet the requirements of certification. Certification provides credibility, ensures proper training, validation of your skills and knowledge and professional satisfaction. It also helps to promote the field of neurofeedback.

Typical certification requirements include 36 hours of didactic neurofeedback coursework, contact hours with a mentor to review personal and client neurofeedback training, a human anatomy/physiology course and a written exam.

BCIA's neurofeedback certification is the only program that is recognized by the three major international membership organizations: the Association for Applied Psychophysiology and Biofeedback (AAPB), the Biofeedback Foundation of Europe (BFE), and the International Society for Neurofeedback and Research (ISNR). BCIA's neurofeedback certification is based on a reading list, *Blueprint of Knowledge, and Professional Standards and Ethical Principles*. It is important to choose a certification process that does not depend on a specific vendor's equipment, databases and protocols.

Besides getting the training you will need to purchase neurofeedback equipment to use in your office with clients. This typically consists of a neurofeedback computer program, a computer, monitor(s), amplifier, sensors and supplies such as alcohol and cotton wipes.

Although the learning curve can be steep, the rewards are great when you can help a client re-regulate their brain and significantly improve their symptoms.

**RESOURCES:**    Visit go.pesi/ADHDworkbook for Handout 10D Neurofeedback Training, Certification and Equipment.

**INTEGRATION:**    Have you thought about becoming a neurofeedback provider? How would it impact your current practice? Could you add it to your work setting? What clients do you have that could benefit from neurofeedback? How long would it take to pay for the equipment? Would you like to provide and supervise home trainers? How would you charge for it?

# Chapter 11
# Mindfulness Skills for Children and Teens with ADHD

Mindfulness has been found to be effective for helping children and teens with ADHD improve concentration, decrease hyperactivity, improve social skills and emotion regulation, as well as decrease anxiety and depression. This chapter includes a variety of mindfulness skills that are particularly helpful for ADHD. Please also refer to my book *Mindfulness Skills for Kids & Teens: A Workbook for Clinicians and Clients with 154 Tools, Techniques, Activities and Worksheets* for a full selection of mindfulness skills, all of which are helpful for ADHD.

Although the mindfulness skills presented here are not based on religious practices, follow appropriate ethical practice by getting specific consent from parents to ensure that teaching mindfulness to their child doesn't conflict with religious or other belief systems of the parent.

## Tool 11-1: Define Mindfulness

**BACKGROUND:**   Most children and teens have no real concept of what mindfulness is or how it could help them. Their parents may not know much about it either. Therefore, it is important to use a simple, basic definition to introduce the concept. As clients use more of the tools in this chapter, they will develop their own personal understanding of what mindfulness means to them and will be able to explain it to you and others. This tool provides several definitions of mindfulness as well as my own simple version that I use with kids.

**SKILL BUILDING:**    Start by asking your client what they think mindfulness is. Review the three definitions in Handout 11-1 Mindfulness Definitions and choose the one that fits your client best. Then use the chosen version to explain what mindfulness is. Break down whichever one you choose and go over each component of the definition. For example with Kabat-Zinn's definition, start with "paying attention to something." This can be anything you choose to pay attention to. It often begins with paying attention to the breath, but it could also be paying attention to your surroundings, doing homework, eating, washing the dishes, your thoughts or emotions, taking a shower, your physical body, or even your parent, teacher or friend. Then go over "in a particular way" and discuss what that means. For example, focusing your attention, closing your eyes and going within, looking at something, listening, tasting, smelling or touching. Next, discuss "on purpose," which simply means that you set the intention and decide to pay attention to this specific "something." "In the present moment" means right now, while dismissing thoughts of the past or future that arise in the present. "Non-judgmentally" means without comparing, judging, or criticizing yourself or what arises while paying attention.

Caution: Many teens are totally put off by the word "meditation," picturing a process of sitting completely still with no thoughts for 20 or 30 minutes. This is a totally overwhelming and unbearable concept for many, especially if they have ADHD or experience anxiety. I typically use the word "mindfulness" and consider meditation to be one of the skills of mindfulness. Most of the mindfulness tools included here teach the process of gradually becoming better at dismissing distracting thoughts and gaining the ability to "meditate." Start small, where the client is, so you don't turn them off to the process. Most of the mindfulness skills in this workbook do not require sitting still for long.

**INTEGRATION:**    Initiate a discussion with your client about their reaction to hearing this definition. Ask them to think of examples of how they might do each part of the definition. For example, ask them to choose something to pay attention to. Ask them how they will focus on it (visual, auditory, tactile senses, etc.) Discuss how once they've set the intention to focus on something, they can then focus "on purpose." Ask how they would stay in the present moment. Discuss judgment and how we all commonly do it, and what it feels like not to judge. Give them examples of being judgmental. Ask them to write their own definition of mindfulness in words that resonate with them.

# MINDFULNESS DEFINITIONS

**Mindfulness Is:**

Paying attention to
something, in a paticular
way, on purpose
in the present moment,
non-judgementally
(Kabat-Zinn, 2003)

Paying attention
to your life,
here and now,
with kindness
and curiosity
(Saltzman, A, 2011)

Being aware
of what's happening
as it's happening
(Kaiser-Greenland, 2006)

Paying attention
to what's going
on right here,
right now, inside of us
or outside of us.
(Burdick, 2013)

## Tool 11-2: Connect Mindfulness Research with Benefits for Client's Condition

**BACKGROUND:**    Despite the fact that many mindfulness practitioners resist setting an intention for any specific result from practicing mindfulness, I have found that helping the client connect the benefit with the practice makes them much more likely to incorporate mindfulness into their lives. Best practice for clinicians also guides us to define treatment goals and track progress, which this tool assists in doing.

Kids tend to accept and participate in mindfulness more readily than some teens, because teens need more understanding of "what's in it for me" for them to "buy into it." See the Confidentiality and Engagement and Buy-in section in Chapter 4, Psychotherapy for ADHD for help with this issue. Use this tool to help older kids, teens and parents understand how practicing mindfulness might help their specific condition.

**SKILL BUILDING:**    Mindfulness has been shown to improve:

- Attention
- Hyperactivity and impulsivity
- Emotional regulation
- Anxiety and depression
- Anger

- Social skills
- Working memory
- Planning and organization
- Self esteem
- Sleep

With the client and parent, look through the list of benefits of practicing mindfulness and find those that pertain to the conditions(s) the client is dealing with. Help them understand how mindfulness practice might be beneficial for them. Ask them if they would be willing to learn some mindfulness exercises like those done in the studies if it would decrease their symptoms. This helps them make a commitment to giving this a try. Use language appropriate to the age of the child. Simplify this step for very young children by using words like "relax our bodies," "calm our busy brains," "smile more," "help us worry less or be less afraid" and "feel happier."

**RESOURCE:**    Visit go.pesi/ADHDworkbook for Handout 11A on Mindfulness Research for Kids and Teens.

**INTEGRATION:**    Explore client and parent understanding of how mindfulness may be helpful to them. Answer questions. Give examples from research and from your practice. This is a good time to write treatment goals with the older child or with the parent. List the specific symptoms they want to improve that mindfulness might positively impact. See Chapter 3 for guidance on defining treatment goals and tracking progress. This sets up the process for monitoring progress and helps ensure accountability during the therapeutic process.

## Tool 11-3: Mindfulness of Intention for ADHD

**BACKGROUND:**    Setting an intention is a first step in any activity or discipline including mindfulness practice. Since not being able to pay attention and being distracted are major issues for clients with ADHD, learning to set an intention can help clients stay on task. It is important for children and teens to learn that in setting an intention they decide what they intend to pay attention to. Doing so helps them to stay focused on a specific goal or task. Most clients have not developed a habit of setting an intention.

In mindfulness we must set an intention every time we practice. For example in the Basic Relaxation Breathing Tool 11-4, we must first set an intention to pay attention to our breath. In the Mindfulness of Tasks Tool 11-6, we set an intention to pay attention to the task at hand such as doing homework.

This tool provides a structured method for helping children and teens define their intention and clarify why they set that particular intention and what they hope to gain from achieving it.

**SKILL BUILDING:** Start by talking about what an intention is. Simply put, an intention is something you plan to do. Use some examples from the present moment to illustrate what an intention is. For instance: "I intend to look at your eyes while I speak to you," "I intend to put my pencil away where it belongs," "I intend to pay attention to doing my homework," "I intend to brush my teeth."

Ask them to name some intentions they might have for the rest of the day. Do they intend to go home after this? Do they intend to eat dinner? When do they intend to do their homework? Who do they intend to talk to tonight? What time do they intend to go to bed? This can be done with kids as young as age five.

Explain to older children and teens that the following exercise provides them with a structured way to figure out what their intention is and why it is important. Ask clients to define an intention and answer the questions provided in Handout 11-3 Mindfulness of Intention. Review the examples on the handout with them. Explain that they will improve their ability to stay on task and complete tasks by setting an intention before they start. This process will help them set an intention and clarify what they are trying to accomplish and why it is important to them.

Remind them that they can use this process for any task or goal such as doing their homework, getting a good grade on a test, sitting still, being on time, or getting ready in the morning.

Once they have set an intention, then every time they notice that they are off-task from what they set as their intention, they can refocus back to the intended task.

**INTEGRATION:** You can help clients reflect on what this process was like for them. Ask them: What was it like to answer the questions? What thoughts or emotions came up for you? Did this exercise help you know why you set an intention to do something like mindfulness or homework? Were any of the questions hard to answer? How will you remind yourself that you set this intention and get back on track if you get side-tracked? What other intentions might you use this process to clarify? Does setting an intention help you stay on task?

# MINDFULNESS OF INTENTION FOR ADHD

**Setting Intention**

**Decide what your intention is. Ask yourself, "What do I want/need to do?"**

To understand why you are setting a particular intention, ask yourself:
- What am I trying to accomplish?
- Why I am I doing this?
- What is the purpose?
- Why do I want this?
- What is my objective?

**Examples for ADHD:**

**Set your intention to pay attention to something in particular.** (Ex. homework)
- Ask: Why do this?
  - To be able to stay focused
  - Reduce daydreaming
  - Avoid distraction
  - Stay more organized
  - Finish tasks
  - Get homework done on time
  - Re-wire my brain to pay attention more easily

**Set your intention to sit still for longer periods of time without getting up.**
- Ask: What is the purpose of this?
  - Reduce hyperactivity and sit still when I need to
  - Reduce distraction
  - Enjoy a whole movie without getting up
  - Sit still in class without feeling antsy
  - Get work done more quickly
  - Stop fidgeting—which annoys my teacher

**Examples for Depression:**
- **Set your intention to notice and dismiss negative thoughts.**
  - Ask: What am I trying to accomplish?
    - Improve mood and feel happier
    - Reduce negative thinking
    - Re-wire my brain so I feel good most of the time

**Examples for Anxiety:**
- **Set your intention to change the channel when feeling anxious.**
  - Ask: What is the purpose of doing so?
    - Replace anxious thoughts with calmer more pleasant thoughts
    - Find thoughts that feel better
    - Reduce anxiety
    - Feel calmer
    - Re-wire my brain to feel calm and less stressed

## Tool 11-4: Basic Relaxation Breath

**BACKGROUND:**　The Basic Relaxation Breath is a great way for children and teens with ADHD to increase their ability to focus their attention and to instantly calm their mind and body. By changing our breathing pattern we indirectly change our physiology.

When we breathe in, or inhale, we activate our sympathetic nervous system, which activates our physiology as well as our stress response. This is often called the "fight or flight" response. When we activate our sympathetic nervous system, our heart rate increases, pupils dilate, blood vessels constrict, sweat increases, and the digestive system slows down. We become more alert and overall tension increases.

When we breathe out, or exhale, we activate our parasympathetic nervous system. The parasympathetic nervous system is responsible for the "rest and digest" activities that occur when the body is at rest. Therefore, when we exhale, our heart rate slows down, intestinal and glandular activity increases, and we generally feel more relaxed.

The practice of focusing on breathing leads to reflective rather than reactive responses. It gives kids control over their responses so they respond rather than react.

**SKILL BUILDING:**　Explain that inhaling or breathing in revs us up and exhaling or breathing out calms us down. Use Handout 11-4 Basic Relaxation Breathing to explain the relaxation breathing technique. Demonstrate the technique, and do it with clients.

If they tell you they already know how to breathe this way ask them to show you how they do it. This is important because often kids have been taught to take a few deep breaths to calm down. However, they tend to take a huge, rapid in-breath, which activates the stress response instead of deactivating it. In my experience, every child that showed me that they already knew how to breathe to calm down did this. Observe them periodically as it can take some weeks for kids to learn this. Teaching their parent how to do it will help the parent de-stress and also get them involved in reminding the child or teen to use the skill and help them do it effectively.

Encourage clients to practice this breathing technique several times a day and to us it any time they realize they are distracted to bring their attention back, or when they are revved up, hyperactive, anxious or stressed out to calm them.

**INTEGRATION:**　This breathing technique quickly calms the physiology of the body and brain. Once children and teens get the hang of doing this skill properly most feel calmer and less anxious within two to three breaths. This is a great place to start most mindfulness exercises and is the basis for the core practice. By practicing this breathing technique, the client will effectively lower their stress response and anxiety, and improve their physical, emotional, and cognitive health. In addition, it will gradually train their brain to pay attention better. Caution clients to inhale slowly while counting to four instead of taking a rapid inhale, which may increase the stress response instead of calming it down.

# BASIC RELAXATION BREATHING

**The Basic Relaxation Breathing technique is very helpful in deactivating the stress response, and can really help kids and teens calm down hyperactivity, anger and anxiety, as well as improve concentration.**

It consists of breathing in through the nose to the count of four and breathing out through the mouth to the count of eight. Thus, we activate the parasympathetic nervous system twice as long as the sympathetic nervous system with a net result of calming our physiology and stress response.

Teach them this simple technique and encourage them to use it during their day as often as they think of it, particularly if they are hyper, angry, stressed out, worried, or distracted. It is an excellent way to increase their ability to self-regulate.

✓ **Breathe** in through your nose to the count of four and out through your mouth to the count of eight. When you breathe out, purse your lips and blow gently like you are blowing a big bubble. This will help you slow down the exhale. Don't worry if your nose is stuffy, just breathe in and out through your mouth instead.

✓ **Inhale** through your nose: 1-2-3-4.

✓ **Exhale** through your mouth with lips pursed, blowing gently, like blowing a bubble: 1-2-3-4-5-6-7-8."

✓ **Repeat** 3–4 times.

Be sure to observe them when they are learning this to make sure they are breathing in slowly and then breathing out twice as slowly. Often, kids will inhale very rapidly to get a big breath. This is counterproductive and may activate them instead of calming them.

## Tool 11-5: Mindfulness of Surroundings

**BACKGROUND:** One of the basic concepts of mindfulness is to increase the ability to be aware in the present moment. This can include self-awareness of body, breath, thoughts, emotions, sounds, smell, and touch. This is particularly helpful for clients with ADHD as it provides a way to bring their attention back when it has wandered. This provides a three-fold benefit:

1. It gives them practice paying attention to their surroundings (or any chosen target of attention) instead of being tuned out and unaware.
2. It gives their brain practice with paying attention which gradually strengthens their ability to do so.
3. This skill is very calming and will help reduce the activity of their "monkey mind" and calm their hyperactivity.

This tool provides a method for leading children and teens to pay attention to what's around them and to stay focused on the present moment.

**SKILL BUILDING:** Older children and teens will benefit from an explanation that this brief mindfulness meditation teaches the ability to stay totally present in this moment, which will help them stay focused, and less distracted or hyperactive. Engage in a discussion about what the present moment is. Ask them to describe the present moment. With younger children, just do the process and then help them reflect on what it was like for them (see below).

Explain to clients that although you will be asking questions, you don't want a verbal response. Explain that clients should just listen to the questions and answer them in their head as they explore their surroundings. Tell them it is normal to be distracted and for thoughts to wander and that as soon as they notice this has happened they can dismiss the thought or distraction and bring their attention back to being aware of their surroundings.

Read Handout 11-5 Mindfulness of Surroundings aloud to lead the client through a guided Mindfulness of Surroundings meditation. Use the same process in any room but change the statements slightly to reflect what is actually in the room. You might say "pay attention to the wall in front of you. Now pay attention to the windows (or pictures, etc.) on the wall." You can do the same process outdoors just noticing the sky, the trees, the grass, or whatever is there.

Encourage kids and teens to practice a brief version of this skill when they are waiting for the bus or when they first arrive in new surroundings such as when they get to school or their part-time job (teens), a store, a friend's house, the movies, each time they change classes, or perhaps when they sit down to do their homework. This skill will help them transition, calm themselves and bring their focus to their present surroundings and the task at hand.

**INTEGRATION:** Ask your client what happened for them during the meditation. Ask them: What did you notice? Did you notice anything new in the room that you never noticed before? How did your body feel? What was going on in your mind? Was it hard to pay attention to the room? Were you distracted and if so, by what? How did you bring your attention back to your surroundings?

# MINDFULNESS OF SURROUNDINGS

**Find yourself a comfortable position in your chair with feet flat on the floor, back resting gently against the back of the chair, thumb and middle finger connected in a loop, and hands resting gently palms up on your thighs. Keep your eyes open and look at what is around you in the room.**

**Look all around.** Pay attention to what you see. Is it bright or dark? Are you alone or with others? Are there windows in the room? Can you see outside? Can you see the sky? Is there light, or sunshine shining in the window? If so, does it light up an area on the floor or the wall? Or if it's dark outside can you see lights or the moon?

**Look at what is in front of you.** Is there a wall, door, window, curtains, artwork, light switches, furniture, or bookshelves? What is beside you? Can you see behind you? Look all the way around you. Observe. When your mind wanders, notice it, accept it, and then bring your attention back to looking around the room again.

**Notice the temperature around you.** Is it warm, cold, just right? Is the air moving or still? Do you smell any odors or smells? Are they comforting or distasteful? Are they new smells or are they familiar?

**What can you hear?** (Pause) Is it quiet? If there is noise what sounds are there? Where are they coming from? Are they loud, soft, sharp, soothing, or annoying? Do you want to keep listening to the sounds or do you want them to stop?

**Is anything moving in the room?** What is moving? What is staying still? Are things moving through the room, coming and going?

**Pay attention to your body sitting in the chair.** Feel where your bottom is touching the chair. Is the chair hard, soft, cushiony, or solid? Is the back supporting your back? Is the chair too big for you? Do your feet touch the floor or swing above it? Do your knees bend at the edge of the chair? Do you fill the seat side to side?

**Look around and find something that particularly attracts your attention.** Notice what shape it is, where it is located, what color it is, its texture, its purpose. Observe why it draws your attention. Does it remind you of something else? Do you know what it is? Is it common, or unusual? When you notice you are not thinking about the room around you and about this present moment, notice these thoughts, accept them, and let them go. Tell them, "not now." Bring your awareness back to your surroundings.

**Become aware of yourself in this space.** How do you feel? Do you feel safe? Do you want to be here? Does this place feel familiar or does everything seem new to you? Have you been someplace else that reminds you of this place? Do you feel good, bad, or neutral here?

Now that you have spent some time completely focused on being in this moment, bring the awareness you have gained back with you as you resume your regular life. Practice this exercise whenever possible to keep yourself present in the moment. You will concentrate better, get more done more quickly and feel calmer.

## Tool 11-6: Mindfulness of Task

**BACKGROUND:**    One important aspect of mindfulness involves being mindful of doing tasks while doing the tasks. This differs from more formal sitting mindfulness meditations in that it is a skill that children and teens with ADHD can incorporate it into their daily routine. It can be done while doing any task or activity. Practicing mindfulness while engaged in daily activities helps with concentration (and therefore memory), efficiency and stress. This tool introduces the concept of being mindful while doing any task.

**SKILL BUILDING:**    Explain to clients that mindfulness of tasks simply means paying attention to what they are doing while they are doing it. As soon as they notice that their mind has wandered (that's normal), they should gently return their attention to the task at hand. Describe how they can practice this skill no matter what they are doing during the day. Ask them about what a task is and then what tasks they do. Some examples are brushing their teeth, eating, washing their hands, taking a shower, going for a walk, doing homework or chores, washing the dishes and getting ready for bed.

Ask the client to close their eyes and imagine they are brushing their teeth. Read Handout 11-6-1 to them. Then help them pick a few tasks they routinely perform during each day such as brushing their teeth and encourage them to use this technique to practice being mindful while doing them.

Use the Dots Concentration Game on Handout 11-6-2 to help clients increase awareness of being off-task and to practice staying on task. Encourage older children and teens to use a timer to figure out how long they can easily stay focused. It may be useful for them to break their homework into chunks that take about that long to complete.

**INTEGRATION:**    Help clients reflect on what it was like to pay such close attention to every detail of a task such as brushing their teeth or drawing. Did their mind wander? Tell them that with 60,000 thoughts a day it's perfectly normal for their mind to wander. Were they able to notice that it wandered and bring their attention back to the task? Ask them what task they practiced being mindful of during the week. What did they notice about their ability to pay attention? Did they do a better job while being mindful? Was it easier to remember what they did? Was their mind calmer as it turned off the busy distracting chatter while they practiced being present? Did they notice any change in their stress level, worry, or ability to stay on task? With practice, is it getting easier to stay on task?

# MINDFULNESS OF TASK

**No matter what task you are doing, you can be more present and aware of the moment by practicing mindfulness of tasks.**

1. Set your intention to do a task.
2. Simply pay attention to what you are doing.
3. As soon as you notice that your attention has wandered and you are paying attention to something else, gently return it to the task at hand.
4. Repeat this process until the task it done.

Here's an example. Use this process no matter what task you are engaged in.

**Mindfulness While Brushing Your Teeth**

- Close your eyes and pretend that you are going to brush your teeth.
- Imagine that you are standing in front of the bathroom sink.
- Look at yourself in the mirror and slowly take a deep belly breath and sigh as you exhale.
- Pick up your toothbrush from wherever it lives.
- As you hold the handle of the toothbrush, pay attention to how it feels in your hand. Is it hard, squishy, warm, cold, sticky, smooth, or rough?
- Now put the toothbrush under the faucet and turn on the water.
- As you do so, notice how the faucet handle feels on your fingers. Is it cool, hot, slippery, smooth, or sticky? Is it shiny or dull? Is it covered with drops of water?
- As the water starts to run into the sink, look at it for a moment. What does it look like? Is it a steady stream? Is it bubbly? Is it dripping or rushing out? Is it going quickly down the drain or starting to fill up the sink?
- Place your toothbrush under the water and notice how your hand feels as the water flows over the toothbrush. Did your hand get wet? What sound do you notice with the water running?
- Pick up the toothpaste container. Notice how much it weighs. Pay attention to how it feels in your hand. Is it warm, cold, smooth, rough, sticky? Is it hard, stiff or flexible?
- Open the toothpaste tube and smell the toothpaste. What do you notice about how it smells? Is it a fresh smell? Is it minty or some other flavor?
- Notice how your hand feels on the toothpaste tube as you put some toothpaste on your brush. Pay attention to the toothpaste as it glides onto the brush. What color is it? Can you smell it?
- Notice how your mouth feels as you put the toothbrush into your mouth and start to brush your teeth. Is there a tingling sensation from the toothpaste? Is your mouth full of toothpaste bubbles? How do the bristles feel on your teeth? How about on your gums or your tongue?
- Now notice how your mouth feels as you rinse it out with water. Run your tongue around your teeth. Do they feel clean, smooth, rough, jagged, bumpy or slippery?
- Pay attention to how the brush looks as you rinse it with water.
- Notice how your hand feels as you put the brush and the toothpaste away.
- Look at yourself in the mirror.
- Take a slow deep breath and give yourself a big smile as you open your eyes.

# DOTS CONCENTRATION GAME

**Use this fun game to help children and teens become more aware of how long they can stay on task as well as how often they are distracted:**

- Give clients paper and markers and ask them to draw a picture of their family, a favorite pet or toy. Or ask older children and teens to make a list of their favorite songs, movies, books or people.

- Tell them that any time you notice they are not paying attention to their drawing you will draw a dot (or a heart) on their paper.

- See how long they can stay focused on the task of drawing before their mind wanders. You might use a timer and record time on task.

- Let them practice and make it fun.

- See if they can get fewer dots with practice until they can do a whole drawing without getting any dots.

- See if they can stay on task for longer periods.

- Reassure them that it is normal for their mind to wander and its okay if they get a few dots.

- Help them avoid self-judgment.

## Tool 11-7: Body Scan for Children and Teens

**BACKGROUND:**    The Body Scan Meditation is customarily included in studies on the effectiveness of mindfulness for adults, teens and children (Biegel, et al., 2009). It is a component of most formal meditation practices such as Kabat-Zinn's Mindfulness-Based Stress Reduction Program. (Stahl & Goldstein, 2010) It involves focusing your full attention on each part of the body, noticing whatever sensations arise, accepting them, and sending kind and compassionate thoughts to each area of the body. Through regular practice, it can help children and teens enter deep states of relaxation, accept their body as it is, work effectively with their body sensations and feelings of discomfort and pain, reduce hyperactivity and increase powers of concentration and mindfulness.

**SKILL BUILDING:**    Explain to children and teens that a body scan is the process of paying attention to each part of their body one area at a time. It is a common part of many formal mindfulness meditation practices. It is designed to help them enter a deep state of relaxation, to accept their body as it is, to work with discomfort and pain, to calm their hyperactivity and increase concentration and mindfulness. Use the script on Handout 11-7 Body Scan for Children and Teens with your client lying on their back if at all possible, or sitting comfortably in a chair. Encourage them to practice this between sessions. If they become uncomfortable or emotional at any point, ask them if they want to continue or to stop. Be prepared to process what comes up with them. Shorten the practice for young children to start and gradually lengthen it. For young children, discuss what the word "notice" means before doing the body scan.

**INTEGRATION:**    Help clients reflect on how they felt during and after practicing the Body Scan Meditation. What did they notice about their body? Were they able to stay focused? Did they fall asleep? Did they become more relaxed or more agitated? What was it like for them to simply observe and accept? Did they feel any pain? Did any pain they felt get better or worse? Did any thoughts or emotions arise when they focused on specific areas of their body? If so, process these and help them connect them to past experiences. It is not uncommon for kids and teens who have experienced trauma to remember deeply buried feelings or thoughts when they focus on certain parts of their body. If they need to stop, process what came up for them. Help them to integrate the past memory with the safety of this moment.

# BODY SCAN FOR CHILDREN AND TEENS

*Guided Script:*

- Let's begin. Breathe in slowly through your nose to the count of 4: 1-2-3-4 and breathe out even more slowly like you are blowing a huge bubble, through your mouth to the count of 8: 1-2-3-4-5-6-7-8. Now just breathe normally.

- Bring your attention to your left foot. Just notice your left foot, including your toes, heel, bottom of your left foot, top of your left foot. Notice what it feels like.

- Then move up to your left ankle. Notice how your left ankle feels. Pay attention to whether there is any pain there, is it cold, or hot, does it feel light or heavy?

- Then pay attention to your left leg starting at the bottom, up to your knees, and thighs, all the way to your hips at the top of your leg. Notice if your left leg feels tight or relaxed, warm or cold, light or heavy.

- Now pay attention to your right foot. Just notice your right foot including your toes, heel, bottom of your right foot, top of your right foot. Notice what it feels like.

- Then move up to your right ankle. Notice how your right ankle feels. Pay attention to whether there is any pain there. Is it cold, or hot, does it feel light or heavy?

- Then pay attention to your right leg starting at the bottom, up to your knees, and thighs, all the way to your hips at the top of your leg. Notice if it feels tight or relaxed, warm or cold, light or heavy.

- Now pay attention to both legs from your toes up to your hips. Be still, breathe and send your legs some kind and loving thoughts.

- Now move your attention to your belly. Just notice what's there. Feel how your belly feels. Let it be the way it is. Send love and kindness to your belly.

- Now pay attention to your back starting with your low back all the way up to your shoulders. Notice how your back feels. Sit for a moment just noticing your back.

- Now give your attention to your fingers, thumbs, wrists, arms and shoulders. Just notice how your arms feel.

- Now pay attention to your neck and throat. Swallow and notice how your neck and throat feel.

- Now pay attention to your face: your chin, your mouth, your cheeks, your eyes, your eyebrows, your forehead and finally your ears.

- Now bring your attention to your head, including your hair and scalp and your brain inside your head.

- Now take a big belly breath and fill your whole body with a cushion of air. Blow the air out gently like you are blowing a huge bubble and let go of anything that needs to go.

- Open your eyes and bring your attention back to the room.

Note: For a shorter body scan do both legs at the same time.

## Tool 11-8: Balancing Chips Game

**BACKGROUND:**    One great way to practice mindfulness for children and teens with ADHD is to help them focus attention on their body. This tool uses the process of balancing chips on the body to see how long the children or teens can stay still without knocking the chips off. It teaches self-awareness and mindfulness of body, concentration and may help hyperactive clients train themselves to be less hyper.

**SKILL BUILDING:**    Use Handout 11-8 Balancing Chips Game to teach clients how to play this mindfulness of body game. Vary the number of chips used depending on the client. Use a timer and challenge them to see how long they can balance the chips before one falls off. Make it fun. Show them how long you can do it, too. Encourage them to practice at home. Suggest that when they notice they are really hyper that they take a breath, say to themselves: "balancing chips," and remember how they felt while balancing the chips.

A brief version of this exercise can be done by placing a chip on the backs of the client's hands and asking them to see how long they can balance them before they fall off.

> *Case Example:*    *A four-year-old boy who was diagnosed with ADHD was extremely hyperactive. We played this Balancing Chips Game one week in session. He loved playing it so much that each time he came in for his therapy session he said, "Miss Deb, can we play that chip game again?" Over the course of several weeks of playing the game in session he was able to calm his body more and more, and each week his time increased before a chip fell off. His mother commented that she noticed he seemed less hyperactive at home.*

**INTEGRATION:**    Help clients process what it was like to play this game: "What did it feel like to balance the chips on your body? Was it hard or easy? Was it fun? Could you feel the chips? How did you know when they were about to fall off? Did you feel how still you kept your body? Did it get easier with practice?"

# BALANCING CHIPS GAME

**Use the chips from a game such as Checkers, Othello or Connect Four. Take them out and place them where you and the child can reach them.**

*Guided Script:*

- We are going to play a mindful body game called Balancing Chips. Please sit down on the floor. Let's get the wiggles out. Do it with me, wiggle every part of your body for a few moments. Wiggle your feet, your legs, your arms, your hands, your fingers, your head, your mouth, and your eyelids. (Do it with them)

- Ok, now take a belly breath in through your nose and blow out like you are blowing a bubble.

- Now I will give you a chip. Take the chip and place it on your leg just above your ankle and balance it there. Now put this next chip on the other leg. Now put this next chip on your leg above your knee and this next chip on the other leg.

- Lie down on the floor on your back with your arms and legs straight. If it is okay with you I will put the rest of the chips on. I will put one chip on the back of each hand and then another chip on each arm between your wrist and your elbow. I will put a chip on each shoulder. Now I will put a chip on each side of your forehead above your eyes. And I will put this last chip on your chin.

- Now I will time how long you can balance all of these chips without moving and knocking any of them off. Pay attention to your breathing. Let yourself relax and sink into the floor. If you feel like you need to move, just let go of that thought and bring your attention back to how it feels to breathe and keep balancing the chips.

Keep track of how long they balance the chips. Let them try several times. Have fun with them and enjoy the process.

Let them play the game for a few minutes each week for a few weeks. Then let them play again later on after learning and practicing more mindfulness skills. They may start to decrease hyperactivity and gain more control over their body movement.

## Tool 11-9: Mindful Movement

**BACKGROUND:**    Moving the body mindfully is a great way to engage active children and teens in being mindful. They love to move. Research shows that movement is a key factor in helping children and teens with ADHD (Hillman, 2014) and (Hoza, 2014). See Chapter 15 Movement to Optimize Brain Function for more information. This tool teaches them to direct their attention to the feeling of the movement using various repetitive movements. It increases their self-awareness and self-regulation.

**SKILL BUILDING:**    Demonstrate each movement on Handout 11-9 Mindful Motions to clients. Lead them in doing each movement slowly and repeat it four times. Then go on to the next movement and repeat it four times. Try to include at least four different movements during each session. Ask children and teens for suggestions of movements they would like to use and incorporate their ideas for variety and fun. The goal is to pay attention to the feeling of each of the movements while breathing slowly in and out.

Encourage parents to make sure their child or teen gets lots of opportunity to move. This might include a sport, dance, karate, yoga, or Tai Chi.

**RESOURCE:**    Thich Nhat Hanh's book, *Mindful Movement,* is a great resource for more detail on this concept (Thich Nhat Hanh, 2008).

**INTEGRATION:**    Help clients reflect on what being mindful while moving was like for them: What did you notice while you moved slowly? How did your body feel? Was this easy or difficult for you? What was it like to breathe slowly while you moved? What happened when you repeated the same motion over and over? What was going on in your mind while you did this? Did you notice any change in your mind before and after doing this exercise? Does your body feel any different after doing this?

# MINDFUL MOTIONS

## SITTING MOTIONS

**Lead the client(s) in doing various movements while seated.**

- Put your hands down to your side. Take a breath in and raise your arms out to the side and straight up over your head. Now breathe out gently like blowing a bubble while lowering your arms back to your side. Repeat four times.

- Place your feet flat on the floor. Now breathe in and raise your feet straight out in front of you. Slowly breathe out and lower your feet to the floor. Repeat four times.

- Take a deep breath in and straighten your neck like a string is pulling your head up to the ceiling. Now blow out gently and lower your chin down to your chest. Repeat four times.

## STANDING MOTIONS

**Stand up and lead the client(s) in these motions.**

- Place both arms at your side. Breathe in slowly and raise your left arm up in front of you until it is level with your shoulders. Blow out gently and lower it back down. Breathe in gently and raise your right arm up in front of you until it is level with your shoulder. Blow out gently and lower it back down. Repeat four times.

- Place your hands on your hips, lean forward, breathe in and circle to the right all the way around. Now breathe out and circle to the left all the way around. Repeat four times.

- Breathe in and raise your right foot out in front of you while pointing your toe. Blow out gently and lower your foot. Breathe in and raise your left foot out in front of you with pointed toe. Blow out gently and lower your foot. Repeat four times.

## Tool 11-10: Meditation for Concentration

**BACKGROUND:**    A number of studies have found that mindfulness improves concentration. Most mindfulness skills can be used to improve concentration. This tool describes a technique that helps children and teens use their imagination to pretend they are in the classroom. It is a guided imagery that leads their attention to notice what's around them that is distracting them and to say "not now" and to bring their attention back to the teacher. This type of practice, when done repeatedly, gradually improves their ability to stay focused when they are doing a task. One special education teacher uses a number of these meditations in class and has found that her students particularly like doing this type of guided imagery.

**SKILL BUILDING:**    Explain to clients that you are going to ask them to use their imagination to pretend they are sitting in their classroom. For older children and teens, explain that this type of exercise helps their brain learn to pay attention, stay focused and be more mindful. Read the meditation on Handout 11-10 In the Classroom to your client and ask them to reflect on what came up for them during the exercise. It will increase the effectiveness of this exercise if you can repeat it a number of times over the course of a few weeks. Recommend that they remember the exercise when they need to concentrate on something to remind themselves to notice when they are distracted and to say "not now" to bring their attention back to what they need to be paying attention to.

**RESOURCE:**    A similar meditation is available on the Meditations for Concentration CD available at www.PESI.com and www.TheBrainLady.com.

**INTEGRATION:**    Explore what this guided imagery was like for your client: Were you able to imagine sitting at your desk? Could you see it in your imagination? What did it feel like to imagine sitting at your desk? What did you notice while you were sitting at your desk? Were you distracted by anything? How did you stay focused on the teacher? Could you feel the desk or hear the teacher? What did you see in the classroom? Were you able to concentrate on pretending you were in the classroom? Did it almost seem real? When have you told yourself "not now" when you are distracted to help yourself pay attention? Were you able to concentrate better in your classroom?

# IN THE CLASSROOM

***Guided Script:***
- Keep your eyes closed and listen to my voice.
- Pretend you are in school.


- Imagine you are sitting in your chair at your desk.
- Can you feel the chair on your bottom and against your back?
- What does the desk feel like when you touch it with your hands?
- Does the desk top lift up?
- What do you keep in your desk?
- Look inside. Can you see what's in your desk?
- Do you have everything you need?


- Imagine what the classroom smells like.
- Does it smell familiar?


- Look at who is sitting next to you.
- Are you friends?
- Do you get along?


- Is the classroom noisy or quiet?


- Where is the teacher?
- Is the teacher talking to the class?
- Listen to the teacher.
- What does the teacher want you to learn?


- If the child next to you tries to talk to you while the teacher is talking, tell them "not now" and look back at the teacher's eyes and lips.
- Pay close attention to what the teacher is saying.


- If there is noise in the hall or outside the window, just notice it and say to yourself "not now" and look right at the teacher's lips and eyes again.
- What does the teacher want you to do?
- If your stomach growls and you feel hungry, say "not now" and bring you attention back to the teacher.
- If you notice yourself daydreaming, say "not now" and bring your attention back to the teacher.


- Continue until the teacher stops talking and tells you what to do next.

## Tool 11-11: Core Practice

**BACKGROUND:** At the heart of mindfulness is the Core Practice. Core Practice is a way to tell our minds to relax and focus and to calm down the "monkey brain." It can be used several times a day, almost like pushing the reset button. It is the perfect way for children and teens with ADHD to increase their ability to pay attention. They can use it to take a quick time-out to calm hyperactivity, refocus their attention, reduce anger or fear, to think before they act, and to make better choices.

**SKILL BUILDING:** Use Handout 11-11 Core Practice to teach clients the basics of Core Practice. The structure of this tool is to Stop, Listen, Breathe, Reflect. Doing this when they are revved up, distracted, upset, angry, afraid, or impulsive can allow children and teens the space in time to calm themselves down, redirect their attention, de-stress and make a better choice than they might otherwise. Modify the length of the silent period to suit the needs of the client and lengthen it as they practice and gain mastery. This might range from 10 seconds for a beginner or hyperactive or anxious client, on up to 15 minutes for a more advanced client.

Normalize their experience—it is normal for the mind to wander. Recommend they practice this several times a day. They might use a short version of the practice (5 or 10 seconds) if they are starting to feel angry or upset or impatient to allow themselves to calm down, stay in control, and make good choices. They might incorporate it into their day to center or ground themselves during transitions or before settling down to start an activity.

Discuss how the Core Practice helps no matter what they are doing. Relate it to making choices when they are being creative, in choosing what to draw or write about, or preparing to take a photo of their lively kitten, or perhaps responding to a bully.

**INTEGRATION:** Teach the client to reflect on the core practice process. Ask them: what was the practice like for you? How did you feel as you breathed? What did you notice about your breathing? How did you stay focused on breathing? What did you do when your mind wandered? Did you feel different after you were finished? What do you think was happening in your brain while you did this? When could you use this during your day? What might it help you with? How could you use this to make better choices?

# CORE PRACTICE

**STOP → LISTEN → BREATHE**

Stop what you are doing.

Close your eyes.

Be still and listen.

Notice how you feel inside.

Pay attention to your breathing.

Breathe slowly in through your nose and out through your mouth.

Imagine the air slowly filling your lungs and belly and then flowing out again.

If you notice that you are thinking about other things, that's ok. Just accept it,
and then bring your attention back to your breath.

Notice your belly moving as you take slow belly breaths.

Ask yourself what am I feeling?

Keep paying attention to your breath.

Continue for a minute in silence (Note: shorten or lengthen as needed).

Open your eyes and return to the room.

## Tool 11-12: Mindfulness Glitter Bottle

**BACKGROUND:**    Practicing with a Mindfulness Glitter Bottle is a great way to help children and teens calm down, de-stress, reduce anger and train concentration. This tool provides a hands-on activity you can do with clients to make their own mindfulness glitter bottle.

**SKILL BUILDING:**    Use Handout 11-12-1 Making a Mindfulness Glitter Bottle to make a mindfulness glitter bottle with your client. Make it for them if they are too young. Then use Handout 11-12-2 Using a Mindfulness Glitter Bottle to do the activity with your client. Use the various recipes to make glitter bottles with various glitter settling times. Start with the shortest times and gradually increase the time as client gains mastery.

**INTEGRATION:**    Help your client reflect on what happened when they shook the bottle and then when they were still. Ask them: were you able to see through the bottle? What happened when you shook it? What did you feel like when you couldn't see through the bottle? What happened when you stayed still? How did you feel when the glitter sank to the bottom of the bottle? When did you use the mindfulness glitter bottle at home? Did it help you calm down and feel better? Can you stay focused longer now?

# MAKING A MINDFULNESS GLITTER BOTTLE

**Ingredients:**
- Clear water bottle with label removed. The smoother the sides of the bottle, the easier it is to see through the bottle. (Can use mason jar but I prefer non-breakable plastic)
- Hot water
- Glitter – be sure to use fine glitter
- Light corn syrup or glycerin (found in the pharmacy section)
- Glitter glue
- Kosher salt
- Dish soap
- Super glue or Gorilla glue to glue the cap back on the bottle

**Recipes:**

The following recipes are general guidelines. The time for the glitter to settle will vary depending on type (or brand) of glitter (finer is better). If the glitter settles too fast, add more corn syrup, glycerin or more salt. If the glitter settles too slowly, add more hot water. Kosher salt will make a clearer solution than table salt. Use different colors for different settling times. Glue the cap on.

**Red (settling time, ~40 seconds)**
1 tbsp glitter glue
1/2 tsp red glitter
1 cup hot water
3-4 drops dish soap

**Purple (about 3 min)**
1/2 cup corn syrup
1/2 cup hot water
1 tsp purple glitter
3-4 drops dish soap

**Blue (about 2 min)**
1/4 cup glycerin
3/4 cup hot water
1 tsp blue glitter
2 tsp salt
3-4 drops dish soap

**Pink (longest settling time, about 20 minutes)**
2 tbsp pink glitter glue
1/4 cup corn syrup
3/4 cup hot water
3-4 drops dish soap

Recipes adapted from http://mommaowlslab.blogspot.com/2012/02/science-thursday-glitter-jars.html?m=1, Retrieved 01-29-15.

# USING A MINDFULNESS GLITTER BOTTLE

**Process:**

• Give the client the empty bottle. Ask them to look through the bottle. What can they see? Can they see their hand that is holding the bottle? Can they see through the bottle?

• Follow the recipe on Handout 11-12-1 Making a Mindfulness Glitter Bottle to help them make the glitter bottle or make it for them. Start with recipes with the shortest settling time and use increasingly longer settling times for older children and teens as they gain mastery and can focus longer.

• Ask them to shake the bottle and watch what happens as the glitter disperses in the water. Ask them to look through the bottle. What can they see now?

• Ask them to shake the bottle and imagine that their mind is revved up, wired, distracted, angry, worried, or busy. Then tell them to hold the bottle completely still and watch what happens inside the bottle.

• Explain that as they become quiet and still in their mind, their busy or angry or worried thoughts calm and clear just like the glitter settles to the bottom and top of the bottle.

• Now ask them to hold the bottle and jump up and down and twirl around and watch what happens in the bottle. Then encourage them to stop and stand completely still as they again watch what happens in the bottle.

• Explain that as they calm their body, their mind quiets and thoughts settle just like the glitter in the bottle. They feel peaceful and clear.

• Encourage them to use their glitter bottle to help them calm their hyperactivity, distractibility, anger or worry.

• Now ask them to watch the glitter settle until the water is clear again. Encourage them to breathe slowly and calmly while they watch.

• Let them take their glitter bottle home and encourage them to hold it, shake it, and then still themselves and watch the glitter settle whenever they feel distracted, upset, angry, afraid, or too revved up.

## Tool 11-13: Changing the Channel

**BACKGROUND:**    Clients with ADHD are easily distracted and tend to daydream. This results in being off-task and missing important information and social cues. Most children and teens don't realize that we can deliberately choose what we want to think about.

This tool uses the concept that the current content of our thoughts is the channel we are watching. Children and teens easily get this concept as most are very familiar with the channels on TV. For example, we may be watching our daydreaming, distracted, worry, anger, sad, or stressed channel. We can change the channel to a focused, on-task, happy, calm, relaxed, or fun channel and thereby change the contents of our thoughts and subsequently our feelings. This aligns with the cognitive behavioral concept that what we think about affects our feelings and our behavior and vice versa. And that we can choose a thought that feels better.

This tool can be used to help clients change the channel to what they are supposed to be paying attention to. It can also be used to help them reduce anxiety, anger, sadness and stress.

**SKILL BUILDING:**    Explain to clients the concept that for this mindfulness skill, their thoughts indicate what channel they are watching, such as the daydreaming, distracted, happy, sad, worried, angry, calm, or stressed channel. Help your client identify the thoughts and the channel they are currently watching.

> ***For concentration:***    Find out when your client has difficulty staying on task or daydreaming. Using a specific situation in which they have trouble, ask them what they are supposed to be paying attention to. Then encourage them to notice if the channel they are watching in their mind is what they are supposed to be paying attention to or is it their daydreaming or distracted channel. For example, in the classroom, are they focused on the work they are doing, or what the teacher is saying, or thinking about something totally different? Encourage them to change the channel to their concentration/paying attention/focused channel and bring their attention back to what they are supposed to be paying attention to.

> Follow the process in Handout 11-13 Changing the Channel. Encourage them to use this tool whenever they need to pay attention and notice they are daydreaming or distracted.

> ***For anxiety, anger, stress, sadness:***    Ask them to think about what they would put on their happy/peaceful/ relaxed channel. Help them come up with at least four positive ideas based on what you know about their interests and hobbies. Children and teens often choose activities such as dance, skateboarding, swimming, or other sports. Help them identify things that feel good to them. Follow the process in Handout 11-13. Encourage them to use this tool whenever they need to shift their thoughts or feelings.

**INTEGRATION:**    Ask clients when they used this tool during their day. How was it helpful? Were they able to identify negative/unpleasant thoughts in the moment? What did they put on their happy/peaceful/relaxed/feel good channel? What did they notice about their thoughts or mood when they used it? Do they need several different positive channels or is one enough? Were they able to notice when they were watching their daydreaming channel? How did they bring their attention back to the paying attention channel? Did it help them stay focused?

# CHANGING THE CHANNEL

**Did you know that you can choose what you want to think about? You can only have one thought at a time so make sure it's a good one.**

**For Concentration:**

Imagine that what you are thinking about or paying attention to is like watching a TV channel.

What are you thinking about right now? What are you supposed to be paying attention to? If you are in school, maybe you should be paying attention to the teacher or your work or your quiz.

If you are paying attention to something else then you are daydreaming or distracted. Then you are watching your daydreaming or distracted channel.

When you notice you are daydreaming or distracted, pretend you are picking up an imaginary remote control and change the channel to your focused, paying attention channel. Then bring your attention to whatever you are supposed to be paying attention to.

Use this process any time you need to pay attention to something to repeatedly bring your attention back.

**For Anxiety, Anger, Sadness, Stress:**

What are you thinking about right now? Are your thoughts calm, happy, sad, worried, angry, painful, helpful or unhelpful? This is the channel you are watching now.

Think about what you would put on your happy/peaceful/relaxed/feel good channel. Be specific. Choose 4 different things you could put on 4 different channels that feel good to you. What are these 4 things? Some examples might be petting your cat or dog, swimming, dancing, playing sports, skateboarding, your favorite music or band, a warm bath, your favorite food, playing your favorite game, or whatever feels good to you. What 4 things could you use for your channels?

If your thoughts feel bad or are negative, then pretend you are picking up an imaginary remote control and using it to "change the channel" to one of your happy/peaceful/relaxed/feel good channels and imagine you are watching what you already decided would be on that channel.

Practice "changing the channel" in your mind to a more positive channel.

Do you feel better watching this channel?

Use this process any time you have negative or unpleasant thoughts or feelings.

## Tool 11-14: Bring Attention To The Present Moment

**BACKGROUND:**   Children and teens that experience symptoms of ADHD often have trouble being grounded in the present moment. They may be easily distracted by their busy mind or by anything in their environment that grabs their attention. This tool provides a very effective technique to quickly and easily help them bring their attention to the present moment.

**SKILL BUILDING:**   Explain to children and teens that you are going to show them how to bring their attention and thoughts to the present moment. For younger children, ask them what the present moment is and engage in a discussion giving them some examples of things in the past, present or future.

Use Handout 11-14 Contact to lead them in an exercise to help them pay attention to where their body makes contact.

Be creative and make this fun.

Encourage them to practice this whenever they notice they are distracted to bring their attention back to the present. It is also a great exercise to help them feel more grounded and relaxed if they feel worried, upset, angry, scared, or tuned out.

**INTEGRATION:**   Help clients reflect on what this exercise was like for them. Did they understand what "contact" means? Were they able to bring their attention to the point of contact? How did they feel after they did it? Did it help them get more present? Were they able to use it when they were distracted or they felt scared, anxious, distressed, or tuned out?

# CONTACT

**Explain to children and teens that you are going to show them how to bring their attention and thoughts to the present moment.**

**For younger children, ask them what the present moment is and engage in a discussion giving them some examples of things in the past, present or future.**

### *Guided Script:*

- Pay attention to, and point to, where your feet are touching the floor. This is a point of contact, where your feet "contact" the floor.
- Repeat after me: "Contact."
- Now pay attention to where your bottom contacts the chair.
- Say, "Contact."
- Now pay attention to where your hands are resting on your legs, lap, or arm of the chair.
- Again, repeat "Contact."
- Now pay attention to where your back contacts the back of the chair.
- Repeat, "Contact."
- Let's stand up and pay attention to where your feet contact the floor.
- Say "Contact."
- Walk slowly and say "Contact" each time one of your feet touches the floor.
- Use your finger to touch your other hand, arm, face and leg.
- Say "Contact" each time you feel the touch.

### Other Options:

- Ask them to hold a small worry stone in their hand and then to say to themselves "Contact" each time they touch it with their fingers.
- Be creative and make this fun.
- You might pass a small toy or other object from person to person and ask them to shout "Contact" when the object touches their hand.
- You might ask them to lie on the floor and say "Contact" as they pay attention to each part of their body that touches the floor.
- Encourage them to practice this if they feel worried, upset, angry, scared, or tuned out to help them relax and bring their attention back to the present.

# Section VII
# Complementary Therapies

# Chapter 12
# Coaching

Tool 12-1: ADHD Coaching

## Tool 12-1: ADHD Coaching

**BACKGROUND:**   Children and teens with ADHD, as well as their parents, often benefit from working with a certified ADHD coach. ADHD coaches combine personal and professional coaching skills with knowledge of ADHD to provide support, structure, and accountability to parents and/or their children. Coaching does not aim to change the ADHD symptoms but makes it much easier to function effectively with the symptoms. This tool provides information about coaching and when to incorporate it into the treatment plan.

### SKILL BUILDING:

An ADHD coach will:

- Help clients understand ADHD and encourage them to clarify and use their strengths, talents, values, and interests rather than focusing on problems, difficulties and limitations.
- Assist them in increasing their self-awareness and self-concept.
- Facilitate the process of planning and setting goals and hold clients accountable to achieving them.
- Help clients understand the concept and practice of self-regulation.
- Fortify the client with strategies that work for them and teach time management and organizational skills that clients with ADHD typically lack.
- Help them through the process of learning how to more effectively manage their life with ADHD.

An ADHD coach will NOT:

- Tell clients what to do
- Provide psychotherapy

After learning about the role an ADHD coach can fill in helping your client, determine if your client could benefit from their services. Could an ADHD coach expand on what you are already providing for this client? What specific issues does this client struggle with that contribute to their sense of failure? Do the therapeutic issues such as anxiety, depression, self-esteem, self-narrative, social skills, self-regulation and parenting skills take up all the session time and leave little time for teaching organizational, time and ADHD management skills and/or providing accountability? Ask yourself if you, the clinician, are able to provide the level of time management and organizational skills building your client needs? If you provide accountability will this change or impair the nature of the therapeutic relationship?

Is the client ready for coaching? Some things to take into account are age, cognitive level, motivation, desire, and ADHD related challenges they need help with. Could the parent use coaching? Find some ADHD coaches that work with children and teens and learn about their approach. Are they willing to work with you as part of the treatment team?

**RESOURCE:**   Visit go.pesi/ADHDworkbook for Handout 12A Finding An ADHD Coach.

**INTEGRATION:**   How do you feel about adding an ADHD coach to the treatment team? Could this client benefit from ADHD coaching? How might an ADHD coach augment the work you are doing with the client? Is the client ready for coaching? How might the parent benefit from coaching?

# Chapter 13
# Frontal Lobe/Working Memory Training

Tool 13-1: Brain Gym®
Tool 13-2: Interactive Metronome®

## Tool 13-1: Brain Gym

**BACKGROUND:** As discussed in Tool 2-5 ADHD Neurobiology and Brain Imaging, ADHD is a brain based disorder. A number of treatment modalities have been developed that address whole brain integration. This tool describes Brain Gym® which is committed to the principle that moving with intention leads to optimal learning. Brain Gym movements, exercises, or activities refer to 26 movements that recall the movements naturally done during the first years of life when learning to coordinate the eyes, ears, hands, and whole body. The 26 activities, along with a program for "learning through movement" were developed by educator and reading specialist Paul E. Dennison.

Brain Gym is being used in 87 countries with significant anecdotal and some clinical evidence of effectiveness. These movements often bring about dramatic improvements (Brain Gym International, 2003) in areas such as:

- Concentration and Focus
- Memory
- Academics: Reading, Writing, Math, Test Taking
- Physical Coordination
- Relationships

- Self-responsibility
- Organization Skills
- Attitude
- Attention
- Hyperactive Behaviors

**SKILL BUILDING:** Brain Gym consists of 26 movements that can be easily taught to children and teens. They are designed to address the physical skills associated with learning, performing, and productivity (posture, fine and gross motor coordination, balance, etc.). By synchronizing all three midlines of the body, Brain Gym activities facilitate increased memory, organization and concentration. See Handout 13-1 Sample Brain Gym Exercises for an example of 4 of these movements.

**RESOURCES:** Visit the Brain Gym website for more information including workshops and courses that teach the 26 movements, the processes, techniques, and the educational theory behind the work as well as how to become a licensed Brain Gym Instructor/Consultant. http://www.braingym.org/

Brown, Kathy, 2012. *Educate Your Brain: Use Mind-Body Balance to Learn Faster, Work Smarter and Move More Easily Through Life*, Balance Point Publishing, LLC, Phoenix, AZ.

**INTEGRATION:** Are you interested in learning more about the full Brain Gym program? How do you think it might help your client? Are there any courses or workshops nearby? Would you like to become a licensed Brain Gym practitioner?

# SAMPLE BRAIN GYM EXERCISES

**The Thinking Cap:** Helps to focus on the important sounds while ignoring distracting sounds. It will help with listening skills, silent speech and thinking.

- Gently massage and unroll your ears

- Begin at the top and gently massage down and around the curve to the ear lobes

- Repeat 3 or more times

**The Cross Crawl:** Synchronizes both sides of the body. May improve concentration and comprehension.

- You can do this either sitting or standing

- Touch your left elbow to you right knee

- Then touch your right elbow to your left knee

- Continue to shift rhythmically back and forth between the two positions for approximately one minute

**Lazy 8s:** Good warm-up for creativity and writing

- Draw a figure 8 lying on its side moving up and to the left first, either in the air with your thumb or on a piece of paper

- Draw the figure 8s slowly so your eyes are tracking the movement

- Use one hand, then the other, and then both together (about three 8s per hand)

**Brain Buttons:** Help to reduce stress and relax eye muscles

- Put one hand in the shape of a "U." Place your index and thumb into the slight indentations below the collar bone on each side of the sternum

- Gently rub for 30 seconds while moving your eyes slowly to the left and right

- At the same time put the other hand over the navel

- Switch hands and repeat

## Tool 13-2: Interactive Metronome®

**BACKGROUND:**   Timing in the brain is critical to successful functioning and has been shown to be impaired in some clients with ADHD. See Tool 2-5 ADHD Neurobiology and Brain Imaging for more information. Timing impacts attention, working memory, and processing speed. This tool describes the Interactive Metronome® (IM) program which uses a game-like auditory-visual platform to engage the client and provide constant feedback at the millisecond level to promote synchronized timing in the brain. IM works to improve the synchronicity of the internal clock and efficiency of neural communication in the brain. It increases the speed and efficiency of communication in the brain, impacts cognitive speed and efficiency and results in a wide variety of skill areas including: visual, motor, cognitive, linguistic, social and behavioral abilities.

One study of the effectiveness of IM for ADHD (Schaffer et al, 2001) showed statistically significant improvements in the following symptoms that clients with ADHD typically need help with:

✓ **Attention**

✓ **Impulsive behavior**

✓ Processing speed

✓ Language processing

✓ Reading

✓ Motor control and coordination

**SKILL BUILDING:**   Explain to clients and parents that the Interactive Metronome program uses button triggers, in-motion triggers and/or a tap mat that the client activates by clapping, stepping or tapping when they hear a reference beat (cow bell sound) on their headphones. The system then gives them feedback about how accurate their timing is in the form of guide sounds that indicate if their timing is right on (high pitch sound), too early (rubber band sound or buzzer for way early – in left ear), or too late or very late (rubber band sound or buzzer in right ear). Then they can adjust their timing until they are getting the high pitch sound consistently indicating accurate timing and neural synchronization.

Use Handout 13-2 Interactive Metronome Fact Sheet to explain the benefits of the IM program to clients and parents.

**RESOURCES:**   For more information about IM and to find or become a certified IM practitioner visit www. interactivemetronome.com.

There are a number of videos about IM posted on YouTube. Simply go to www.YouTube.com and search for Interactive Metronome ADHD.

**INTEGRATION:**   Could the client benefit from the Interactive Metronome program? Is there an IM practitioner nearby? Are you interested in adding this treatment modality to your practice? Has the client already used the IM program and what results did they obtain?

# INTERACTIVE METRONOME FACT SHEET

**The goal of IM is to:**

- Drive functional neuroplasticity
- Improve mental (doing)/interval (planning) timing
- Improve the brain's efficiency and performance

**Neural synchronization is critical for:**

- Attention
- Executive Function
- Working Memory
- Processing Speed
- Speech & Language
- Social Skills
- Reading & Other Academic Skills
- Motor Control & Coordination
- Sensory Processing & Integration

**Study showed improved:**

- Attention
- Impulsive Behavior
- Processing Speed
- Language Processing
- Reading
- Motor Control and Coordination

**Resources:** For more information about IM and to find a certified IM practitioner visit www.interactivemetronome.com. There are a number of videos about IM posted on YouTube®. Simply go to www.YouTube.com and search for "Interactive Metronome ADHD".

# Chapter 14
# Vestibular/Cerebellar Exercises

Tool 14-1: Sensory Integration Therapy
Tool 14-2: Breakthrough Learning Program®

## Tool 14-1: Sensory Integration Therapy

**BACKGROUND:**   Sensory processing problems in children with ADHD are more common than in typically developing children (Ghanizadeh, 2010). Children and teens with ADHD symptoms may have sensory processing disorder (SPD) instead of, or in addition to ADHD. These two disorders have strikingly similar symptoms. In one study 46% of the children with ADHD also had sensory over-responsiveness (Lane et al, 2010). Another study found 69% of the boys with ADHD had tactile defensiveness, a deficit in somatosensory function (Parush, et al, 2007).

Although sensory processing disorder was excluded from the DSM-5 it still makes sense to compare the client's symptoms with those of SPD, as well as ADHD, because the treatment for each may vary and in fact both treatment strategies may be needed.

This tool reviews the characteristics of SPD and outlines the basics of therapy for sensory integration.

**SKILL BUILDING:**   Explain to clients and parents that there is an overlap of symptoms of sensory processing disorder (SPD) and ADHD which sometimes makes it difficult to differentiate between the two. Therefore, it is helpful to look at the symptoms the client is experiencing and see if they are experiencing too much or too little stimulation through their senses and have trouble integrating, regulating and organizing a response to the information they're getting (Miller, 2012), (Mangeot et al, 2001).

Use Handout 14-1-1 Symptoms Common to ADHD and SPD to review the symptoms that overlap between SPD and ADHD and to find out if the client experiences these.

If sensory integration, processing or modulation difficulties are suspected then it may be helpful to refer the client to an occupational therapist (OT) who specializes in sensory integration (SI) therapy. SI therapy is a fun, play-based intervention that takes place in a sensory-rich environment sometimes called a "sensory gym." Private clinics and practices, hospital outpatient departments, and university occupational therapy programs are typical places where treatment for SPD or for sensory issues in disorders such as ADHD may be found.

The theory behind SI therapy is that specific movement activities, resistive body work, and even brushing of the skin can help a child with sensory problems experience an optimal level of arousal and regulation. This, according to OTs, can actually "rewire" the brain so that kids can appropriately integrate and respond to sensory input, allowing them to both make sense of and feel safer in the world. Research shows that subjects participating in sensory integration therapy performed significantly better than members in the control groups who did not receive sensory integration therapy (Ottenbacker, 1982).

If the child or teen appears to be experiencing sensory issues, explore options for treatment. Review Handout 14-1-2 Sample School Accommodations with parents and encourage them to work with the school to put these accommodations in place. These will help the client with ADHD whether or not they have SPD.

**RESOURCES:**   Visit the Sensory Processing Disorder Foundation website for more information and to locate a practitioner that provides treatment for SPD. http://spdfoundation.net/index.html

Aune, B., Bert B., and Gennaro, P., 2010, *Behavior Solutions for the Inclusive Classroom: A Handy Reference Guide that Explains Behaviors Associated with Autism, Asperger's, ADHD, Sensory Processing Disorder, and other Special Needs*, Future Horizons, Arlington, Texas.

Biel, L and Peske, N., 2009. *Raising a Sensory Smart Child, The Definitive Handbook for Helping Your Child with Sensory Processing Issues,* Penguin Books, New York, NY.

**INTEGRATION:**   Does the client have symptoms of sensory processing disorder? Work with an occupational therapist (OT) who specializes in sensory integration therapy to help determine if the symptoms are truly sensory based or ADHD based or both. If SPD is present refer client to an OT. If a client is already receiving OT for SPD, how is it impacting their ADHD symptoms?

# SYMPTOMS COMMON TO ADHD AND SPD/SMD

**Sensory Processing Disorder**

- Response to sensory input from environment and body is maladaptive

- Challenges with responding to sensory stimuli appropriately will affect:

  - Motor function
  - Emotional, affective state
  - Arousal and attention

**Symptoms of Sensory Processing Disorder That Look Like ADHD**

- Distractibility and inattentiveness

- Poor impulse control

- Hyperactivity

- Inappropriate movement and touch

- Sensory over-responsivity

- Sensory under-responsivity

- Being unaware when spoken to or asked to follow directions

- Difficulty with self-control

- Emotional instability

- Poor peer relations and social interaction

- Low self-image

- Weak expressive and receptive language

- Poor handwriting

- Poor organizational skills

Visit the Sensory Processing Disorder Foundation website for more information and to locate a practitioner that provides treatment for SPD. http://spdfoundation.net/index.html

# SAMPLE SCHOOL ACCOMMODATIONS FOR SPD AND ADHD

**Walk** Get up and take a short walk at specified intervals, perhaps with an aide.

**Desk Accommodations:** Place a band of stretchy material around front chair legs that you can push your shins and ankles against. Attach a carpet square or piece of soft cloth to the underside of the desk to touch. Or sit on an inflatable cushion.

**Fidget with Objects:** Use "fidgets" such as a Koosh ball, fabric tab sewn in to a pocket, or bracelet, small plastic figures, anything that keeps your hands busy so you can focus better.

**Listen to Calming Music:** Use headphones and listen to music that helps calm you.

**Chew:** Use objects to chew on such as a Pencil Topper, ChewEase, or Chewable Jewel which provide soothing oral input to keep you focused on learning rather than sensory cravings.

**Push-ups and Jumping Jacks:** Periodically stand up and do jumping jacks or push-ups done in a chair or against a wall provide organizing proprioceptive input.

**Stretch:** Stretch often.

**Move Often:** All children—especially those with ADHD and/or sensory challenges —need to *move* before, during, and after school: run, jump, swing, hang from monkey bars, throw, push and pull objects. **Ask teachers not to keep students in from recess to catch up on work as this is counterproductive to their ability to concentrate and sit still.**

**Brush:** Go into a bathroom stall, and brush yourself using the deep touch pressure technique for sensory defensiveness.

Adapted from http://sensorysmarts.com/working_with_schools.html

## Tool 14-2: Learning Breakthrough Program

**BACKGROUND:**   The Learning Breakthrough Program™ uses balance and physical movements to integrate auditory, visual, motor planning, tactile, balance, body positioning and feedback systems in order to strengthen neurotransmission and calibrate the brain's functions. It is being used to improve learning, attention and balance-challenged physical disorders. Research is limited to case studies and anecdotal evidence but for some who have used it, improvements have been dramatic. Well known ADHD psychiatrist, Dr. Hallowell uses it at his Hallowell ADHD Centers and states that it greatly helped his son as well as many of his patients. This tool describes the program and gives resources to access it.

**SKILL BUILDING:**   Use Handout 14-2 to explain the Learning Breakthrough Program and to help clients learn where to find out more about it. Discuss the possible benefits, the absence of risk of harm from trying it and whether or not this might be a good addition to their treatment plan.

**RESOURCE:**   For more information visit the Learning Breakthrough Website at: https://learningbreakthrough.com/

**INTEGRATION:**   Consider whether this type of exercise program might be helpful given the needs of the client. Discuss the pros and cons of investing in this tool considering the lack of evidenced- based research. Encourage the client/parent who is interested to learn more about it from the website above and if possible to talk to some people who have completed the program to discuss how it helped them. If you are interested, visit the website to learn about offering the program in your practice.

# LEARNING BREAKTHROUGH PROGRAM™

**The Learning Breakthrough Program**

- Designed to improve attention, impulse control, grades, reading abilities, math and science skills and overcome a wide variety of learning problems

- Research is limited but improvements noted by individuals are significant

- Offered and endorsed by Dr. Hallowell at the Hallowell Centers

- Consists of a series of exercises that are done for 15 minutes twice a day for a period of 9-12 months

- The exercises involve balance, eye-hand coordination, visual and motor planning

- The exercises combine activation of the vestibular system, sensory integration and balance

- The program involves integration of both hemispheres of the brain and practices timing and sequencing

- Improvement is seen gradually over time

- Equipment used:

    - Belgau Balance Board
    - Visual Motor Control Stick
    - Pendulum Ball
    - Target Stand/Target Pins
    - Bean Bags
    - Toss Back Board with 4 Super Balls
    - Program Instruction Handbook
    - Program Activity Work-along DVD

# Chapter 15
# Movement to Optimize Brain Function

Tool 15-1: Movement Techniques for ADHD

## Tool 15-1: Movement Techniques for ADHD

**BACKGROUND:** According to Dr. Ratey, in his book *Spark. The Revolutionary New Science of Exercise and the Brain*, "exercise is the single most powerful tool you have to optimize brain function." A number of studies have shown that exercise enhances cognitive performance and brain function, attention, memory, hyperactivity, impulsivity, behavioral, emotional, and social functioning, and reduces the need for ADHD medications — all of which clients with ADHD can benefit from.

**SKILL BUILDING:**

*Exercise:* Explain to parents, children and teens the importance of movement, exercise, and physical activity for improving attention, cognitive control, impulse control, emotional control, behavioral control and social functioning. Discuss the fact that exercising and moving their body exercises the brain and makes it work better. Explain that they might think of exercise as administering the transmission fluid for the basal ganglia, which is responsible for the smooth shifting of the attention system. This area is the key binding site for stimulants, and brain scans show it to be abnormal in children with ADHD (Ratey, 2008). Let them know that although exercise doesn't typically make the symptoms of ADHD totally disappear, overall it can be very helpful and there are some who no longer need ADHD medications since they adopted a regular routine of physical exercise.

Ask the client (and their parent for younger children) what type of physical activity they enjoy. Use Handout 15-1 Physical Exercise for ADHD to help them find a way to participate in some form of exercise every day. Encourage parents to exercise with their child or teen.

*Classroom:* Encourage parents to ask their school to incorporate a program of short bursts of activity throughout the day such as the ABC for Fitness program or GoNoodle. Make sure their classroom teacher is not keeping the client inside during recess to catch up on work as this will be counterproductive for the client. Become or help them find a Brain Gym® practitioner who can teach the client simple exercises that are part of an integrated movement program (see the next page for resources).

*Yoga:* Discuss the benefits of yoga with parents. Explain that yoga is a mind-body practice that can help children and teens with ADHD release physical tension, frustration and excess energy; improve their self-awareness and physical self-control; and help them learn to slow down and gain control over their physical activity (Brown and Gerberg, 2012). Most parents will agree that their child could benefit from all these improvements, but find it hard to believe their hyperactive child could ever sit still. Yoga is particularly helpful for children and teens with hyperactivity as they need and love to move, and yoga allows them to move while teaching them self-control and self-awareness. Consider the developmental readiness of the child before suggesting they practice yoga. I have seen children as young as two-years-old learn and hold yoga positions and practice breathing techniques.

Before using yoga and/or meditation therapy for children with ADHD follow appropriate ethical practice by getting specific consent from parents to ensure that teaching yoga or mindfulness to their child doesn't conflict with religious or other belief systems of the parent.

***Karate:***   Karate is another way to incorporate movement and physical activity into a child or teen's life. Although the research is preliminary, there is a lot of anecdotal evidence that karate helps with self-control and academic success. According to Dr. Ratey, the martial arts demand a kind of concentration that forces coordination of the attention centers in the brain: the frontal cortex, the cerebellum and the limbic system. (Saulny, 2000) Find out if the client and their parents might be interested in finding a karate instructor.

***Dance and Gymnastics:***   Dance and gymnastics, similarly to karate, can provide physical exercise while teaching concentration, memorization and self-control.

***Team Sports:***   Team sports provide an opportunity for exercise as well as mastery, team building and social skills. Help clients figure out if there is a team sport they might be interested in. Caution them that sometimes during the season, team members may not be getting much actual exercise if they are sitting on the bench a lot or waiting for their turn to play. If that happens, they will need to add other types of exercise to their day.

## RESOURCES:

**ABC for Fitness**, developed by David Katz, co-founder of the Yale University Prevention Research Center, is offered free to school districts through Dr. Katz's nonprofit, Turn the Tide Foundation. The program helps teachers use short bursts of activity of three to ten minutes to accumulate thirty minutes a day. http://www.davidkatzmd.com/ abcforfitness.aspx

**GoNoodle** is an online program that leads students in what it calls "brain breaks." A two-minute program might lead the children in forming letters with their bodies, and a ten-minute session might run through a Zumba dance routine. The product, offered in both free and premium versions, is currently being used by 130,000 elementary school teachers. https://www.gonoodle.com/

**Brain Gym®** is an integrated movement program consisting of simple exercises designed to activate the brain, increase blood flow, short-term memory, and concentration, to facilitate learning and to calm and center the client. See Tool 13-1 Brain Gym for more information. http://www.braingym.org/

**INTEGRATION:**   Review Handout 15-1 Physical Exercise for ADHD with the client (and parent). What exercise is the client already getting? What do they notice about their ADHD symptoms when they do or don't exercise? What might they incorporate to get more regular exercise? Have they increased their activity level since discussing the importance of exercise to managing and decreasing their ADHD symptoms? Are they being held inside to complete work during recess? Is their school open to including "exercise/brain breaks" throughout the school day? If they are doing a team sport, are they sitting on the bench too often to get the benefits of exercise?

# PHYSICAL EXERCISE FOR ADHD

**List your current exercise/physical activity:**

**Exercise/Activity**                                                **How Often**

_____

_____

_____

_____

_____

_____

_____

_____

_____

**List exercise you enjoy or you are interested in trying**

Examples: team sports, bicycling, running, swimming, dancing, karate, yoga, skateboarding, skiing, gymnastic, tai chi

_____

_____

_____

_____

_____

_____

_____

_____

_____

- Make it a habit
- Schedule exercise on your calendar
- Plan on at least 3-4 times per week for at least 30 minutes
- **WEAR A HELMET** on your bicycle, scooter, skateboard, skis etc.

Tool 16-1: Physical Body Work

## Tool 16-1: Physical Body Work

**BACKGROUND:**  Some clients with ADHD may benefit from several types of body work including massage, chiropractic treatment, acupuncture and repetitive transcranial magnetic stimulation. This tool provides a brief review of the the benefits and effectivness of these treatment modalities.

**SKILL BUILDING:**  Review the different types of physical bodywork for ADHD and discuss the possible benefits of these types of body work for clients with ADHD. Although none of them have been exhaustively studied for ADHD, many of them have been found to have a significant improvement on symptoms of ADHD.

### Physical Body Work for ADHD

**Massage:** In one study, adolescents with ADHD were provided massage therapy or relaxation therapy for ten consecutive school days (Field, Quintino, & Hernandez-Reif, 1998). The massage therapy group, compared with the relaxation therapy group, showed less fidgeting behavior following the sessions. In addition, after the two-week period, their scores on the Conners Scale (Conners, 1989 and 1990) completed by their teachers (who were unaware of the group assignments) suggested that the children spent more time on-task and were less hyperactive in the classroom.

In another study adolescents with ADHD received massage therapy for twenty-minutes, twice-per-week, for one month which resulted in improved mood, anxiety, daydreaming and hyperactivity. The massage therapy group had significant improvements in self-ratings of mood and significant improvements in teacher ratings of classroom behavior (Khilnani et al. 2003).

**Chiropractic Treatment:** Chiropractic treatment is not specifically tailored for ADHD. It does not treat disease but relieves spinal nerve stress to allow the body to function normally via manipulation and pressure. One small case study of chiropractic treatment for children ages 9-13 showed improvement in ADHD symptoms (i.e., hyperactivity, impulsivity, and inattentiveness), as well as behavioral, social, or emotional difficulties (Alcantra, 2010).

**Repetitive Transcranial Magnetic Stimulaton (rTMS):** rTMS is a form of brain stimulation therapy developed in 1985 that uses magnetic pulses to activate parts of the brain. The magnetic pulses are delivered via small electromagnets. rTMS has been studied for and is FDA approved for depression but not yet for ADHD. rTMS affects dopaminergic secretion in the prefrontal cortex. Since ADHD has been suggested to involve dopaminergic prefrontal abnormalities it seems reasonable that rTMS might improve ADHD symptoms. Thus far, some studies showed overall improvements in functioning but did not specifically improve ADHD symptoms (Weaver et al, 2008, 2012). One study showed a beneficial effect on attention ten minutes after treatment (Bloch et al, 2010). More studies are needed.

***Acupuncture:*** Acupuncture is a component of traditional Chinese medicine (TCM). TCM holds that there are as many as 2,000 acupuncture points on the human body, which are connected by twenty pathways (twelve main, eight secondary) called meridians. These meridians conduct energy, or qi (pronounced "chi"), between the surface of the body and its internal organs. Each point has a different effect on the qi that passes through it. Qi is believed to help regulate balance in the body influenced by the opposing forces (positive, negative) of yin and yang. Acupuncture is believed to keep the balance between yin and yang thus allowing for the normal flow of qi throughout the body to restore health to the mind and body.

There appears to be no evidence base as of yet of randomized or quasi randomized controlled trials to support the use of acupuncture as a treatment for ADHD in children and adolescents. A meta-study done by Li et al (Li, 2011) found that due to the lack of trials, no conclusions can be reached about the efficacy and safety of acupuncture for ADHD in children and adolescents.

This doesn't mean it doesn't work for ADHD, but rather shows we cannot reach any conclusions about its efficacy and safety for children with ADHD. Some acupuncture practitioners find that acupuncture is extremely grounding and calming even for young children.

**INTEGRATION:**   Has the client already tried any of these treatment modalities and if so, were they helpful? Which ones do they have easy access to? Which ones have been shown to help the symptoms this client experiences? Does it make sense to add any of these treatment modalities to the treatment plan?

# Section VIII
# Environmental Influences

# Chapter 17

# Effects of Screen Time on Attention

Tool 17-1: Assess and Limit Screen Time

## Tool 17-1: Assess and Limit Screen Time

**BACKGROUND:** Studies show that children and teens often spend huge amounts of time in front of some type of screen, whether it is a TV, computer, tablet, smartphone or gaming console. A Kaiser Family Foundation study found that kids ages –eight to eighteen in the U.S. spend an average of 7.3 hours a day in front of a screen or listening to audio. Since they may be multi-tasking, this adds up to nearly 11 hours per day (Rideout et al, 2010).

In 2002, Hill and Castro found that TV negatively affects:

- Cognitive function and lower IQ's
- Attention
- Neurological function
- Violence and aggression

- Physical underdevelopment and obesity
- Visual and language problems
- Social problems

One study showed that early television exposure is associated with attentional problems at age seven (Christakis, 2004). Another study showed that educational television watched before the age of three is not significantly associated with attention problems. However, non-violent and violent programs (non-educational) watched before the age of three are significantly associated with attention problems five years later. Each hour per day spent viewing violent programs, doubled the odds for attention problems later on (Zimmerman et al, 2007).

Those with ADHD may use more screen time (internet and games) than those without and some become addicted to the short periods of activity with instant rewards in computer games. This may exacerbate ADHD symptoms and reduce time spent on developmentally challenging tasks (Weiss et al, 2011).

Therefore the amount and type of screen time children and teens are exposed to may have a significant impact on their ADHD symptoms. This tool provides a structured process for helping parents monitor screen time and make good decisions about its use.

**SKILL BUILDING:** Find out how much screen time the child or teen is exposed to by asking them to list:

- TV shows they watch
- When they use the computer and what for
- How much time they spend playing computer games
- How much they use their tablet and smartphone

Asking them about their favorite computer game may help get this discussion started. Most are enthused to tell you all about the game, how it works and how well they do on it.

Engage parents in a discussion of the family TV habits. Review Handout 17-1 Monitoring Screen Time with them to discuss how TV may be impacting their child or teen's attention problems. Ask them if they see any of these issues in their child's behavior or symptoms. Encourage them to use the suggestions on the handout to monitor and limit screen time.

Not all screen time is negative. There are plenty of positive and educational TV shows available. And let's face it, games are fun. Children and teens need to use the internet for information, school, and connecting. So the goal is not to completely avoid screen time, but rather to be mindful of its use and to limit the daily amount and content.

**INTEGRATION:**   Is screen time an issue? How are ADHD symptoms being impacted? How are behaviors impacted? Is the parent open to monitoring and limiting screen time? Are they aware of how much screen time their child or teen is being exposed to? Do they realize how screen time may be negatively affecting their child or teen? Are they able to find positive TV shows that encourage attention and learning?

# MONITORING SCREEN TIME

**Why Monitor Screen Time?**

- TV negatively affects:
  - Cognitive function and lower IQ's
  - Attention
  - Neurological function
  - Violence and aggression
  - Physical underdevelopment and obesity
  - Visual and language problems
  - Social problems

- Early television exposure
  - Is associated with attentional problems at age 7

- Educational television watched before the age of three
  - Not significantly associated with attention problems

- Non-violent and violent programs (non-educational) watched before the age of three
  - Significantly associated with attention problems five years later

- Each hour per day spent viewing violent programs, accounted for double the odds for attention problems later on

**How to Monitor Screen Time**

- ALWAYS monitor what your child or teen watches on TV – ALWAYS
  - Watch what they watch
  - Have a discussion with them about what they watched
  - Avoid letting them choose shows while you are busy with chores

- Keep a TV diary to know what your family watches

- Create a list of acceptable shows and who can watch them
  - Choose educational programs
  - Choose non-violent programs
  - Watch shows before allowing children and teens to watch them

- Put TV on the family calendar

- Limit hours spent in front of a screen: TV, computer, tablet, smartphone

- Avoid stimulating shows before bedtime

- Evaluate other screen time: computer games, social media, tablet use

# Chapter 18
# Environmental Toxins

Tool 18-1: Second-hand Smoke
Tool 18-2: Lead Poisoning
Tool 18-3: Chemical Sensitivity

## Tool 18-1: Second-hand Smoke

**BACKGROUND:**    Many children and teens with ADHD are exposed to second-hand smoke. A review of the literature regarding prenatal tobacco and postnatal second-hand smoke exposure shows that both are associated with increased rates of behavior problems including:

• ADHD

• Irritability

• Oppositional Defiant Disorder

• Conduct Disorder

 Another study suggests that prenatal tobacco exposure accounts for 270,000 excess cases of ADHD (Braun, 2006). Also, smoking begins at an earlier age in those with ADHD, they tend to smoke more and have more trouble quitting. Since ADHD is heritable, more parents of children with ADHD may smoke. This means that children and teens with ADHD might be exposed to more smoke.

Therefore, it is important to consider options for limiting exposure to second-hand smoke. This tool provides information on the research and options for increasing awareness about the effects of smoke on ADHD.

**SKILL BUILDING:**    Discuss the impact of smoke on ADHD with clients and parents. Explore options for decreasing and preferably eliminating exposure to smoke.

**RESOURCES:**    Visit go.pesi.com/ADHDworkbook for Handout 18A on the Effects and Guidance on Reducing Exposure to Second-hand Smoking.

**INTEGRATION:**    Is the child or teen being exposed to second-hand smoke? Have they been in the past? If there is current exposure from a parent or relative, are they open to limiting or eliminating exposure? Is the child or teen smoking? Are they wishing they could quit? If so, discuss options for getting them some help to do so.

## Tool 18-2: Lead Poisoning

**BACKGROUND:**    Studies are showing a link between lead exposure and ADHD. In one study, higher blood lead levels were associated with combined ADHD, but not inattentive ADHD. Another study found that blood lead was associated with symptoms of hyperactivity-impulsivity (parent rating) and inattention (teacher rating) (Nigg et al. 2010). Another study found that the risk of ADHD symptoms increased with blood lead concentration (Ha et al, 2009). Lead exposure accounts for 290,000 excess cases of ADHD in the United States (Braun, 2006). Therefore, it is important to make sure that symptoms of ADHD are not being caused by or exacerbated by lead exposure. Lead poisoning can cause a host of health problems including poor concentration seen in ADHD. This tool provides guidance on the connection between lead poisoning and ADHD, how to get lead blood levels tested and how to limit exposure.

### Common Sources of Lead Exposure:

- Lead may be inhaled, swallowed and (rarely) absorbed through the skin
- Lead based paint used in older homes or before 1970s
    - Can be found in dust, soil, peeling paint chips
- Contaminated soil around older homes (from lead based paint) or busy streets (gas contained lead until 1970s)
    - Soil can remain contaminated long after the lead paint or leaded gas is gone
- Water that flows through old lead pipes or faucets, if the pipes begin to break down
- Food stored in bowls glazed or painted with lead, or imported from countries that use lead to seal canned food
- Some toys, jewelry, hobby and sports objects (like stained glass, ink, paint, and plaster)

**SKILL BUILDING:**    Research has found a link between lead exposure and symptoms of ADHD. Explain the possibility that ADHD symptoms may be caused or exacerbated by lead exposure, how to get blood levels tested if appropriate, and where to look for possible sources of lead.

Find out if there is a possibility that lead exposure is present. If so, encourage parents to get blood levels checked. If blood levels are higher than normal, try to identify possible sources of lead and encourage them to seek help in eliminating the lead from the child or teen's environment.

### How to Find Out If Lead Exposure Is Present:

- Talk to your doctor about a blood test to measure lead blood levels
- Get water tested for lead in older homes and schools

**INTEGRATION:**    Is lead exposure possibly present? Is the lead blood level above normal? If yes, what is the parent doing to eliminate lead exposure? What local resources can you connect them with for doing so?

## Tool 18-3: Chemical Sensitivity

**BACKGROUND:** Some children and teens are sensitive to chemicals in their environment that may exacerbate symptoms of ADHD such as hyperactivity and poor concentration. They may have multiple chemical sensitivities (MCS) which cause their body and brain to react to chemicals and toxins normally found in the environment with an array of symptoms. Although the medical community often considers MCS to be controversial, I have previously experienced the effects of MCS on concentration and memory myself and have seen a number clients for whom this was a significant issue. This tool provides information on possible sensitivities and how to address them.

**SKILL BUILDING:** A small percentage of children and teens react to low exposures of chemicals found in their environment. This can include but is not limited to fragrances, cleaning products, fumes from additives in gasoline, chemicals used in building materials, and chemicals used on lawns as pesticides or weed killers. Therefore, when a child or teen has symptoms of ADHD it can be helpful to discover if they are having reactions to any of these chemicals and then reduce their exposure. Although they may experience such symptoms as headache, fatigue, dizziness, congestion, muscle pain, rash, heart rate changes, or nausea, they may also have increased trouble with concentration and memory.

If there is any indication of such sensitivity, encourage parents to look for possible culprits. Help them track any worsening of symptoms after certain activities where there may have been an exposure to a chemical. Encourage them to use unscented cosmetics, soap, shampoo, laundry detergent, dryer sheets and to avoid anything that contains fragrance. Remind them to use low chemical cleaning products and to have plenty of outside ventilation whenever they use any cleaning products, paint or glue inside the home. Wash new clothes before wearing to remove chemicals used to treat the fabrics. Be wary of new or newly renovated buildings where new construction materials are still out-gassing.

**RESOURCES:** Visit go.pesi.com/ADHDworkbook for Handout 18B on Limiting Chemicals and Toxins In The Environment.

**INTEGRATION:** Is there any evidence that chemical sensitivity is present? If so, how does it impact symptoms of ADHD? Has the culprit(s) been identified? How is the family doing at eliminating chemical exposure? Is it helping?

# Section IX
# Nutrition for the ADHD Brain

# Chapter 19

# Common Food Sensitivities May Mimic or Increase ADHD Symptoms

Studies repeatedly demonstrate the importance of eating a healthy diet. A client's diet can have a significant impact on his brain, health, concentration, behavior and sleep. This includes what he eats and when he eats it. Children and teens with ADHD are often found to be deficient in some important nutrients. Others have food sensitivities that result in poor concentration and/or hyperactivity. Some foods additives have been linked to increased hyperactivity.

This chapter provides tools for helping clients figure out what foods might be mimicking ADHD or making their ADHD symptoms worse. It reviews common nutritional deficiencies found in ADHD and how to assess and address them. It also provides guidelines for an optimal ADHD diet.

## Tool 19-1: Is Sugar the Culprit?

**BACKGROUND:** Many foods today that clients love to eat are loaded with sugar. Eating foods high in sugar results in a surge of sugar in the bloodstream followed by a dumping of energy a short time later. The hyperactive client may be sensitive to the effects of sugar and may become extremely hyper when they have it.

Besides increasing hyperactivity, sugar may have the opposite effect when the body responds to a rapid surge in blood sugar. A sudden increase in blood sugar will trigger an increase in insulin which will rapidly lower the sugar level in the blood. A low sugar level worsens the already low brain arousal level of the ADHD child or teen and can aggravate behavioral problems. Then you will have a cranky, irritable, and unmotivated child or teen who cannot concentrate well.

Studies are contradictory about the effects of sugar on hyperactivity and behavior and many indicate no change in symptoms (Wolriach, ML, 1994). My own daughter became incredibly hyperactive when she had sugar or artificial colors. (I guess she didn't read those studies!) Many of my clients have discovered that sugar was a culprit in making symptoms worse. It is definitely worth looking at the effects of sugar consumption on your clients.

**SKILL BUILDING:** Find out how much sugar your client consumes. Help them keep track by using Handout 19-1-1 Food Diary to write down everything they eat for 1-2 days. Review it with them to see what food choices they are making and how much sugar they are eating. Teach them to look at food labels and show them where the sugar content is listed. Discuss with parents and older children and teens the effects of sugar on the symptoms of ADHD. Explain that sugar affects some people with ADHD by increasing hyperactivity and then increasing poor concentration and irritability. If they consume a lot of sugar use the Food/Symptom Diary on Handout 19-1-3 (example on Handout 19-1-2) to determine if sugar is increasing and/or decreasing their ADHD symptoms.

Explain that the glycemic index is a scale that indicates how fast the body will convert a particular food to glucose. The higher the number, the faster the rise in blood sugar will be. A low GI value is 55 or less, medium is 56 – 69 and high 70 or more. Encourage them to serve foods that have a low glycemic index. You can help them find a glycemic index chart online be searching for "glycemic index chart."

Encourage them to replace high sugar content foods with lower sugar content alternatives. One 20-ounce bottle of a popular orange soda contains 83 grams of sugar. That translates to 21 teaspoons of sugar. That's a huge amount! They might replace that with a flavored water such as 0 calorie SoBe® LifeWater Fuji Apple Pear which is sweetened with a stevia extract and has 0 grams of sugar. (At the time of this writing stevia has been found to be safe and non-toxic but as always, encourage clients to consult with their doctors before use.) Or they could replace candy with fruit or cheese, or use fruit-sweetened jelly. Beware of fruit juices that contain a lot of sugar. Use only fruit juice sweetened juices and limit the amount consumed daily due to the large amount of sugar they contain. Make a healthy drink by putting a wedge of fruit such as an apple, lemon, lime or orange into a glass of water.

Discuss the importance of avoiding the replacement of sugar with artificial sweeteners such as aspartame. See Tool 19-2 Food Additives for more information on this. At this writing stevia appears to be a safe alternative.

**INTEGRATION:** How much sugar is the client consuming? How much impact is sugar having on the client's ADHD symptoms? Were they able to complete the Food Diary? Did they discover a pattern of increased ADHD symptoms following consumption of sugar when they completed the Food/Symptom Diary? Are they finding ways to decrease sugar intake?

# FOOD DIARY

**Write down everything you put in your mouth today including food and drinks.**

| Time | Food or Drink |
|------|---------------|
|      |               |
|      |               |
|      |               |
|      |               |
|      |               |
|      |               |
|      |               |
|      |               |
|      |               |
|      |               |
|      |               |
|      |               |
|      |               |
|      |               |
|      |               |
|      |               |
|      |               |
|      |               |
|      |               |
|      |               |
|      |               |
|      |               |
|      |               |
|      |               |
|      |               |
|      |               |
|      |               |
|      |               |
|      |               |

# FOOD / SYMPTOM DIARY EXAMPLE

**Instructions:** Write the symptoms above the columns. Write down the date and time, what was eaten (include drinks and everything eaten), and circle the number to rate the symptom. 0 is no problem, 1 = a little, 2=some, 3=often, 4=very often, 5 = a huge problem. So for example if they are revved up and really hyper and can't sit still, rate hyperactivity a 5. After a day or two see if there are any patterns where ratings go up or down within 3-4 hours of eating certain food or within 24 hours of eating certain foods.

(Circled rating shown in parentheses.)

| Date/Time | Food/Drink Eaten | Hyperactivity | Concentration | Irritability | On Task | Sleep |
|---|---|---|---|---|---|---|
| 1/28 9AM | Egg, OJ, WhlWhtToast | (0) 1 2 3 4 5 | (0) 1 2 3 4 5 | 0 (1) 2 3 4 5 | 0 1 2 3 (4) 5 | 0 1 2 3 4 (5) |
| | Butter, Milk | 0 (0) 2 3 4 5 | (0) 1 2 3 4 5 | 0 (0) 2 3 4 5 | (0) 1 2 3 4 5 | 0 1 (2) 3 4 5 |
| 11AM | 2 candy bars | 0 1 (2) 3 4 5 | 0 1 2 (3) 4 5 | 0 1 2 (3) 4 5 | 0 1 2 3 (4) 5 | 0 (1) 2 3 4 5 |
| 12:30PM | Rye Bread, Tuna, Mayo | 0 1 2 (3) 4 5 | 0 (0) 2 3 4 5 | 0 (1) 2 3 4 5 | 0 1 (2) 3 4 5 | 0 1 2 3 (4) 5 |
| | Water, Banana | (0) 1 2 3 4 5 | 0 1 2 (3) 4 5 | 0 (0) 2 3 4 5 | 0 1 2 (3) 4 5 | 0 (1) 2 3 4 5 |
| 3:30 PM | Twizzlers/Soda | 0 1 2 3 4 (5) | 0 1 2 3 (4) 5 | 0 1 2 3 (4) 5 | 0 1 2 (3) 4 5 | 0 (1) 2 3 4 5 |
| 6:00 PM | Flounder with Lemon | 0 1 (2) 3 4 5 | 0 (1) 2 3 4 5 | 0 (1) 2 3 4 5 | 0 (1) 2 3 4 5 | 0 1 (2) 3 4 5 |
| | Broccoli | 0 1 (2) 3 4 5 | 0 (1) 2 3 4 5 | 0 (1) 2 3 4 5 | 0 (1) 2 3 4 5 | (0) 1 2 3 4 5 |
| | Sweet Potato, Butter | 0 (1) 2 3 4 5 | 0 1 2 (3) 4 5 | 0 1 2 (3) 4 5 | 0 (1) 2 3 4 5 | 0 1 (2) 3 4 5 |
| | Milk | 0 1 2 (3) 4 5 | 0 (1) 2 3 4 5 | 0 (1) 2 3 4 5 | 0 1 2 3 (4) 5 | 0 1 2 3 (4) 5 |
| | Choc Chip Cookies 4 | 0 1 2 (3) 4 5 | 0 1 2 3 (4) 5 | 0 1 2 3 (4) 5 | 0 1 2 3 (4) 5 | (0) 1 2 3 4 5 |
| | | 0 1 2 3 4 5 | 0 1 2 3 4 5 | 0 1 2 3 4 5 | 0 1 2 3 4 5 | 0 1 2 3 4 5 |
| | | 0 1 2 3 4 5 | 0 1 2 3 4 5 | 0 1 2 3 4 5 | 0 1 2 3 4 5 | 0 1 2 3 4 5 |
| | | 0 1 2 3 4 5 | 0 1 2 3 4 5 | 0 1 2 3 4 5 | 0 1 2 3 4 5 | 0 1 2 3 4 5 |
| | | 0 1 2 3 4 5 | 0 1 2 3 4 5 | 0 1 2 3 4 5 | 0 1 2 3 4 5 | 0 1 2 3 4 5 |
| | | 0 1 2 3 4 5 | 0 1 2 3 4 5 | 0 1 2 3 4 5 | 0 1 2 3 4 5 | 0 1 2 3 4 5 |
| | | 0 1 2 3 4 5 | 0 1 2 3 4 5 | 0 1 2 3 4 5 | 0 1 2 3 4 5 | 0 1 2 3 4 5 |

# FOOD / SYMPTOM DIARY

**Instructions:** Write the symptoms above the columns. Write down the date and time, what was eaten (include drinks and everything eaten), and circle the number to rate the symptom. 0 is no problem, 1 = a little, 2=some, 3=often, 4=very often, 5 = a huge problem. So for example if they are revved up and really hyper and can't sit still, rate hyperactivity a 5. After a day or two see if there are any patterns where ratings go up or down within 3-4 hours of eating certain food or within 24 hours of eating certain foods.

| Date/Time | Food/Drink Eaten | | | | | | |
|---|---|---|---|---|---|---|---|
| | | 0 1 2 3 4 5 | 0 1 2 3 4 5 | 0 1 2 3 4 5 | 0 1 2 3 4 5 | 0 1 2 3 4 5 | 0 1 2 3 4 5 |
| | | 0 1 2 3 4 5 | 0 1 2 3 4 5 | 0 1 2 3 4 5 | 0 1 2 3 4 5 | 0 1 2 3 4 5 | 0 1 2 3 4 5 |
| | | 0 1 2 3 4 5 | 0 1 2 3 4 5 | 0 1 2 3 4 5 | 0 1 2 3 4 5 | 0 1 2 3 4 5 | 0 1 2 3 4 5 |
| | | 0 1 2 3 4 5 | 0 1 2 3 4 5 | 0 1 2 3 4 5 | 0 1 2 3 4 5 | 0 1 2 3 4 5 | 0 1 2 3 4 5 |
| | | 0 1 2 3 4 5 | 0 1 2 3 4 5 | 0 1 2 3 4 5 | 0 1 2 3 4 5 | 0 1 2 3 4 5 | 0 1 2 3 4 5 |
| | | 0 1 2 3 4 5 | 0 1 2 3 4 5 | 0 1 2 3 4 5 | 0 1 2 3 4 5 | 0 1 2 3 4 5 | 0 1 2 3 4 5 |
| | | 0 1 2 3 4 5 | 0 1 2 3 4 5 | 0 1 2 3 4 5 | 0 1 2 3 4 5 | 0 1 2 3 4 5 | 0 1 2 3 4 5 |
| | | 0 1 2 3 4 5 | 0 1 2 3 4 5 | 0 1 2 3 4 5 | 0 1 2 3 4 5 | 0 1 2 3 4 5 | 0 1 2 3 4 5 |
| | | 0 1 2 3 4 5 | 0 1 2 3 4 5 | 0 1 2 3 4 5 | 0 1 2 3 4 5 | 0 1 2 3 4 5 | 0 1 2 3 4 5 |
| | | 0 1 2 3 4 5 | 0 1 2 3 4 5 | 0 1 2 3 4 5 | 0 1 2 3 4 5 | 0 1 2 3 4 5 | 0 1 2 3 4 5 |
| | | 0 1 2 3 4 5 | 0 1 2 3 4 5 | 0 1 2 3 4 5 | 0 1 2 3 4 5 | 0 1 2 3 4 5 | 0 1 2 3 4 5 |
| | | 0 1 2 3 4 5 | 0 1 2 3 4 5 | 0 1 2 3 4 5 | 0 1 2 3 4 5 | 0 1 2 3 4 5 | 0 1 2 3 4 5 |
| | | 0 1 2 3 4 5 | 0 1 2 3 4 5 | 0 1 2 3 4 5 | 0 1 2 3 4 5 | 0 1 2 3 4 5 | 0 1 2 3 4 5 |
| | | 0 1 2 3 4 5 | 0 1 2 3 4 5 | 0 1 2 3 4 5 | 0 1 2 3 4 5 | 0 1 2 3 4 5 | 0 1 2 3 4 5 |
| | | 0 1 2 3 4 5 | 0 1 2 3 4 5 | 0 1 2 3 4 5 | 0 1 2 3 4 5 | 0 1 2 3 4 5 | 0 1 2 3 4 5 |
| | | 0 1 2 3 4 5 | 0 1 2 3 4 5 | 0 1 2 3 4 5 | 0 1 2 3 4 5 | 0 1 2 3 4 5 | 0 1 2 3 4 5 |
| | | 0 1 2 3 4 5 | 0 1 2 3 4 5 | 0 1 2 3 4 5 | 0 1 2 3 4 5 | 0 1 2 3 4 5 | 0 1 2 3 4 5 |
| | | 0 1 2 3 4 5 | 0 1 2 3 4 5 | 0 1 2 3 4 5 | 0 1 2 3 4 5 | 0 1 2 3 4 5 | 0 1 2 3 4 5 |

## Tool 19-2: Food Additives

**BACKGROUND:**    Children and teens today often unknowingly eat a diet loaded with additives, chemicals, preservatives, pesticides, artificial sweeteners, artificial colors and antibiotics. This tool provides a framework for identifying food additives that may be worsening the symptoms of ADHD.

**SKILL BUILDING:**    Use Handout 19-2 Food Additive Guidelines to explain to parents, older children and teens that sometimes foods contain additives that may make their symptoms worse. Use the Food/Symptom Diary on Handouts 19-1-1 & 19-1-2 to help them discover if their symptoms worsen after eating certain foods. Use Handout 19-3 Reading Food Labels to explain what to look for on labels.

> *Artificial Sweeteners:*    One common artificial sweetener is aspartame, marketed as Nutrasweet, Equal, and Spoonful (in the UK). It is found in over 9,000 food and beverage products including some you wouldn't think of like juice products, cereal, yogurt and gum. Some of my clients have had significant health problems from eating aspartame including migraine headaches, poor concentration, body pain and feeling generally ill. Although one study found no link between aspartame and ADHD symptoms, (Wolraich, ML, et al, 1994) other studies of the effects of the amino acids in aspartame indicate they can interfere with mood, panic, and alter seizure thresholds. Candice Pert, in her book, *Everything You Need to Know to Feel Go(o)d*, states that aspartame breaks down into methanol (wood alcohol-which can cause blindness), which is broken down into formaldehyde with is listed as a carcinogen by the EPA and causes death in large doses. She and other brain experts state that aspartame should never have been approved by the FDA and describes it as a neurotoxin. Splenda, another artificial sweetener, also has some negative effects for some people. Some experts say that although sugar is not a health food, they would rather someone use sugar than an artificial sweetener like aspartame.

Use the handouts in this chapter to help clients find out if their symptoms are impacted by eating food with artificial sweeteners. Encourage clients to avoid artificial sweeteners if they notice a change in symptoms when they eat it. If the product label says "sugar-free" it is probably artificially sweetened. Show them a label with artificial sweetener to help them know what to look for. Look for aspartame, Nutrasweet or sucralose.

> *Pesticides:*    Children are generally considered to be at greatest risk from pesticide toxicity, because the developing brain is more susceptible to neurotoxicants (Weiss, B., 2000) and the dose of pesticides per body weight is likely to be larger for children. Children six to eleven years of age have the highest urinary concentrations of markers of pesticide exposure, compared with other age groups in the U.S. population (Barr, DB, et al, 2004).

Researchers at the Harvard School of Public Health found that the urine of children with ADHD had significantly higher levels of byproducts of insecticides. Children with levels higher than the median of detectable concentrations had twice the odds of ADHD, compared with children with undetectable levels. These kids were exposed to "normal" levels of pesticides (Bouchard, M.F. et al, 2010).

Another study found that increased levels of PCBs in umbilical cord blood samples were associated with a higher risk for AHDH-like behaviors in children (Sagiv et al., 2010).

Use Handout 19-2 Food Additive Guidelines for ADHD to encourage parents to limit exposure to pesticides by buying locally grown fresh produce in season and then washing it carefully. Thorough scrubbing of produce in cold water can eliminate 50% of pesticide residues. Suggest that they consider choosing organic for produce that tends to contain the most pesticide residues. These include peaches, apples, strawberries, blueberries, nectarines, cherries, imported grapes, potatoes, carrots, green beans, celery, bell peppers, spinach, kale, and collard greens. When possible peel fruits and vegetables, which may lower the exposure to pesticides.

Avoid fish that are high in PCBs: Atlantic or farmed salmon, bluefish, wild striped bass, flounder and blue crab.

Buy certified organic meats, organic milk, low-fat milk, and organic produce.

Also avoid exposure to pesticides applied to lawns and farm fields and use organic products in your own yard. Encourage schools to do the same.

**Artificial Colors:**   Studies have shown that artificial colors added to foods can cause allergic hypersensitivity reactions that can aggravate hyperactive behavior. The three worst offenders are Red 40 (allura red AC), yellow 5 (tartrazine) and yellow 6 (sunset yellow).

Encourage parents to look foods labeled "no artificial colorings or preservatives." Show them where the artificial colors are listed on a food label. Use Food/Symptom Diary on Handouts 19-1-2 & 19-1-3 to discover if certain artificial colors are causing or increasing ADHD symptoms.

For a review of studies done over the past 35 years on the relationship of diet to ADHD symptoms see state-of-the-art review article, The diet factor in attention-deficit/hyperactivity disorder. Millichap JG & Yee MM (2012). *Pediatrics*, 129 (2), 330-337.

**Antibiotics:**   A research study found that 69% of children being evaluated for school failure who were receiving medication for hyperactivity gave a history of greater than ten ear infections. By contrast, only 20% of non-hyperactive children had more than ten infections. Another study suggests that middle ear disease in school-age children may also be associated with hyperactivity and/or inattention, independently of learning disability (Adesman, AR, et al, 1990).

Some experts correlate ear and other infections with the systemic effects of repeated doses of antibiotics. Some suggest that this can result in a yeast overgrowth in their intestinal track and that yeast overgrowth can cause symptoms of ADHD. Also, as discussed in Tool 2-7 ADHD Mimics and Contributors, inner ear fluid has been shown to be a factor related to infections and allergies which are more common in children with ADHD and may need to be evaluated.

Find out if your client has taken repeated doses of antibiotics and if so encourage their parent to find a homeopathic physician who can ascertain if their ADHD symptoms might be related to or worsened by an imbalance in their body created by antibiotics.

**INTEGRATION:**   Explore the possible connection of food additives with ADHD symptoms with your client and/or their parent. Is the parent open to finding out what additives might make their child's symptoms worse? What additives have they already eliminated? What have they found has the most impact, if anything? Is organic really necessary?

# FOOD ADDITIVE GUIDELINES FOR ADHD

**Artificial Sweeteners:**

- Use the Food/Symptom Diary Handouts 19-1-1 – 19-1-3 to find out if your child's symptoms are impacted by eating food with artificial sweeteners.

- If yes, avoid artificial sweeteners.

- Read product labels. If it says "sugar-free" it is probably artificially sweetened. Watch out for and avoid aspartame, Nutrasweet, Splenda, Equal or sucralose.

**Pesticides:**

- Children are generally considered to be at greatest risk from pesticides, because the developing brain is more susceptible to neurotoxicants (Weiss, B., 2000)

- Children with higher levels of the most commonly detected pesticide had twice the odds of ADHD, compared with children with undetectable levels

- **Limit Pesticide:**
  - Buy locally grown fresh produce in season and then wash it carefully
  - Choose organic produce as much as possible but definitely for these foods that tend to contain the most pesticide residues
    - Peaches, apples, strawberries, blueberries, nectarines, cherries, imported grapes, potatoes, carrots, green beans, celery, bell peppers, spinach, kale, and collard greens
  - Peel fruits and vegetables whenever possible
  - Avoid or limit fish that are high in PCBs: Atlantic or farmed salmon (buy wild-caught), bluefish, wild striped bass, flounder, and blue crab
  - Buy certified organic meats, organic milk, low-fat milk, and organic produce
  - Thorough scrubbing of produce in cold water can eliminate 50% of pesticide residues
  - Avoid exposure to pesticides applied to lawns and farm fields

**Artificial Colors:**

- Studies have shown that artificial colors added to foods can cause allergic hypersensitivity reactions that can aggravate hyperactive behavior

- Use Food/Symptom Diary on Handouts 19-1-1 – 19-1-3 to discover if certain artificial colors are causing or increasing ADHD symptoms. Look for increased hyperactivity and irritability

- Look for foods labeled "no artificial colorings or preservatives"

- Read food labels and avoid the worst offenders; Red 40, Yellow 5 and Yellow 6; or other colors your child is sensitive to
  - Example: Certified colors: "FD&C Red No. 40" or "Red 40"
    Non-certified colors: List as "artificial color," "artificial coloring"

**Antibiotics:**

- Studies suggest that middle ear disease in school-age children may also be associated with hyperactivity and/or inattention, or school failure, independent of learning disability.

- Has your child had repeated infections and/or taken repeated doses of antibiotics?

- Was there any change or increase in ADHD symptoms after doing so?

- If so, find a holistically oriented pediatrician or naturopathic physician to find out if your child's ADHD symptoms might be related to or worsened by an imbalance in their body created by antibiotics

- Use organic beef, chicken and bison to avoid added antibiotics

- Read food labels and look for "no antibiotics used"

## Tool 19-3: Reading Food Labels

**BACKGROUND:**    Most children and teens, and even some parents, do not know how to read a food label. In order to make healthy food choices they must read the food labels and understand how to compare different foods. This tool provides guidance on what to look for on the label and in the ingredients list based on the avoidance of food additives and sugar discussed in the previous Tools 19-1 and 19-2.

**SKILL BUILDING:**    Use the reading Food Labels Handout 19-3 as a guide. Ask clients to bring in some labels from foods that they eat regularly and point out where to look for fats, sugars, calories, artificial colors and other food additives. Show them a variety of food labels and ingredients lists from foods they love or from offending foods and compare them with healthier alternatives.

**RESOURCES:**

• The FDA website provides guidance on how to read the nutrition label at http://www.fda.gov
• Many restaurant chains list the nutrition facts online. Simply search for "restaurant name nutrition." Do this in session with clients and look up their favorite foods to help them make better choices.
• Visit go.pesi.com/ADHDworkbook for Handout 19A on Preservatives.

**INTEGRATION:**    How did clients (or their parents) react to learning about food labels and ingredients list? Were they able to find foods they like that have healthier ingredients? Were they surprised by the amount of sugar they eat? Encourage them to read the label for every food they eat to make sure it is low in sugar, artificial colors, and food additives. Has this exercise helped their symptoms improve?

# READING FOOD LABELS

**Where to Find the Nutrition Label and Ingredient Label:**
> The nutrition label is usually found on the back or side of the package. The ingredient label is normally found on the back of the package and lists ingredients in the order of their quantity in the food.

**What to Look for on the Nutrition Label and Ingredients List:**

**Calories:** Choose products with lower calories to prevent obesity

**Sodium:** Choose products with lower sodium content

**Protein:** Be sure to include plenty of protein in each meal

**Sugar:** Choose foods with less than 15 grams of sugar. Note that 4 grams is equivalent to 1 teaspoon. Ingredients that end in the word "ose" are all forms of sugar, such as:

- sucrose, maltose, dextrose, fructose, glucose, galactose, lactose, high fructose corn syrup, glucose solids.

**Also be on the lookout for:**
- Cane juice, dehydrated cane juice, cane juice solids, cane juice crystals, dextrin, maltodextrin, dextran, barley malt, beet sugar, corn syrup, corn syrup solids, caramel, buttered syrup, carob syrup, brown sugar, date sugar, malt syrup, diatase, diatastic malt, fruit juice, fruit juice concentrate, dehydrated fruit juice, fruit juice crystals, golden syrup, turbinado, sorghum syrup, refiner's syrup, ethyl maltol, maple syrup, yellow sugar, honey and corn sweeteners

**Fats:** The American Heart Association recommends choosing vegetable oils and margarines with liquid vegetable oil as the first ingredient and no more than 2 grams of saturated fat per tablespoon.

**Whole-grain Foods:** Should deliver at least 3 grams of fiber per serving and ideally even more.

**Artificial Colors:** Will list the color: Example: Yellow 5, Yellow 6, Red 40, Red 3, Blue 1, Blue 2, Green 3, and Orange B. Or they may be listed as:

- FD&C Blue No. 1 (brilliant blue FCF)
- FD&C Blue No. 2 (indigotine)
- FD&C Green No. 3 (fast green FCF)
- FD&C Red No. 40 (allura red AC)
- FD&C Red No. 3 (erythrosine)
- FD&C Yellow No. 5 (tartrazine)
- FD&C Yellow No. 6 (sunset yellow)
- Orange B (restricted to use in hot dog and sausage casings)

**Artificial Sweeteners:** as in sucralose, saccharin, aspartame, acesulfame
**Monosodium Glutamate (MSG):** may be listed as MSG or as "hydrolyzed soy protein" and "autolyzed yeast"

## Tool 19-4: Food Allergies/Sensitivities

**BACKGROUND:**    Food allergies and/or sensitivities can cause or aggravate symptoms of ADHD for some children and teens. Allergists can perform food allergy testing such as skin testing, blood testing and food challenges. Allergy tests for food allergies can give a starting point for what foods might be causing symptoms. Eliminating a suspected problem food for seven days, tracking symptoms, and then challenging by eating the food, and again tracking symptoms, is the most effective process available to tell if any particular food is contributing to ADHD symptoms. This tool does not replace the expertise provided by a medical doctor but provides the framework for how to determine if a particular food is causing symptoms.

**SKILL BUILDING:**    Discuss with parents, older children and teens how food allergy or sensitivity might be making their symptoms worse. Ask them if they have ever noticed feeling bad, sleepy, more hyperactive, less focused, or more irritable after eating any particular food. Encourage them to use the Food/ Symptom Diary on Handout 19-1-1 – 19-1-3 to write down everything they eat and drink for two to three days and rate their symptoms. Help them write up to five symptoms they experience across the top of the chart. See Handout 19-1-2 for an example of a completed Food/ Symptom Diary.

Explain that sometimes it can be difficult to track down the possible culprit. The effects of food allergy/sensitivity from eating a particular food can take up to four days to clear the system. Reactions can occur any time between immediately after eating a particular food until three to four days later. Sometimes the ingredients label doesn't contain every ingredient so you may be unaware that you're eating an offending food.

> ***Rain Barrel Analogy:***    My allergist used this rain barrel analogy to explain that allergy tends to be cumulative. If there is a little water in the bottom of the rain barrel and it rains, no problem. The water level just comes up. But if the rain barrel is already full of water and it rains, then the water spills over the top.

Allergies tend to work this way, too. You may be exposed to something you are allergic to, but if you haven't been exposed to many other things your body handles it without a reaction. But if you have been exposed to a number of things you are allergic/sensitive to, the last thing you eat may cause your rain barrel to overflow and you have a reaction. But it might not have been just that one last thing that caused the reaction but rather the background load you were already dealing with. Therefore, it is crucial to keep the background level of exposure to allergens or triggers low to prevent a reaction.

Review the client's Food/Symptom Diary with them. Look at when symptoms increased (if they did) and look for patterns of what they ate before this occurred. Remember, it may take up to three days for a reaction to occur. Pay attention to what they ate repeatedly. Is their diet loaded with sugar, artificial colors, processed foods and food additives? Notice if they are eating any of the eight foods that account for 90% of all food-allergic reactions in the United States (Food Allergy Research and Education, 2015). These foods are:

| | |
|---|---|
| • Peanuts | • Wheat |
| • Tree nuts | • Soy |
| • Milk | • Fish |
| • Eggs | • Shellfish |

If you find a suspected culprit encourage the client's parent to eliminate all forms of that food from their child or teen's diet for seven days and continue tracking symptoms. For example, if they suspect milk, they must read all labels and avoid foods that contain milk or any ingredients that contain milk in any form.

It may take a few days for the symptoms to ease but if this is a problem food, the symptoms should gradually decrease. Keep in mind that it may be a combination of foods that are contributing to the problem. After eliminating a food for seven days, serve a small and then larger serving of the food and see if symptoms worsen. If there is no change in symptoms, then add the food back into the diet. Eliminating food from the diet can be challenging and you need to be careful to avoid an unnecessarily restricted diet that becomes unhealthy.

Repeat the process with other suspected foods. Some experts contend that avoiding a food for a year will lower the allergic response. Therefore, it may be possible to add back some of these foods in time.

Develop professional relationships with naturopathic physicians and allergists who specialize in helping clients with food allergy and sensitivity. Encourage the client's parents to work with these practitioners to assist with this process.

> **Case Example:**   *Julie, at five -years -old, was experiencing intense irritability, temper tantrums for no apparent reason, very low frustration tolerance and extreme hyperactivity. These episodes happened many times every day. After keeping the Food/Symptom Diary it appeared that Julie's symptoms were worse after she drank milk, ate cheese or had ice cream. Julie's parents removed all milk products from her diet for a week. By the end of the week Julie seemed like a new child. She was even-tempered, calmer, happier, could concentrate better and her meltdowns were gone.*
>
> *When her mom gave her a serving of milk at the end of the week, within a half-hour Julie was lying on the floor screaming, and having an intense temper tantrum.*
>
> *Julie never indicated that she was in any kind of pain such as a stomach ache or headache, so her parents never suspected that milk products were contributing to her behavior.*
>
> *Even with the elimination of milk from her diet Julie's symptoms still met the criteria for ADHD. But the level of her symptoms decreased significantly and her temper tantrums resolved. Julie is now an adult and still feels best when she limits dairy. She no longer needs ADHD medication nor meets the ADHD criteria since she completed neurofeedback treatment. See Chapter 10 for more information on neurofeedback.*

**RESOURCES:** Visit go.pesi.com/ADHDworkbook for Handout 19B on Foods that Contain Milk.
The Food Allergy Research and Education website is a great resource. http://www.foodallergy.org/allergens

**INTEGRATION:**   Was the client able to discover any connection between certain foods and symptoms? Are they working with an allergist or naturopathic physician? What symptoms, if any, have improved? Is the client less hyperactive, more focused, more successfully regulating their emotions? Is there more than one food contributing to their symptoms? Are they able to avoid the culprit foods? Is the child or teen able to notice the difference when they eat an offending food and when they don't? Do they still meet the criteria for the diagnosis of ADHD?

## Chapter 20
# Healthy ADHD Diet

Tool 20-1: Common Mineral and Fatty Acid Deficiencies
Tool 20-2: Optimal Diet for ADHD
Tool 20-3: Supplements/Nutraceuticals

## Tool 20-1: Common Mineral and Fatty Acid Deficiencies

**BACKGROUND:** Studies show that children with ADHD are commonly found to be deficient in zinc (Brown, Gerbarg, 2012), magnesium, (Starobrat-Hermelin, 1997), omega-3 fatty acids (Sinn & Bryan, 2007) and iron (Konofal, et al, 2004). This tool explains why these are important and provides food sources of these nutrients.

**SKILL BUILDING:** Explain to clients and parents that studies show that children with ADHD are often found to be deficient in zinc, magnesium, Omega-3 fatty acids, and/or iron. Use Handout 20-1 Common Mineral and Fatty Acid Deficiencies in ADHD to explain the research and provide them with food sources of these nutrients.

Encourage them to have their child or teen tested to determine if they are deficient in any of these before supplementing, as too much may be just as harmful as too little. Encourage parents to see a holistic doctor who routinely assesses for these deficiencies. Some tests are blood tests. Magnesium may be assessed from a hair sample to get a more accurate level.

If the client is deficient, encourage the parent to talk to their holistic medical practitioner about proper supplementation doses specific to their child's age, size and deficiency. Encourage parents to include foods in the child's or teen's diet that are rich in the deficient nutrient. Engage older child and teen clients in a discussion about options for including these foods in their diet. Remind parents to have the levels retested at a later date to make sure the levels have normalized after changing the diet or supplementing.

**INTEGRATION:** Are the parents open to having their child tested for these possible deficiencies? Is the client deficient? Are they using foods to incorporate more of the deficient nutrients? Are they using supplements? How are symptoms improving as the deficiency is being rectified?

# COMMON MINERAL AND FATTY ACID DEFICIENCIES IN ADHD

**OMEGA-3 FATTY ACIDS**

- **Studies**
  - A number of studies involving children with ADHD have shown **deficient Omega-3 fatty acids** such as eicosapentaenoic acid (EPA) and docosahexaenoic acid (DHA) which are essential to proper brain functioning.
  - Various studies report that an EPA and DHA containing supplement with Omega-3 fatty acids is effective in reducing ADHD symptoms including significant inattention and hyperactivity and behavior.

- **Omega-3 Function**
  - Cell membrane flexibility and function
  - Transmission efficiency
  - Mood, cognitive function, memory

- **Omega-3 Fatty Acids Can Be Found Naturally In**
  - Cold water fish (sardines, salmon, halibut, albacore tuna, swordfish, herring, etc.)
  - Flaxseeds, walnuts
  - Soybeans, scallops, shrimp
  - Tofu, algae, and primrose oil

**ZINC**

- **Studies**
  - Some studies suggest that children with inattentive ADHD may **have lower than normal levels of zinc** in their body
  - Several studies have shown a reduction in **hyperactivity and impulsivity** with zinc supplementation.
  - A 2005 study in the *Journal of Child and Adolescent Psychopharmacology*, showed a correlation between zinc levels and teacher- and parent-rated **inattention** in children.

- **Zinc Function**
  - Immune System
  - Neuronal activity
  - Neurogenesis
  - Learning impairment

- **Foods High in Zinc Include**
  - Oysters and other seafood
  - Red meat, poultry, lamb
  - Dairy products
  - Beans, nuts
  - Whole grains and fortified cereals

## MAGNESIUM

- **Studies**
  - Studies show a correlation between **hyperactivity and magnesium deficiency**
  - In one study a group of children was given magnesium supplementation for six months. This resulted in an increase in magnesium content in hair and a **significant decrease of hyperactivity**

- **Magnesium Function**
  - Calming the brain
  - Sleep
  - Concentration
  - Mood

- **Foods Containing the Most Magnesium**
  - Spinach
  - Squash and Pumpkin Seeds
  - Nuts
  - Wheat bran
  - Whole grain
  - Soybeans
  - Oatmeal

## IRON

- **Studies**
  - Studies show that low ferritin (an indirect measure of iron level) in kids with ADHD is correlated to more severe cognitive deficits and ADHD ratings.

- **Iron Function**
  - Needed for dopamine synthesis often impaired in ADHD
  - Needed for improved memory, learning and ADHD Symptoms

- **Foods Containing the Most Iron**
  - Red meat
  - Egg yolks
  - Dark, leafy greens (spinach, collards)
  - Dried fruit (prunes, raisins)
  - Iron-enriched cereals and grains (check the labels)
  - Mollusks (oysters, clams, scallops)
  - Turkey or chicken giblets
  - Beans, lentils, chick peas and soybeans
  - Liver
  - Artichokes

## Tool 20-2: Optimal Diet for ADHD

**BACKGROUND:**    Most children and teens with ADHD will benefit from eating a nutritious diet that supports overall brain health. This tool provides guidance on helping clients assess their current diet and make positive changes that aid in reducing ADHD symptoms.

**SKILL BUILDING:**    Use the Food Diary on Handout 19-1-1 to find out what your client is currently eating and to assess what if anything could be improved. Look over the completed Food Diary with the client and their parent when appropriate. Encourage them to continue with the foods that are healthy and that support their overall brain function. Review the guidelines on the Optimal Diet for ADHD Handout 20-2-1 with them and discuss what changes they can make to create a healthier diet. Use the Sample Meals on Handout 20-2-2 to help them design a menu of healthy foods that they enjoy eating for the next week. Refer to Tools 19-1 and 19-2 on sugar and food additives.

If you are working with a teen client, encourage them to include their parent in this process so they will make sure the healthy foods are available in the house each week.

Many clients are running on empty as they don't eat nutritious foods that support and fuel their brain. Some go all day without eating, especially if they are taking stimulant medications. Teach them that food is fuel for their brain like gas is fuel for the car. Ask them how far the car would go if it was out of gas. Encourage them to eat breakfast and help them design a fast, portable and healthy breakfast if they are always running late. Explore options for making sure they get healthy snacks, a good lunch and dinner. They should not go more than three hours without eating something.

> *Case Example:*    *When Terry, a nine-year-old boy with ADHD would arrive in my office after school for his neurofeedback session he was routinely lethargic, irritable and uncooperative. One day, when I asked him what he had for lunch he said he had some ice cream. His mother said he refused a snack on the way to see me. I had a mixture of nuts, raisins, and pumpkin seeds in my office. With his mother's permission I offered some to him. He said, "Yuck, I don't like those." So I said, "that's okay, they are here if you want to try them." I had a few and he started munching on some. Pretty soon he was wolfing them down. By about half way through the session he perked up, was cooperative, attentive and motivated.*

**INTEGRATION:**    Where is there room for improvement in the client's diet? Does it appear that their current diet might contain foods, pesticides, artificial colors and additives that might be impacting their symptoms? Are they eating breakfast and if so is it loaded with sugar? Are they skipping lunch or just eating potato chips and milk like one of my clients was doing? Are they eating often enough? Are they and their parents able to make healthy changes to their diet? Are symptoms improving as they transform to a healthier diet?

# OPTIMAL DIET FOR ADHD

- Eat breakfast that is low in sugar, contains protein such as eggs, nut butter, milk, or a protein smoothie and organic whole grains and fruit.

- Use organic food whenever possible to avoid pesticides, antibiotics, food additives, artificial colors.

- Use organic whole grains.

- Limit sugar. Replace sugary snacks with fruit or cheese and crackers. Replace soda with filtered water, milk, flavored water, limited no-sugar-added juice or water with fruit slices such as apple, lemon, lime, orange, or strawberry.

- Avoid artificial sweeteners. Instead, use stevia, fruit juice, small amounts of molasses or local honey.

- Include a variety of proteins, fruits and vegetables, whole grain (organic), water, dairy.

- Avoid caffeine, including sodas, energy drinks and chocolate.

- Avoid margarine.

- Avoid additives such as artificial colors, flavors, stabilizers, and binders.

- Avoid MSG (listed as: hydrolyzed vegetable protein, yeast extract, autolyzed yeast and sometimes natural flavorings).

- Use only monounsaturated fats (olive oil, nut butters) or small amounts of butter.

- Serve a good amount of protein at each meal. Follow the rule of a half a gram of protein per pound of body weight. (Example: 40 lb child needs 20 grams of protein)

- Use supplements for zinc, magnesium, and/or iron if deficient.

- Include a well-rounded multi-vitamin containing minimum daily requirements.

- Use fish oil, two servings of cold water fish per week, or Omega-3 supplements if deficient in Omega-3.

- Serve breakfast, lunch, dinner and 2-3 healthy snacks.

# SAMPLE MEALS

**Always serve water.** Also, serve milk, cider, fruit juice sweetened juice, flavored water (no sweetener, just water), water with fruit slices.

**Serve organic food to avoid pesticides, antibiotics, artificial colors and food additives.**

**Breakfast:**
- ✓ Whole grain toast with unsweetened nut butter (peanut, almond, cashew, soy nut) and fruit juice sweetened jelly (Simply Fruit and Polaner are two brands). This can be eaten as a sandwich on the way to the bus.
- ✓ Two eggs, whole grain toast with Simply Fruit jelly and half a pink grapefruit
- ✓ Protein powder shake with blueberries, bananas or strawberries
- ✓ Luna bar or other protein bar and a piece of fruit
- ✓ Plain yogurt with nuts, berries or Simply Fruit or Polaner jelly
- ✓ Oatmeal with cinnamon, sunflower seeds, raisins or nuts
- ✓ Left-over dinner

**Lunch:**
- ✓ Cheese on whole wheat bread, carrot sticks with low fat dressing, an apple, healthy chips or popcorn
- ✓ Left- over dinner
- ✓ Salad with spinach, carrots, tomato, tuna, organic turkey, or hardboiled egg and blueberries
- ✓ Beef barley soup, peanut butter and jelly (Polaner or Simply Fruit) on whole wheat bread and an orange
- ✓ Tuna with light mayo on whole grain bread with lettuce and tomato, Sun Chips and an apple

**Dinner:**
- ✓ Turkey burgers, green beans, brown rice, fruit cup
- ✓ Hamburger, broccoli, baked sweet potato, juice pop
- ✓ Pizza, small salad, an orange
- ✓ Pasta and meat/tomato sauce, peas and salad
- ✓ Wild caught salmon, brown rice and Brussel sprouts

**Snack:**
- ✓ An apple, orange, banana, berries
- ✓ Carrot sticks
- ✓ A piece of low fat cheese
- ✓ Red peppers
- ✓ Juice pops – no added sugar
- ✓ Yogurt – plain with fruit sweetened jelly or some fruit
- ✓ Nut butter on raw veggies
- ✓ Walnuts, pecans or almonds
- ✓ Whole wheat crackers

## Tool 20-3: Supplements/Nutraceuticals

**BACKGROUND:** If the client is deficient in zinc, magnesium, iron, or Omega-3 fatty acids, it may be helpful to use supplements or nutraceuticals to correct the deficiency. Other supplements are sometimes recommended as well. This tool provides a look at the issues involved in finding good quality products and gives a list of some of the more common nutraceuticals being recommended. I do not prescribe supplements but I refer clients to holistic or naturopathic physicians who do.

### SKILL BUILDING:

*Safety and Effectiveness:* Before recommending dietary supplements or nutraceuticals, explain to clients and their parents, that because these are not regulated as drugs by the FDA, their manufacturers are not required to prove that supplements are safe and effective (FDA, 2015). Consequently, few supplements have been studied rigorously for safety and effectiveness, although some may eventually be shown to be safe and effective. Also, supplements, unlike drugs, are not regulated to ensure that they are pure or that they contain the ingredients or the amount of active ingredient they claim to contain. As a result, the supplement may contain other substances, and the amount of active ingredient in a dose may vary.

Encourage parents and clients to talk with their holistic or naturopathic physician about recommendations for brands that are safe and from a well-known manufacturer. They will also need to ask for specific doses needed to correct any deficiency that is present. Make sure that they understand the possibility that supplements could interact with prescription and non-prescription drugs, which might intensify or reduce the effectiveness of a drug, or cause a serious side effect.

*Supplements/Nutraceuticals Commonly Used for ADHD:* As discussed in Tool 20-1, and Handout 20-1 Common Mineral and Fatty Acid Deficiencies in ADHD, the following have been found to be deficient in children with ADHD and symptoms have improved with supplementation. Recommend that parents work with a holistic or naturopathic physician to test their levels and follow their recommendations for supplementation.

- Zinc

- Magnesium

- Iron

- Omega-3

Encourage clients to ask their holistic or naturopathic physician about the following supplements that can be helpful in reducing symptoms of ADHD.

- Acetyl-l-carnitine

- B vitamins

- Meclofenoxate

- Picamilo

- Pycnogenol

- SAMe

- Discuss supplementing with a multi-vitamin containing minimum daily requirements.

During the intake process you found out what supplements they are already taking, right? Make sure they are not using anything that might be contra-indicated.

**Case Example:**     *One of my 12-year-old clients had abnormally large alpha brainwaves (as shown on her QEEG – see Tool 2-3 QEEG) and the supplement she was taking, l-theanine, made them even larger. Although this was prescribed to calm her anxiety it was effectively impairing her ability to pay attention. When discontinued, she was better able to stay focused and learn although she still met the criteria for ADHD. She then learned mindfulness skills and did neurofeedback training which reduced her anxiety significantly and improved her ability to concentrate to normal levels.*

**RESOURCES:**     Richard Brown, MD and Patricia Gerbarg, MD include a chart of recommended doses in their excellent book *Non-Drug Treatments for ADHD*.

**INTEGRATION:**     Do the client's parents understand the safety concerns about using supplements or nutraceuticals? Are they already using supplements and if so, are they helping? Are they using anything that is contraindicated? Have you connected them with a holistic or naturopathic physician who can test for deficiencies and recommend safe supplements?

# Section X
# Sleep and ADHD

# Chapter 21
# Assess and Improve Sleep

## Tool 21-1: The Impact of Sleep on ADHD and Vice Versa

**BACKGROUND:**   An estimated 25-50% of children and teens with ADHD have trouble sleeping. (Weiss et al, 2010) This can include taking longer to fall asleep, resistance to going to bed or falling asleep, being extra tired upon waking and daytime tiredness. Also, restless leg syndrome, limb movement disorder and sleep-disordered breathing problems are more common in children and teens with ADHD. One study found that stimulant medication for ADHD was more effective in poor sleepers than in good sleepers (Cortese, 2006). This may indicate that children and teens with ADHD may be chronically tired and the stimulants make them more alert. This tool provides guidance on assessing the client's sleep habits.

**SKILL BUILDING:**   During the intake process and periodically thereafter ask clients and their parents about sleep habits. Use Handout 21-1-1 Are You Sleeping? to help them be as specific as possible about when they:

- Go to bed
- Go to sleep
- Wake up
- Get up

Ask them:

- How do you feel upon waking?
- How sleepy are you during the day?
- How restless are you?
- Do you snore? (Ask the parent if they hear their child snore.)

If they are unsure about how much time they are actually sleeping they might use something that monitors movement to find out how long they were still during the night. Although these don't actually measure sleep they can give a good idea of how long the wearer lays still. They also increase the user's mindfulness about sleep by helping them focus on when they went to sleep and woke up. Some are more accurate than others. Here are some brands: Philips Actiwatch Spectrum ($600), Basis Chrome ($199), Jawbone Up ($115), FitBit Flex ($99).

Use the chart on Handout 21-1-3 Sleep Required By Age to find out if they are getting about the right amount of sleep for their age. Since every child is different it is important to help them figure out the amount of sleep that makes them feel the best the next day. Use Handout 21-1-2 Get the Sleep You Need to help them figure out how much sleep they need to function the best.

Explain that poor sleep can worsen and even mimic symptoms of ADHD such as poor concentration and hyperactivity. Children without enough sleep are often cranky, easily irritated, and need more parental attention. They may fall asleep in class because they are they tired. They may have more trouble concentrating due to fatigue and brain fog. Their hyperactivity may increase as they try to keep themselves awake and alert by moving. Ask the child or teen and the parent how they know when they or their child or teen did not get enough sleep.

**INTEGRATION:** Based on the assessment of sleep does it appear that the client might have a sleep issue that is worsening or perhaps mimicking symptoms of ADHD, such as concentration, hyperactivity, and impulsivity? If there are signs of a primary sleep disorder or of sleep apnea, encourage them to consult with a sleep neurologist. Perhaps a sleep study would help define the problem.

# ARE YOU SLEEPING?

**Current Sleep Pattern:**

What time do you go to bed?_____

What time do you fall asleep?_____

How many times do you wake up during the night?_____

How long before you fall back to sleep?_____

What time do you wake up?_____

How tired are you when you wake? (0 = Fully rested->10 = Exhausted) _____

Are you a restless sleeper? (How do your blankets look in the AM?)_____

How tired/sleepy are you during the day (0 = Not at all->10 = Extremely)_____

Has anyone ever told you that you snore? Yes_____ No_____

# GET THE SLEEP YOU NEED

**Determine how much sleep you need:**

- What's the most sleep you ever get?_____
- How tired are you when you sleep this much? (0-10)_____
- What's the least amount of sleep you ever get?_____
- How tired are you when you sleep this much? (0-10)_____
- How many hours of sleep per night make you feel the best?_____

**Determine your ideal bedtime:**

- What time do you need to get up in the morning?_____
- How much sleep do you need (from above)?_____
- Subtract the number of hours of sleep from the time you need to get up._____
- Example:
    - You need to get up at 6:30AM
    - You need 9.5 hours of sleep
    - Your bedtime is 6:30AM – 9 hours = 9:30PM

Note: Think about how you know you are tired. Do you fall asleep during the day, in class, while reading, while riding in the car? Do you have extra trouble concentrating? Do you fidget and have more trouble sitting still? Are you cranky and grumpy, easily annoyed and quickly frustrated? Do you have trouble motivating yourself to do things? These can all be signs that you are tired.

# SLEEP REQUIRED BY AGE

The amount of sleep a child needs will vary depending on the age of the child and tends to decrease with age. Every child is different. Use this as a general guideline.

| Age | Total Hours of Sleep Needed |
|---|---|
| 0-3 months | 10.5-18 |
| 4-11 months | 9-12 |
| 1 -2 years | 11-14 |
| 3 - 5 years | 11-13 |
| 6 -13 years | 9-11 |
| Teens | 8-10 |

Example: If your child is 7-years-old and they need to get up at 7:00 AM, then make sure they are in bed between 8:00 and 8:30 PM to get the required hours of sleep 9-11 hours.

## Tool 21-2: Setting Up the Bedroom

**BACKGROUND:**   In order to promote good sleep, the bedroom should be dark, quiet, and designed specifically for sleeping - and nothing else. The client will go to sleep more easily if there is nothing in the bedroom that is fun or activating to distract them from sleeping. This tool provides guidance on how to set up the bedroom.

**SKILL BUILDING:**   Review Handout 21-2 Tips for the Bedroom with clients and parents to help them set up the bedroom so it is peaceful, safe, comfortable, quiet and dark. Emphasize that the bedroom should be set up for sleep and nothing else. This will help them learn to associate the bedroom with sleep which will subconsciously improve their sleep. Otherwise the child or teen will be easily distracted and activated by all the things vying for their attention while they are trying to sleep.

**INTEGRATION:**   Does the client or parent understand the importance of making the bedroom be for sleep and nothing else? Was the client or parent able to identify things they could change in the bedroom to make it more sleep friendly? Were they able to make some positive changes? Are the changes helping? Do they need help organizing the stuff in the bedroom so it feels calm?

# TIPS FOR THE BEDROOM

**Set up the bedroom for sleep**

- ✓ Get a comfortable bed
- ✓ Make the bedroom peaceful: clean, organized, not cluttered
- ✓ Organize the stuff in the room, as it's hard to sleep in chaos
- ✓ Make sure the bedroom is quiet
- ✓ Keep the bedroom cool and dark
- ✓ Use a sound screen to block outside noise
- ✓ Darken room with room darkening shades
- ✓ Remove, turn around or cover lights from electronics such as clocks
- ✓ Remove TV, computers, tablets, phones, games, projects, crafts
- ✓ Provide books (or e-books with dim light) to read at bedtime
- ✓ Make your child's room feels comfortable and safe with favorite stuffed animals, favorite sheets, favorite posters, etc.
- ✓ Give them a stuffed animal with pretend powers that keeps monsters away if scared
- ✓ Provide a variety of alarm clocks and/or clock radios

**Make a list of things that need changing or rearranging in the room**

_____

_____

_____

_____

_____

_____

_____

_____

## Tool 21-3: Getting to Bed on Time

**BACKGROUND:**    Children with ADHD often avoid going to bed. One reason is they are not able to organize themselves well enough to get through their nightly routine without getting distracted. Another reason is that they want their parent's attention. Once they are in bed, they'll want a drink of water or anything else that will keep parents engaged with them.

Teens with ADHD typically struggle with time management and may put off doing their homework and stay up late to get it done. Additionally, they may have trouble stopping their social media interactions. My own daughter would stay up all night if left to her own devices, and many of my teen clients do the same.

Stimulant medication can double the rate of insomnia and is often a reason the client must stop taking it (Efron and Pearl, 2001).

Children and teens may not get enough hours of sleep for their age, get up late and feel exhausted the next day.

This tool provides guidance on how to get to bed on time.

**SKILL BUILDING:**    Find out if the client is having trouble getting to bed in time to get enough sleep. Ask the client (or their parents) to tell you about what they do during the evening between dinner and bedtime. Explore what might be getting in their way of getting to bed at the best time. Show parents how to use Tool 21-1-3 to figure out the ideal bedtime. Ask them to list all the things they need to do in the evening. Help them organize and pare down their list.

Explain that they will fall asleep more easily if they go to bed and get up at the same time every day, even on weekends. Use Handout 21-3-1 Nighttime Routine for Sleep to help them design a nighttime routine that ensures the client will be in bed at the best time. Post the schedule where they can refer to it every night. If they get distracted and forget to go to bed, encourage them to use an alarm clock to remind them and leave it set for the same time every night.

If they are taking stimulant medication, encourage them to talk with their prescriber to schedule the last dose so it doesn't interfere with sleep by making them feel wide awake when it is bedtime. Use the Medication/Sleep Diary on Handouts 21-3-2 and 21-3-3 to help your prescriber determine the best time to take the last dose.

Use Handout 21-3-4 to determine if eating certain foods is impacting sleep. Foods containing sugar, caffeine and certain additives may activate the brain too much, making it difficult to fall asleep.

Use Handout 21-3-5 Prepare to Sleep to help clients and parents prepare to go to bed and fall asleep.

**INTEGRATION:**    Was the client able to create an evening schedule that works for them? Are they getting to bed at the same time on a regular basis? If not, what is getting in their way? Do they need to unload their evening schedule? Are they following their schedule? If not, discuss what else would help them. Are they using an alarm clock? Is a sleep meditation helping them fall asleep faster?

# NIGHTTIME ROUTINE FOR SLEEP

My ideal bedtime is: _____

If I take stimulant medications it is worn off by then: **Y/N**

In order to be in bed on time I must complete homework by:_____

I must start my homework by: _____

I will shut off my computer, TV, Tablet and/or Phone 1 hour before bedtime. **Y/N**

I'll have a low sugar, caffeine-free snack an hour or more before bedtime. **Y/N**

I will use an alarm to remind me when to get ready for bed. **Y/N**

I will turn down the lights, listen to music, read (dim the brightness on tablet) **Y/N**

I will listen to a sleep meditation to fall asleep. **Y/N**

**Fill in the schedule below and post it where you can see it every night:**

**Time:**          **Task/Activity:**

_____

_____

_____

_____

_____

_____

_____

_____

_____

_____

**Sample schedule:**

| Time: | Task/Activity |
|---|---|
| 6:30-8:30 pm | Homework |
| 8:00 pm | Snack while completing homework |
| 8:30 pm | Alarm goes off, get ready for bed |
| 8:45 pm | Read, listen to music |
| 8:55 pm | In bed with lights out |
| 9:30 pm | Listen to Sleep Meditation CD/mp3 and fall asleep |
| 6:30 am | Alarm goes off, wake up and get out of bed |

# MEDICATION / SLEEP DIARY - SAMPLE

**Instructions:** Write the symptoms above the columns. Write down the date and time, what medication was taken and circle the number to rate the sleep symptom that night and the next morning. 0 is no problem, 1 = a little, 2 = some, 3 = often, 4 = very often, 5 = a huge problem. For example if they are revved up and can't fall asleep, rate "fall asleep" a 5. See if sleep symptoms improve or get worse after taking various doses of medications at certain times.

| Date/Time | Medication and Dose | Fall Asleep | Stay Asleep | Up On Time | Fatigue | Concentration |
|---|---|---|---|---|---|---|
| 3/25 7AM | Adderall 10mg | 0 ①2 3 4 5 | ⓪1 2 3 4 5 | 0 1 2 3 ④5 | 0 1 2 ③4 5 | 0 ①2 3 4 5 |
| noon | Adderall 10mg | 0 1 ②3 4 5 | 0 1 2 ③4 5 | 0 ①2 3 4 5 | 0 1 2 3 4 ⑤ | 0 1 2 3 4 ⑤ |
| 5PM | Adderall 10mg | 0 1 2 ③4 5 | 0 1 ②3 4 5 | ⓪1 2 3 4 5 | ⓪1 2 3 4 5 | 0 1 ②3 4 5 |
| | | 0 1 2 3 4 5 | 0 1 2 3 4 5 | 0 1 2 3 4 5 | 0 1 2 3 4 5 | 0 1 2 3 4 5 |
| 3/26 8AM | Adderall XR 20mg | 0 1 2 3 ④5 | ⓪1 2 3 4 5 | 0 1 2 3 4 5 | 0 1 ②3 4 5 | 0 1 2 3 ④5 |
| | | 0 1 2 3 4 5 | 0 1 2 3 4 5 | 0 1 2 3 4 5 | 0 1 2 3 4 5 | 0 1 2 3 4 5 |
| | | 0 1 2 3 4 5 | 0 1 2 3 4 5 | 0 1 2 3 4 5 | 0 1 2 3 4 5 | 0 1 2 3 4 5 |
| | | 0 1 2 3 4 5 | 0 1 2 3 4 5 | 0 1 2 3 4 5 | 0 1 2 3 4 5 | 0 1 2 3 4 5 |
| | | 0 1 2 3 4 5 | 0 1 2 3 4 5 | 0 1 2 3 4 5 | 0 1 2 3 4 5 | 0 1 2 3 4 5 |
| | | 0 1 2 3 4 5 | 0 1 2 3 4 5 | 0 1 2 3 4 5 | 0 1 2 3 4 5 | 0 1 2 3 4 5 |
| | | 0 1 2 3 4 5 | 0 1 2 3 4 5 | 0 1 2 3 4 5 | 0 1 2 3 4 5 | 0 1 2 3 4 5 |
| | | 0 1 2 3 4 5 | 0 1 2 3 4 5 | 0 1 2 3 4 5 | 0 1 2 3 4 5 | 0 1 2 3 4 5 |
| | | 0 1 2 3 4 5 | 0 1 2 3 4 5 | 0 1 2 3 4 5 | 0 1 2 3 4 5 | 0 1 2 3 4 5 |
| | | 0 1 2 3 4 5 | 0 1 2 3 4 5 | 0 1 2 3 4 5 | 0 1 2 3 4 5 | 0 1 2 3 4 5 |
| | | 0 1 2 3 4 5 | 0 1 2 3 4 5 | 0 1 2 3 4 5 | 0 1 2 3 4 5 | 0 1 2 3 4 5 |
| | | 0 1 2 3 4 5 | 0 1 2 3 4 5 | 0 1 2 3 4 5 | 0 1 2 3 4 5 | 0 1 2 3 4 5 |
| | | 0 1 2 3 4 5 | 0 1 2 3 4 5 | 0 1 2 3 4 5 | 0 1 2 3 4 5 | 0 1 2 3 4 5 |
| | | 0 1 2 3 4 5 | 0 1 2 3 4 5 | 0 1 2 3 4 5 | 0 1 2 3 4 5 | 0 1 2 3 4 5 |
| | | 0 1 2 3 4 5 | 0 1 2 3 4 5 | 0 1 2 3 4 5 | 0 1 2 3 4 5 | 0 1 2 3 4 5 |
| | | 0 1 2 3 4 5 | 0 1 2 3 4 5 | 0 1 2 3 4 5 | 0 1 2 3 4 5 | 0 1 2 3 4 5 |
| | | 0 1 2 3 4 5 | 0 1 2 3 4 5 | 0 1 2 3 4 5 | 0 1 2 3 4 5 | 0 1 2 3 4 5 |

# MEDICATION / SLEEP DIARY

**Instructions:** Write the symptoms above the columns. Write down the date and time, what medication was taken and circle the number to rate the sleep symptoms that night and the next morning. 0 is no problem, 1 = a little, 2 = some, 3 = often, 4 = very often, 5 = a huge problem. For example if they are revved up and can't fall asleep, rate "fall asleep" a 5. See if sleep symptoms improve or get worse after taking various doses of medications at certain times.

| Date/Time | Medication and Dose | | | | |
|---|---|---|---|---|---|
| | | 0 1 2 3 4 5 | 0 1 2 3 4 5 | 0 1 2 3 4 5 | 0 1 2 3 4 5 |
| | | 0 1 2 3 4 5 | 0 1 2 3 4 5 | 0 1 2 3 4 5 | 0 1 2 3 4 5 |
| | | 0 1 2 3 4 5 | 0 1 2 3 4 5 | 0 1 2 3 4 5 | 0 1 2 3 4 5 |
| | | 0 1 2 3 4 5 | 0 1 2 3 4 5 | 0 1 2 3 4 5 | 0 1 2 3 4 5 |
| | | 0 1 2 3 4 5 | 0 1 2 3 4 5 | 0 1 2 3 4 5 | 0 1 2 3 4 5 |
| | | 0 1 2 3 4 5 | 0 1 2 3 4 5 | 0 1 2 3 4 5 | 0 1 2 3 4 5 |
| | | 0 1 2 3 4 5 | 0 1 2 3 4 5 | 0 1 2 3 4 5 | 0 1 2 3 4 5 |
| | | 0 1 2 3 4 5 | 0 1 2 3 4 5 | 0 1 2 3 4 5 | 0 1 2 3 4 5 |
| | | 0 1 2 3 4 5 | 0 1 2 3 4 5 | 0 1 2 3 4 5 | 0 1 2 3 4 5 |
| | | 0 1 2 3 4 5 | 0 1 2 3 4 5 | 0 1 2 3 4 5 | 0 1 2 3 4 5 |
| | | 0 1 2 3 4 5 | 0 1 2 3 4 5 | 0 1 2 3 4 5 | 0 1 2 3 4 5 |
| | | 0 1 2 3 4 5 | 0 1 2 3 4 5 | 0 1 2 3 4 5 | 0 1 2 3 4 5 |
| | | 0 1 2 3 4 5 | 0 1 2 3 4 5 | 0 1 2 3 4 5 | 0 1 2 3 4 5 |
| | | 0 1 2 3 4 5 | 0 1 2 3 4 5 | 0 1 2 3 4 5 | 0 1 2 3 4 5 |
| | | 0 1 2 3 4 5 | 0 1 2 3 4 5 | 0 1 2 3 4 5 | 0 1 2 3 4 5 |
| | | 0 1 2 3 4 5 | 0 1 2 3 4 5 | 0 1 2 3 4 5 | 0 1 2 3 4 5 |
| | | 0 1 2 3 4 5 | 0 1 2 3 4 5 | 0 1 2 3 4 5 | 0 1 2 3 4 5 |
| | | 0 1 2 3 4 5 | 0 1 2 3 4 5 | 0 1 2 3 4 5 | 0 1 2 3 4 5 |
| | | 0 1 2 3 4 5 | 0 1 2 3 4 5 | 0 1 2 3 4 5 | 0 1 2 3 4 5 |
| | | 0 1 2 3 4 5 | 0 1 2 3 4 5 | 0 1 2 3 4 5 | 0 1 2 3 4 5 |

# FOOD / SLEEP DIARY

**Instructions:** Write the symptoms above the columns. Write down the date and time, what was eaten (include drinks and everything eaten), and circle the number to rate the symptom. 0 is no problem, 1 = a little, 2 = some, 3 = often, 4 = very often, 5 = a huge problem. For example, if they are revved up and really hyper and can't sit still, rate hyperactivity a 5. After a day or two see if there are any patterns where ratings go up or down within 3–4 hours of eating certain food or within 24 hours of eating certain foods.

| Date/Time | Medication and Dose | | | | |
|---|---|---|---|---|---|
| | | 0 1 2 3 4 5 | 0 1 2 3 4 5 | 0 1 2 3 4 5 | 0 1 2 3 4 5 |
| | | 0 1 2 3 4 5 | 0 1 2 3 4 5 | 0 1 2 3 4 5 | 0 1 2 3 4 5 |
| | | 0 1 2 3 4 5 | 0 1 2 3 4 5 | 0 1 2 3 4 5 | 0 1 2 3 4 5 |
| | | 0 1 2 3 4 5 | 0 1 2 3 4 5 | 0 1 2 3 4 5 | 0 1 2 3 4 5 |
| | | 0 1 2 3 4 5 | 0 1 2 3 4 5 | 0 1 2 3 4 5 | 0 1 2 3 4 5 |
| | | 0 1 2 3 4 5 | 0 1 2 3 4 5 | 0 1 2 3 4 5 | 0 1 2 3 4 5 |
| | | 0 1 2 3 4 5 | 0 1 2 3 4 5 | 0 1 2 3 4 5 | 0 1 2 3 4 5 |
| | | 0 1 2 3 4 5 | 0 1 2 3 4 5 | 0 1 2 3 4 5 | 0 1 2 3 4 5 |
| | | 0 1 2 3 4 5 | 0 1 2 3 4 5 | 0 1 2 3 4 5 | 0 1 2 3 4 5 |
| | | 0 1 2 3 4 5 | 0 1 2 3 4 5 | 0 1 2 3 4 5 | 0 1 2 3 4 5 |
| | | 0 1 2 3 4 5 | 0 1 2 3 4 5 | 0 1 2 3 4 5 | 0 1 2 3 4 5 |
| | | 0 1 2 3 4 5 | 0 1 2 3 4 5 | 0 1 2 3 4 5 | 0 1 2 3 4 5 |
| | | 0 1 2 3 4 5 | 0 1 2 3 4 5 | 0 1 2 3 4 5 | 0 1 2 3 4 5 |
| | | 0 1 2 3 4 5 | 0 1 2 3 4 5 | 0 1 2 3 4 5 | 0 1 2 3 4 5 |
| | | 0 1 2 3 4 5 | 0 1 2 3 4 5 | 0 1 2 3 4 5 | 0 1 2 3 4 5 |
| | | 0 1 2 3 4 5 | 0 1 2 3 4 5 | 0 1 2 3 4 5 | 0 1 2 3 4 5 |
| | | 0 1 2 3 4 5 | 0 1 2 3 4 5 | 0 1 2 3 4 5 | 0 1 2 3 4 5 |
| | | 0 1 2 3 4 5 | 0 1 2 3 4 5 | 0 1 2 3 4 5 | 0 1 2 3 4 5 |
| | | 0 1 2 3 4 5 | 0 1 2 3 4 5 | 0 1 2 3 4 5 | 0 1 2 3 4 5 |
| | | 0 1 2 3 4 5 | 0 1 2 3 4 5 | 0 1 2 3 4 5 | 0 1 2 3 4 5 |
| | | 0 1 2 3 4 5 | 0 1 2 3 4 5 | 0 1 2 3 4 5 | 0 1 2 3 4 5 |
| | | 0 1 2 3 4 5 | 0 1 2 3 4 5 | 0 1 2 3 4 5 | 0 1 2 3 4 5 |
| | | 0 1 2 3 4 5 | 0 1 2 3 4 5 | 0 1 2 3 4 5 | 0 1 2 3 4 5 |

# PREPARE FOR SLEEP

**How to Get Ready for Sleep**

- **Stop activities that activate your brain an hour before bedtime**

    - Stop exercise at least two hours before bedtime

    - Avoid violent or activating TV shows (please don't let children watch violent shows at all)

    - Avoid devices with bright light such as TV, computers or tablets at least 2 hours before bed

- **Start the bedtime routine at the same time every night**

    - Set an alarm to remind you to start getting ready for bed

- **Follow a routine that calms you and prepares your brain for sleep**

    - Turn the lights down low a half-hour before bedtime

    - Take a warm and relaxing bath

    - Put on favorite pajamas

    - Read a bedtime story or book (use books vs. e-books to avoid light activation or dim the brightness on tablets)

    - Say goodnight to pets or stuffed animals

    - Climb into a comfortable bed (maybe with favorite sheets)

## Tool 21-4: Staying in Bed

**BACKGROUND:**    Many children with ADHD have trouble calming down their mind and body enough to fall asleep. They may avoid going to bed, and once in bed they may keep calling their parent or getting out of bed. This tool provides suggestions on how to help children learn to self-soothe and stay in bed.

**SKILL BUILDING:**    If the child keeps getting out of bed it may be helpful to use a reward system for motivating them to stay in bed and fall asleep. Handout 21-4 Teach Your Child to Stay In Bed contains time-tested options to teach parents how to get their child to stay in bed, including the process of simply putting them back in bed over and over again. Make sure they do not interact with their child during the process, as doing so will reward the child with parental attention. This will teach the child to keep getting out of bed to get their attention – the opposite of what they need.

**INTEGRATION:**    Does the client keep getting out of bed or calling parents? Are the parents learning to use the methods described on Handout 21-4 to teach their child to stay in bed? Be prepared to fortify parents with encouragement and let them know that as difficult as it is at first, if they are consistent in putting their child to bed at the same time every night, and putting them back into bed over and over without interacting with them, eventually (after three to five nights) their child will stay in bed. Help them tolerate their child's crying without responding to it when it is simply because they are unhappy that they are being put to bed or back into bed.

# TEACH YOUR CHILD TO STAY IN BED

- **You may find it helpful to use a reward system for motivating your child to stay in bed and fall asleep.** Give them a star on a reward chart for every ten minutes they stay in bed quietly. When they earn a certain number of stars reward them with something like an extra fifteen minutes of computer time the next day or with an extra half hour of one on one time with you over the weekend.

- **Another reward system works in reverse.** Depending on their age, give them five or ten pennies (or nickels or dimes) when they go to bed. Each time they call for you, you take one coin from them. They get to keep all the coins that you give them if they don't call at all. The less they call you, the more money they keep. If they lose all the coins, and still call you again, then give them a consequence such as an extra chore, or going to bed five minutes earlier the next day.

- **If your child is crying, tell them you will check on them in five minutes, leave the room and let them cry.** Be sure to show up in five minutes, but don't interact with them. Just let them see that you checked on them and tell them you will be back in ten minutes. Show up in ten minutes, and repeat up to about 20 minutes. Children will eventually wear themselves out and fall asleep – if you let them. Once they learn that crying doesn't get your attention anymore, eventually they will be able to fall asleep faster.

- **Use the same concept if they won't stay in bed.** Just keep putting them back in bed. Do it until they fall asleep. Exhausting and annoying? You bet. But you are the adult and you can outlast your child. You will only need to do this for several nights in a row until your child learns that his old habits of getting your attention don't work anymore. Use the Be A Robot technique in Chapter 7 and do your best not to show your annoyance. Simply put them back in bed. Don't say anything. Let your actions speak for you.

- **Teach them to sleep in their own bed.** Some parents allow their kids to come into their bed if they wake up or even to go to sleep in the first place. This varies in different cultures and expert opinion varies on this. Children need to learn to soothe themselves to sleep, and back to sleep if they wake up. Eventually, this needs to be done in their own bed (even if you need to lie down with them for a few minutes.) They will learn what you teach them or reward them for doing. Be careful not to teach them that when they wake up it is okay for them to wake you up too early, ruin your sleep, or keep you up all night! Instead help them soothe themselves and feel comfortable in their own bed. Give them a favorite stuffed animal or a musical mobile to help them feel safe.

## Tool 21-5: Falling Asleep

**BACKGROUND:**    Good sleep is essential for optimal brain function. Many children and teens with ADHD have trouble settling down to go to sleep. Their brains often have trouble quieting down enough to stop thoughts from zooming and/or their body from moving. Additionally, they may be too activated by medication, food or activity to readily fall asleep. This tool provides guidance on helping children and teens with ADHD fall asleep faster.

**SKILL BUILDING:**

Explain the information on Handout 21-5-1 Tips for Falling Asleep.

> ***Set Up the Bedroom for Sleep:***    Remind clients/parents that their bedroom should be associated with sleep and nothing else. Nothing else! No TV, no computer, tablet, video games, crafts or toys. A favorite stuffed animal is fine. Some kids feel safer with a dim night light, but the brain rests better in complete darkness. Refer to Tool 21-2 Setting Up the Bedroom to make sure the bedroom is set up properly for sleeping.

> ***Medication:***    Explain to clients and parents that stimulant medication can double the rate of sleep problems in children with ADHD (Efron & Pearl, 2001). Therefore, if medication is part of the treatment plan, use Handout 21-5-2 Is Medication Interfering with Sleep? and Handout 21-3-2 Sleep/Medication Diary to help the parent and the medication prescriber determine if it is making it harder to fall asleep.

> ***Foods:***    Explore what clients eat during the evening and encourage them to limit sugary or high carbohydrate snacks or drinks, as well as food or drinks that contain caffeine. Caffeine shows up in popular soft drinks, ice tea, coffee, candy, chocolate, and even some 'healthy' bottled water. Sugar can also activate the brain, so it should be limited, especially after dinner. Artificial colors have also been shown to activate some brains as discussed in Tool 19-2 Food Additives, so encourage the client (or parent) to limit these if they appear to be impacting the client Encourage them to use a Food/Sleep Diary on Handouts 21-3-4 to figure out if what they are eating is preventing them from falling asleep.

> ***Activity:***    Remind clients/parents to stop all activating activities such as homework, TV, phone calls, playing, computer or internet time at least an hour before bed. Stop exercise two hours before.

> > ***Case Example:***    *As a teen my daughter liked to be online with her friends late at night. I used to tell her to go to bed and then go to bed myself only to discover she was still up hours later. I finally learned that she would not go to bed unless I stood behind her where I could read her computer screen and waited for her to turn off the computer. She got very angry with me but it only took a couple of nights of being very firm, staying put, letting her know I meant what I said, and not letting her stay on the computer any longer. Some parents have success with taking the power cords to the computer or video game or TV. Some put the cords in their car trunk, their briefcase, or even take them to their office. Then the kids can earn them back.*

> ***Routine:***    Help clients/parents to set a bedtime and stick with it consistently every night. Then follow the same routine nightly. Children and teens with ADHD do best with a predictable structure and lots of reminders to follow the routine. See Tool 21-3 Getting to Bed On Time.

> ***Self-Soothing:***    Explain to clients and their parents that they need to learn to soothe themselves and calm themselves enough to fall asleep. If they have trouble calming down their busy "monkey mind" when they get in bed, encourage them to use techniques that calm such as relaxation breathing (Tool 11-4) and Body Scan (Tool 11-7). Encourage them to use a sleep meditation to help them let go of their busy thoughts, progressively relax

their mind and allow the body to fall asleep. Clients as young as three have successfully used this. One client's whole family reported relaxing and falling asleep faster when they listened to their child's sleep meditation CD.

**Put Children to Bed When Still Awake:**    Encourage parents to teach their child to go to sleep in the same situation/environment they will find themselves in if they wake up. Aim to put them in their own bed, turn out the light, leave the room and close the door. Explain that if their child gets used to falling asleep while being rocked, or perhaps in front of the TV, it will be much harder for them to fall back asleep if they wake up during the night alone in their room. These habits often become established during infancy when we work so hard to get our baby to go to sleep by rocking them, rubbing their back, letting them fall asleep in the living room with the TV on, etc. If you must rub their back or lie down with them, do it in their bed. This will help them be comfortable soothing themselves back to sleep alone in their own room.

**Neurofeedback:**    This is a great option for clients who have ADHD, not only to help them self-regulate their brains enough to fall asleep, but also to improve all the symptoms of ADHD. See Chapter 10 Neurofeedback for more information.

**Case Example:**    *I worked with a four-year-old boy who had ADHD and who could keep himself and his parents up all night. He was hyperactive and anxious. I gave him a progressive relaxation sleep meditation CD that I recorded for him with my voice. Within four nights he was falling asleep regularly within fifteen to twenty minutes. He was so proud of himself, too!*

**INTEGRATION:**    Is the client having trouble falling asleep? If so, do they seem too activated? Is there anything that might be activating them above and beyond the symptoms of ADHD such as food, medications, or activity? What changes are they making that are helping? It may take some time for clients to learn to fall asleep faster so remind them to be patient and not to give up too soon.

# TIPS FOR FALLING ASLEEP

**Set Up the Bedroom for Sleep:** The bedroom should be associated with sleep and nothing else. Nothing else! Refer to Tool 21-2 Setting Up the Bedroom and Handout 21-2 to make sure the bedroom is set up properly for sleeping.

**Medication:** Use a Medication/Sleep Diary to help your medication prescriber determine if medication is making it harder (or easier) to fall asleep.

**Foods:** Make a list of foods eaten during the evening. Avoid high carbohydrate or sugary foods, caffeine and artificial colors. Use a Food/Sleep Diary to determine if foods are interfering with sleep.

**Activity:** Stop all activating activities such as homework, TV, phone calls, playing, computer or internet time at least an hour before bed. Stop exercise two hours before.

**Routine:** Set a bedtime and stick with it consistently every night. Then follow the same routine nightly. Children and teens with ADHD do best with a predictable structure and lots of reminders to follow the routine.

**Put Children to Bed When Still Awake:** Teach them to go to sleep in the same situation/environment they will find themselves in if they wake up, their own bed.

**Self-Soothing:** Use calming, self-soothing techniques such as:
- Warm Bath
- Bedtime Story
- Mindfulness of Surrounding
- Basic Relaxation Breath
- Body Scan
- Core Practice
- Soothing Music
- Sleep Meditation

**Neurofeedback:** Use neurofeedback to help the brain self-regulate enough to fall asleep and also to improve all the symptoms of ADHD.

# IS MEDICATION INTERFERING WITH SLEEP?

Taking stimulant medication may interfere with your child's or teen's ability to fall asleep. On the other hand, some fall asleep faster because the medication helps them lie still long enough to fall asleep.

See what works best for your child and work with your medication prescriber to adjust the timing of the medication if necessary. Some children cannot take stimulant medication at all because the impact on their ability to fall asleep is unacceptable. Use a medication/sleep diary to track the effects of medications on your child's or teen's ability to fall asleep, stay asleep, wake on time, and on their daytime energy.

✓ Does your child or teen have more trouble falling asleep when/if they take stimulant medication?

✓ Does your child's or teen's energy level increase or decrease when they take stimulant medication?

✓ Do they seem revved up or wired at bedtime?

✓ Do they have trouble lying still long enough to fall asleep?

✓ Do they fall asleep faster on days they don't take medication?

✓ Does changing the timing of when they take their medication help them fall asleep faster?

## Tool 21-6: Getting Up In the Morning

**BACKGROUND:**    Some children and teens wake up way too early. Others are still deeply asleep when it is time to get up, especially if they had trouble going to sleep or stayed up too late. This tool provides options for helping children who wake up too early stay asleep a bit longer and for helping those who are still "dead to the world" when they need to get up be able to get up on time.

**SKILL BUILDING:**

*Getting Up Too Early:*    If a child or teen gets up too early (rarely have I met a teen who gets up too early) encourage parents to consider the possibility that their child is going to bed so early that they wake up too early having had enough sleep. Use Handout 21-6 Getting Up In the Morning to help them consider possible ways to help their child sleep later or perhaps fall back to sleep instead of getting up as soon as they awake.

*Trouble Getting Up:*    Many children and teens have trouble waking up on time in the morning. This might be because they simply aren't getting enough hours of sleep because they had trouble going to sleep the night before. If they are having trouble getting up, start by looking at their bedtime routine first. Make sure they are getting enough sleep, make their bedtime earlier, and use all techniques described throughout this chapter to help them get to sleep.

Some children and teens have trouble transitioning from a sleep state to an awake state even if they got enough sleep. Or, they would just rather stay asleep than wake up. In this case, encourage them to explore options that help them wake up. Ask the child or teen what they think would help them wake up on time. One six-year-old told me that he thought an alarm clock would help him. His mother got him one and she stopped having to wake him up and battle with him to get him out of bed.

Tell clients who are older than six or so that it is their job to wake up and get out of bed on time. Make it their responsibility, not the parent's. Use a series of alarms that go off at different times with different sounds to gradually wake the client. Use an alarm that is on wheels and rolls off the nightstand and around the room making the client get out of bed and chase it to turn it off (look for one online). Put some lights on timers to turn them on in sequence before the client needs to wake up to help them wake up naturally.

Help parents motivate the child or teen to get up on time. Discuss "what's in it for them" if they get up on time. Perhaps a teen will have time to do their hair, or there will be time to have their favorite breakfast. Set up a reward system to earn rewards for getting up on their own, on time. Younger children can earn stars on a reward chart. Or remove privileges if they oversleep such as no electronics, sports or friends over that day. These techniques can help clients take responsibility for getting up on their own and can help them get in the habit of doing so. My daughter had a huge problem getting up until she learned how to fall asleep on time. When her therapist recommended that we make her stay in her room after school with no electronics if she overslept and missed the bus, she never missed the bus again!

Parents often get into stressful power struggles trying to get their kids to wake up and get up each morning. Encourage parents to use the Be A Robot technique to avoid this. State the facts using statements such as: "It is time to get up." "You have 45 minutes before the bus comes." "Get up now and I will make your favorite breakfast." "Remember how you felt when you were late for class yesterday." "It is your responsibility to get up so this is the last time I'm coming in here this morning."

Review Handout 21-6 Getting Up In the Morning with clients and parents to help them figure out why the client is having trouble getting up on time and to explore and try out options to make it easier to get up on time.

**INTEGRATION:** Is the client getting enough sleep? Do they need a later or an earlier bedtime? Are they having trouble waking up because they have difficulty going to sleep on time? Is the client taking more responsibility for waking up and getting up? Does an alarm clock help? Does changing the light in the bedroom impact their wake-up time?

# GETTING UP IN THE MORNING

## Getting Up Too Early

- Do they appear to have had enough sleep?
- If they slept enough hours for their age, does setting bedtime later help?
- Do they wake up when it gets light?
- Do room darkening shades that totally block outside light help?
- Can they go back to sleep?
- Will they stay in their bed even if they are awake?
- Will they play in their room quietly if you reward them for doing so?
- Will they go back to sleep if you don't interact with them?

## Trouble Getting Up

- After they wake up and get going does it seem like they had enough sleep?
- What time did they fall asleep?
- Did they get enough hours of sleep for their age?
- Do they need an earlier bedtime to get more hours of sleep?
- Did they wake up during the night?
- Use multiple alarm clocks.
- Make getting up on time their responsibility.
- Let the alarm wake them and avoid calling them over and over.
- Open the shades or leave them open overnight to let the light in.
- Set up a timer to turn on a light in their room 5 minutes before wake up time.
- Ask a friend or family member to call them on the phone.
- Send the dog or cat in to wake them up.
- Motivate them to get up on time with rewards or privileges.
  - Time for favorite breakfast, time to do their hair, time to play before school, stickers on reward chart.
- Let them pay the consequences of being late – don't keep rescuing them.
  - If they miss the bus – they must pay you to drive them to school.
  - No sports, after school activities or friends over on days they sleep late.
  - Lose electronics for the rest of the day.
- Can you let them sleep in occasionally or is this an everyday event?
  - Until they are getting to sleep well, you may need to let them sleep sometimes.

# Section XI
# Strategies for Success at School

# Chapter 22
# School and ADHD

Tool 22-1: Getting the School Involved
Tool 22-2: Organizational Strategies for Homework

## Tool 22-1: Getting the School Involved

**BACKGROUND:**   The symptoms of ADHD typically make success in the school setting challenging for the student. Once a child or teen has been diagnosed with ADHD he or she may qualify for special accommodations at school to assist them in being successful. This tool outlines the process of getting the client's school involved in giving them the in-school support they need to thrive.

**SKILL BUILDING:**

*504 Plan:*   Section 504 of the Rehabilitation Act and Americans with Disabilities Act of 1973 provides for specific accommodations in the classroom for students with ADHD. Accommodations for students as per this act are defined in a 504 Plan. This act specifies that no one with a disability can be excluded from participating in federally funded programs or activities, including elementary, secondary or postsecondary schooling. Children with ADHD are often categorized under this act as "Other Health Impaired." They will receive accommodation under a 504 Plan only if the school feels their disorder is affecting their academic success. A child or teen with ADHD whose academic success is not being affected may still be working twice as hard as those without ADHD. Encourage the school to consider this in deciding whether to provide accommodations.

Typical accommodations provided in accordance with Section 504 of this act include physical arrangement of the room, lesson presentation, assignments, test modifications, organization and behavior management. Help clients and parents determine which of these would assist the client in being more successful in school. Talk to the parent, the client's teacher, school social worker and school psychologist to help them define the best plan for your client. Refer to Handout 22-1 for a checklist of common accommodations.

Sometimes parents are reluctant to involve the school, fearing that their child will be stigmatized. Encourage them to explore the options and explain that expecting their child or teen to do well without taking advantage of any of the support available to them at school is like asking a child who cannot see the board without glasses to go to school without them.

***Pupil Planning Team (PPT):***   Encourage parents to request that the school assess their child or teen so that appropriate accommodations and special education can be provided to them if warranted. Children and teens with ADHD are likely to have specific learning disabilities in areas such as math, reading and writing in addition to the classic ADHD symptoms of difficulty concentrating, staying on task, finishing work on time, etc. Parents can request a Pupil Planning Team meeting (PPT) to start the process of having their child evaluated. This is called different things in different states but the process is similar, so encourage parents to ask their school what it is in their school.

The PPT typically starts with a meeting with everyone involved, including parents, teachers, special education staff, school psychologist, the student if old enough, and often the student's psychotherapist or coach. If possible, I recommend that clinicians attend these meetings for two reasons. First, you will learn more about the specific areas the child or teen struggles with which will help you be more targeted in your work with them. Second, you will be able to make recommendations for accommodations that may be instrumental in the client's academic and/or social success.

If the team determines that there is evidence of academic difficulty, a variety of tests can be ordered to look for learning disabilities, psychological and behavioral functioning and ADHD symptoms.

***Individualized Education Plan (IEP):***   If the results of the testing show that ADHD symptoms are contributing to difficulty in school or if any learning issues are discovered, an Individualized Education Plan (IEP) will be created tailored to the student's academic and social needs. This will have specific goals for the student and will include any special accommodations being made, special education services, counseling, or social skills groups being provided by the school. It will be reviewed periodically, with progress tracked and updated as need be. It provides a means for the school, the teachers, parents and you to stay on track with the student's progress.

## RESOURCES:

- 504 Plan: https://www.understood.org/en/school-learning/special-services/504-plan
- U.S. Department of Education: www.ed.gov

**INTEGRATION:**   Is the parent open to involving the school? Has the client been evaluated at school? How is ADHD impacting their school experience academically, emotionally or socially? Are they receiving accommodations? Are these helping them to get better grades? Are they helping the client feel less stressed about school? Are there other accommodations that might help?

# ACADEMIC ACCOMMODATIONS

**Examples of accommodations and modifications include modifying rules, policies or practices, removing architectural or communication barriers, providing aids, services, or assistive technology.**

### Physical Room Arrangement
- Seat the student near the teacher
- Seat student near a positive role model and away from distracting peers
- Seat the student away from distractions (window, door, motors)
- Increase distance between student's desk and their classmates
- Remove nuisance objects (rubber bands, toys)
- Teacher to stand near student when giving directions or presenting lessons
- Lower the noise level

### Lesson Preparation
- Pair students to check accuracy of work
- Provide peer tutoring
- Write key points on the board
- Provide visual aides
- Provide peer note taker
- Provide written outline
- Allow tape recording lessons
- Have student review key points orally
- Use computer assisted instruction
- Allow word processing technology to take notes
- Make sure the student understands the directions
- Include a variety of activities during each lesson
- Divide long presentations into shorter ones

### Assignments
- Allow extra time to complete tasks
- Simplify complex directions
- Hand out worksheets one at a time
- Reduce the reading level of an assignment
- Require fewer correct responses to achieve goals
- Require fewer repetitions of practice work
- Reduce the number of homework assignments
- Allow the student to tape record homework
- Allow student to use word processor, computer, or tablet
- Provide structural guides for completing assignments
- Provide study skills training
- Give frequent short quizzes and avoid long tests
- Shorten assignments, divide work into smaller pieces
- Do not grade handwriting or spelling except for a spelling test

### Test Modification
- Allow extra time to complete test
- Permit test to be taken in a low distraction setting
- Permit use of assistive technology to record answers (recorder, computer, tablet, word processor)
- Read test items to the student
- Read directions to the student, confirm understanding directions
- Give exam orally
- Give take home tests
- Use more objective questions
- Give frequent short quizzes versus long tests
- Allow periodic breaks during testing
- Allow interaction with teacher to promote attention to task

### Organization
- Provide peer assistance with organizational skills
- Set up a homework buddy
- Provide an extra set of books at home
- Color coded folders
- Send daily/weekly progress reports listing missing assignments or behavior concerns
- Use a reward system for class work and homework
- Provide an assignment book to student
- Check accuracy of daily assignment notebook
- Remind student what to bring home
- Remind student to turn in homework
- Provide clock or wristwatch

### Behavior
- Teacher to design and use behavior management system
- Praise specific behaviors immediately
- Tie privileges and rewards to specific behaviors
- Make appropriate use of negative consequences
- Clear and simple classroom rules
- Allow short breaks between assignments
- Use non-verbal cues to help student stay on task
- Mark correct answers versus mistakes
- Allow time out of seat to move around
- Allow movement that does not distract others
- Develop "contracts" with student
- Use time out
- Ignore negative behavior that is not way outside classroom norm

## Tool 22-2: Organizational Strategies for Homework

**BACKGROUND:**   Children and teens with ADHD typically struggle with organizational skills. They often don't know what the homework assignment is, they don't have the right book at home, they may do their homework but not turn it in or they may lose their schoolwork. Therefore, they need to be taught systems that help them keep track of assignments, homework and books. This tool provides some basic skills to get them started.

**SKILL BUILDING:**   Find out if the client is having trouble with getting their homework done and turned in on time. Use Handout 22-2-1 Homework Challenges with the client and parent to determine what areas need help. You may need to put on your detective hat to discover a good solution as described in the case example included in the Strategies Tailored to Their Needs section of Tool 4-4 Ingredients of Effective Psychotherapy Sessions.

Use Handout 22-2-2 Checklist for Homework Success to help clients organize homework, and set up distraction free homework space.

If the client procrastinates or avoids doing homework, use the behavior management skills discussed in Chapter 7 Parenting Skills Tailored for ADHD to help them take responsibility and to avoid power struggles and homework battles.

**INTEGRATION:**   Does the client have trouble getting their homework done? Were you able to sort out what is getting in their way? Is the family giving priority to homework? What changes might help? Have they made changes and if so what changes are helping the most? Are headphones helping filter out distractions? Is the family having homework battles because the client procrastinates or avoids doing homework?

# HOMEWORK CHALLENGES

| | Never | Sometimes | Often | Always |
|---|---|---|---|---|
| **HOMEWORK** | | | | |
| I know what the homework assignment is. | 0 | 1 | 2 | 3 |
| I have the right textbook to do my homework. | 0 | 1 | 2 | 3 |
| I do my homework. | 0 | 1 | 2 | 3 |
| I can find the worksheets I have for homework. | 0 | 1 | 2 | 3 |
| I remember to do my homework. | 0 | 1 | 2 | 3 |
| I break big projects into small tasks. | 0 | 1 | 2 | 3 |
| I understand my homework. | 0 | 1 | 2 | 3 |
| I can do my homework without help. | 0 | 1 | 2 | 3 |
| I get my homework done in a reasonable time. | 0 | 1 | 2 | 3 |
| I know where my homework is. | 0 | 1 | 2 | 3 |
| I remember to turn in my homework. | 0 | 1 | 2 | 3 |
| I turn my homework in on time. | 0 | 1 | 2 | 3 |
| I am up to date on turning in my homework. | 0 | 1 | 2 | 3 |
| I get good grades on my homework. | 0 | 1 | 2 | 3 |
| I do my homework willingly. | 0 | 1 | 2 | 3 |

# CHECKLIST FOR HOMEWORK SUCCESS

☐ **Give Homework Priority in the Household**
- Set aside homework time **every** night
- Help children and teens organize their homework
- Buy color coded homework folders for each subject
  - Put homework to be done on the right, and homework that is ready to turn in on the left
- Look over the finished work

☐ **Get a Planner**
- Use a paper assignment book or an electronic calendar loaded on the child or teen's smartphone
- Get a homework app for their smartphone or tablet to keep track of assignments (search online for "Homework apps")
- Make sure it's convenient to use and hard to lose
- Remind them to use it
- Ask their teacher to remind them to write down and type in assignments
- Find out if their assignments are available online

☐ **Get a Second Set of Textbooks to Keep at Home**
- Avoid not having the right textbook to do the homework

☐ **Turn Off the TV**
- Some children do well with instrumental music playing which covers distractions
- Provide headphones with music that blocks out noise distraction but doesn't keep grabbing their attention
- Some do best lying in front of the TV – but rarely. See what works best!

☐ **Set Aside "Cell Phone-free, Electronics-free" Homework time.**
- Place cell phones and other electronics in a basket or bin unless they are being used for homework

☐ **Find a Good Spot for Doing Homework**
- If possible find a desk or table
  - Flat, cleared off
  - Room for a computer
- Where you can monitor them
  - In the child's own room unless they are too easily distracted alone
  - Near you
  - Out of traffic flow
  - Minimize sound and activity distractions
- Room to hold supplies: paper, pens, pencils, markers, scissors, ruler, index cards, paper clips, calculator, highlighter, sticky notes, tape, glue, stapler
- Adjustable chair to grow with your child

☐ **Schedule Homework Computer Time for Each Child**
- Ask how much computer time they each need
- Divide the time up between the kids
- Get them involved in planning
- Help each child plan around their scheduled time

☐ **Clean Out Backpack Once a Week**
- Throw out food, wrappers, and papers no longer needed
- Organize graded homework by subject in files in room for future reference
- Do this at the end of every school week

☐ **An Excellent Resource:**
- Goldberg, Donna. *The Organized Student*, Fireside, NY, 2005

# About The Author

**Debra Burdick, LCSW, BCN**, also known as "The Brain Lady," is a Licensed Clinical Social Worker and board certified neurofeedback practitioner who recently retired from private practice to slow down and focus on writing and speaking. She is a national speaker and #1 bestselling author who provided outpatient psychotherapy and mindfulness skills to her clients for 25 years and neurofeedback for 16 years. She is an expert author on SelfGrowth.com.

Debra specializes in ADHD, depression, anxiety, stress, pain, sleep, and healing. She teaches all-day workshops including: *Childhood ADHD: Advanced Non-drug Treatments That Change the Brain, 100 Brain-changing Mindfulness Strategies for Clinical Practice, A Holistic Approach to Success with ADHD* and more. You can find DVDs of her workshops at www.pesi.com. Besides her private practice, Debra worked at the Child Guidance Clinic, Family Services, Child and Family Agency, and Lawrence and Memorial Hospital in New London, CT.

Debra has extensive experience helping children and adults thrive with ADHD. In addition to counseling and training the brains of hundreds of clients with ADHD over the past 25 years, she parented a daughter who has ADHD, was married to a man with ADHD, and was business partners with someone with ADHD. She combines knowledge gained from her own personal healing journey, her parenting experience, her clients, and her professional study of ADHD, brain dysregulation and neurofeedback into her holistic, non-medication approach.

Her books and CDs include:
- *Mindfulness Skills for Kids & Teens. A Workbook for Clinicians and Clients with 154 Tools, Techniques, Activities & Worksheets*
- *Mindfulness Skills Workbook for Clinicians and Clients: 111 Tools, Techniques, Activities and Worksheets*
- *Is It Really ADHD? Only ADHD? How to Get an Accurate Diagnosis for You or Your Child*
- *ADHD and Sleep—Children and Adults; Sleep Better Tonight*
- *ADHD Treatment Options. How to Choose the Right Treatment for You or Your Child*
- *A Holistic Approach to Successful Children with Attention Deficit/ Hyperactivity Disorder—A Home Study System for Parents*
- *Meditations for Concentration CD/mp3*
- *Mindfulness Toolkit CD/mp3*
- *Mindfulness Toolkit for Kids and Teens CD/mp3*
- *Meditation for Sleep mp3*

Debra continues to write books and teach presentations, workshops, and teleseminars. She is often interviewed on Internet radio and her work has been featured on Doctors of the USA, Attention Talk Radio and ADHD Support Talk Radio, *The Day* newspaper and *Self-Improvement* magazine, plus *Parenting Powers* and *Restoring Health Holistically* television shows.

For more information visit www.TheBrainLady.com.

# References

For your convenience, you may download a PDF version of the handouts in this book from our dedicated website: go.pesi.com/ADHDworkbook

Adesman, A., Altshuler, L., Lipkin, P., Walco, G.. (1990). Otitis media in children with learning disabilities and in children with attention deficit disorder with hyperactivity. *Pediatrics. 85*(3 Pt 2), 442-6.

Alcantara, J., Davis, J. (2010). The chiropractic care of children with attention-deficit/hyperactivity disorder: a retrospective case series. *Explore (NY). 6*(3), 173-82.

Amen, D. (1998). *Change your brain change your life.* New York: Three Rivers Press.

Amen, D. (2001). *Healing ADD, the breakthrough program that allows you to see and heal the 6 types of ADD.* New York, NY: G. P. Putnam's Sons.

American Academy of Pediatrics, (2011, revised October 2012). The original document was included as part of *Addressing Health Concerns in Primary Care: A Clinician's Toolkit.* Retrieved on Feb. 25, 2015 from http://sharpbrains.com/blog/2012/10/05/biofeedback-now-a-level-1-best-support-intervention-for-attention-hyperactivity-behaviors/ and http://www.sharpbrains.com/wp-content/uploads/2014/12/Blue-Menu-2014_02_18.pdf

American Psychiatric Association, (2013). *Diagnostic and Statistical Manual of Mental Disorders, 5th Edition: DSM-5.* Washington, DC: Author.

Analayo, S. (2003). *The direct path to realization.* Birmingham, UK: Windhorse Publications.

Anderson, S. (2005). Stimulants and the developing brain. *Trends in Pharmacological Sciences, 26(5), 237-243.*

Antshel, K., Farone, S., Gordon, M. (2012). Cognitive behavioral treatment outcomes in adolescent ADHD. *Journal of Attention Disorders*, 18, 483-495.

Arns, M., de Ridder, S., Strehl, U., Breteler, M. & Coenen, A. (2010). Efficacy of neurofeedback treatment in ADHD: The effects on inattention, impulsivity and hyperactivity: A meta-analysis. *Clinical EEG and Neuroscience, 40*(3), 180-189.

*Attention Deficit Disorder Association (ADDA),* Web. 21 Dec 2011. http://www.add.org/.

Aune, B., Bert B., and Gennaro, P. (2010). *Behavior solutions for the inclusive classroom: A handy reference guide that explains behaviors associated with autism, Asperger's, ADHD, sensory processing disorder, and other special needs.* Arlington, Texas: Future Horizons.

Barkley, R. (1997) Behavioral inhibition, sustained attention, and executive functions: Constructing a unifying theory of ADHD. *Psychological Bulletin, 121,* (1), 65-94.

Barr D, Bravo R, Weerasekera G, et al. (2004). Concentrations of dialkyl phosphate metabolites of organophosphorus pesticides in the US population. *Environmental Health Perspectives. 112*(2), 186 –200.

Barry RJ, Clarke AR, McCarthy R, Selikowitz M. (2002). EEG coherence in attention-deficit/hyperactivity disorder: a comparative study of two DSM-IV types. *Clin Neurophysiol.* 113(4):579-85.

Beauregard, M., & Levesque, J. (2006). Functional magnetic resonance imaging investigation of the effects of neurofeedback training on neural bases of selective attention and response inhibition in children with attention-deficit/hyperactivity disorder. *Applied Psychology and Biofeedback, 31,* 3–20.

Biegel, G, Brown, K, Shapiro, S, Schubert, C. (2009). Mindfulness-based stress reduction for the treatment of adolescent psychiatric outpatients: A randomized clinical trial. *Journal of Consulting and Clinical Psychology, 77,* (5), 855–866.

Biel, L and Peske, N. (2009). *Raising a sensory smart child. The definitive handbook for helping your child with sensory processing issues.* New York: Penguin Books.

Bilici M, Yildirim F, Kandil S, Bekaroğlu M, Yildirmiş S, Değer O, Ulgen M, Yildiran A, Aksu H. (2004) Double-blind, placebo-controlled study of zinc sulfate in the treatment of attention deficit hyperactivity disorder. *Progress in Neuropsychopharmacology and Biological Psychiatry. 28*(1), 181-190.

Bloch Y, Harel EV, Aviram S, Govezensky J, Ratzoni G, Levkovitz Y. (2010). Positive effects of repetitive transcranial magnetic stimulation on attention in ADHD subjects: A randomized controlled pilot study. *World Journal of Biological Psychiatry. 11*(5), 755-8.

Bouchard, M.F, Bellinger, D.C, Wright, R.O., & Weisskopf, M.G. (2010). Attention-deficit/hyperactivity disorder and urinary metabolites of organophosphate pesticides. *Pediatrics,* 125(6), 1270-1277.

Brain Gym® International, (2003) Research: A chronology of Annotated Research Study Summaries in the Field of Educational Kinesiology. The Educational Kinesiology Foundation, Ventura, CA. Retrieved 2/2/2015 from http://www.braingym.org/brochures/BG_Research.pdf

BrainTrain, IVA-2. Retrieved 4/6/15 from http://www.braintrain.com/iva2/

Braun JM, Kahn RS, Froehlich T, Auinger P, Lanphear BP. (2006). Exposures to environmental toxicants and attention deficit hyperactivity disorder in U.S. children. *Environmental Health Perspectives. 114* (12), 1904-9.

Brown, R., Gerbarg, P. (2012). *Non-drug treatments for ADHD*. New York: W.W. Norton & Company, p 116.

Burdick, D. (2014). *Mindfulness skills for kids & teens. A workbook for clinicians and clients with 154 tools, techniques, activities and worksheets*. Eau Claire, WI: PESI Publishing & Media.

Casey, B.J. & Durston, S. (2006). From behavior to cognition to the brain and back: What have we learned from functional imaging studies of attention deficit hyperactivity disorder? *American Journal of Psychiatry*. 163 (6), 957-960.

Chabot R.J. & Serfontein, G. (1996). Quantitative EEG profiles of children with attention deficit disorder. *Biological Psychiatry*, 40, 951–963.

Charach A, Fernandez R. (2013). Enhancing ADHD medication adherence: Challenges and opportunities. *Current Psychiatry Reports*. 15(7):371.

Christakis, D., Zimmerman, F., DiGiuseppe, D., McCarty, C. (2004). Early television exposure and subsequent attentional problems in children. *Pediatrics,* 113 (4*), 708 -713*.

Clark, Lynn (2005). *SOS help for parents: A practical guide for handling common everyday behavior problems*. Bowling Green, KY: SOS Programs and Parents Press.

Clay, R. (2013). Easing ADHD without meds. *American Psychological Association Online*. 44(2). Retrieved 3/24/14 from: http://www.jpeds.com/article/S0022-3476(12)00994-8/abstracthttp://www.jpeds.com/article/S0022-3476(12)00994-8/abstract

Conner, K. (1989, 1990). Conners Rating Scales Manual.

Connolly, A. (2007) KeyMath™ 3 Diagnostic Assessment. Retrieved 4/6/15 from: http://www.pearsonclinical.com/education/products/100000649/keymath3-diagnostic-assessment.html

Cooper-Kahn, J., Dietzel, L. (2008). *Late, lost, and unprepared*. Bethesda, MD: Woodbine House.

Cortese, S., Konofal, E., Yateman, N., Mouren, M., Lecendreux, M. (2006). Sleep and alertness in children with attention-deficit/hyperactivity disorder: A systematic review of the literature. *Sleep: Journal of Sleep and Sleep Disorders, 29* (4), 504-511.

Davidson RJ, Kabat-Zinn J, Schumacher J, Rosenkrantz M, Muller D, Santorelli SF. (2003). Alterations in brain and immune function produced by mindfulness meditation. *Psychosomatic Medicine*, 65,564–570.

del Campo, N, Fryer, T, Hong, Y, Smith, R, Brichard, L, Acosta-Cabronero, J. (2013). A positron emission tomography study of nigro-striatal dopaminergic mechanisms underlying attention: implications for ADHD and its treatment. *Brain, 136* (11), 3252-3270;

DeBoo, G.M. & Prins, P.J. (2007) Social incompetence in children with ADHD: possible moderators and mediators in social-skills training. *Clinical Psychology Review*, 27: 78-97.

Demos, J (2005). *Getting started with neurofeedback*, New York, NY: W. W. Norton & Company, Inc.

Efron, L., & Pearl, P. (2001). Sleep Disorders in Children with ADHD. *ADVANCE for Respiratory Care Practitioners, 14*, Retrieved Jan 15, 2003, from: http://www.advanceforrcp.com/editorial/rc/8-27-2001/aug27_rcp26.html?frominc=editorial.

Epstein, S. (2012) Over 60 techniques, activities & worksheets for challenging children & adolescents. Eau Claire, WI: Premiere Publishing and Media.

Farb NAS, Segal ZV, Mayberg H, Bean J, McKeon D, Fatima Z, Anderson AK. (2007). Attending to the present: Mindfulness meditation reveals distinct neural modes of self-reference. *Social Cognitive and Affective Neuroscience*, 2, 313–322.

FDA, U.S. Food and Drug Administration. FDA 101: Dietary Supplements. Retrieved on 02/04/15 from: http://www.fda.gov/ForConsumers/ConsumerUpdates/ucm050803.htm

Field, T, Quintino, O., & Hernandez-Reif, M. (1998). Adolescents with attention deficit hyperactivity disorder benefit from massage therapy. *Adolescence, 33*, 103-108.

Food Allergy Research & Education (FARE). Retrieved on 02/04/15 from http://www.foodallergy.org/allergens

Fuchs, T., Birbaumer, N., Lutzenberger, W., Gruzelier, J. H., & Kaiser, J. (2003). Neurofeedback treatment for attention deficit/hyperactivity disorder in children: A comparison with methylphenidate. *Applied Psychophysiology and Biofeedback, 28*, 1-12.

de Boo, G., Prins, P. (2007). Social incompetence in children with ADHD: Possible moderators and mediators in social-skills training. *Clinical Psychology Review, 27* (1), 78–97.

Gevensleben, H., Holl, B., Albrecht, B., Vogel, C., Schlamp, D., et al. (2009). Is neurofeedback an efficacious treatment for ADHD?: A randomized controlled clinical trial. *Journal of Child Psychology and Psychiatry*, 50, 780–789.

Ghanizadeh, A. (2011). Sensory processing problems in children with ADHD: A systematic review, *Psychiatry Investig*ation, 8(2),89–94.

Ghaziri, J., Tucholka, A., Larue,V., Blanchette-Sylvestre, M., Reyburn, G., Gilbert, G., Lévesque, J., and Beauregard, M. (2013). Neurofeedback induces changes in white and gray matter. *Journal of Clinical EEG and Neuroscience*, 44, (4), 265-272.

Gilliam M, Stockman M, Malek M, Sharp W, Greenstein D, et al. (2011). Developmental trajectories of the corpus callosum in attention-deficit/hyperactivity disorder. *Biological Psychiatry*. 69(9),839–46.

Greenberg, L, Leark, R, Kindschi, C, Dupuy, T, Hughes, S. (2008, 2011, 2013) TOVA Test of Variables of Attention Professional Manual. Retrieved 4/6/15 from: http://files.tovatest.com/documentation/8/Professional%20Manual.pdf and http://www.tovatest.com/

Gruber R; Grizenko N; Schwartz G; Bellingham J; Guzman R; Joober R. (2007). Performance on the continuous performance test in children with ADHD is associated with sleep efficiency. *SLEEP 30*(8),1003–1009.

Guan, L., Wang, B., Chen, Y., Yang, L., Li, J., and Qian, Q. (2009). A high-density single nucleotide polymorphism screen of 23 candidate genes in attention deficit hyperactivity disorder: Suggesting multiple susceptibility genes among Chinese Han population. *Molecular Psychiatry*, 14(5),546–554.

Ha, M., Kwon, H., Lim, M., Jee, Y., Hong, Y., Leem, J., et al. (2009). Low blood levels of lead and mercury and symptoms of attention deficit hyperactivity in children: A report on the children's health and environment research (CHEER), *NeuroToxicology* 30(1):31-36.

Haffner J, Roos J, Goldstein N, Parzer P, Resch F. (2006). [The effectiveness of body-oriented methods of therapy in the treatment of attention-deficit hyperactivity disorder (ADHD): results of a controlled pilot study]. [Article in German] *Z Kinder Jugendpsychiatr Psychother, 34*(1),37-47.

Hak, E, de Vries, T, Hoekstra, P, Jick, S. (2013). Association of childhood attention-deficit/hyperactivity disorder with atopic diseases and skin infections? A matched case-control study using the General Practice Research Database. *Annals of Allergy, Asthma and Immunology, 111*, (2), 102–106.

Hall, T., Gerard Kaduson, H., Schaefer, C. (2002). Fifteen Effective Play Therapy Techniques Professional Psychology: Research and Practice Copyright 2002 by the American Psychological Association, Inc. 33(6), 515–522. Retrieved 01-22-15 from http://pegasus.cc.ucf.edu/~drbryce/Play%20Therapy%20Techniques.pdf

Hallowell, E., Ratey, J. (2005) *Delivered from Distraction*, (pp 132-134). New York: Ballantine Books.

Herrmann, M., King, K., and Weitzman, M. (2008). Prenatal tobacco smoke and postnatal secondhand smoke exposure and child neurodevelopment. *Current Opinion in Pediatrics* 20(2):184-190.

Hernandez-Reif, M., Field, T. & Thimas, E. (2001). Attention deficit hyperactivity disorder: benefits from Tai Chi. *Journal of Bodywork and Movement Therapies, 5*, 120-123.

Hill, R, PhD, & Castro, E, M.D. (2002). *Getting Rid of Ritalin*. Charlottesville, VA: Hampton Roads Publishing Company, Inc.

Hillman, C., Pontifex, M., Castelli, D., Khan, N., Raine, L., Scudder, M., et al. (2014). Effects of the FITKids randomized controlled trial on executive control and brain function. *Pediatrics, 134*(4):1063 -1071.

Hirshberg, L., Chiu, S., & Frazier, J. (2005). Emerging interventions. *Child and Adolescent Psychiatric Clinics of North America*. 14, 1-176.

Hoedlmoser, K., Pecherstorfer, T., Gruber, E., Anderer, P., Doppelmayr, M., Klimesch, W., & Schabus, M. (2008). Instrumental conditioning of human sensorimotor rhythm (12-15 Hz) and its impact on sleep as well as declarative learning. *Sleep*, 31(10), 1401-1408.

Hölzel, BK., Ott, U., Gard, T., Hempel, H., Weygandt, M., Morgen, K., Vaitl, D. (2007). Investigation of mindfulness meditation practitioners with voxel-based morphometry. *Social Cognitive and Affective Neuroscience, 3,55–61.*

Hoza, B., Smith, A., Shoulberg, E., Linnea, K., Dorsch, T., Blazo, J., et al. (2014). A randomized trial examining the effects of aerobic physical activity on attention-deficit/hyperactivity disorder symptoms in young children, *Journal of Abnormal Child Psychology*, 43:655-667.

Hyatt, K. J. (2007). Brain Gym®: Building stronger brains or wishful thinking? *Remedial and Special Education, 28*(2), 118 -124.

Jensen, P., Hinshaw, S., et al. (2001). Findings from the NIMH Multimodal Treatment Study of ADHD (MTA): Implications and applications for primary care providers, *Developmental and Behavioral Pediatrics, 22*(1), 60-73.

Kabat-Zinn J. (2003) Mindfulness-based interventions in context: Past, present, and future. *Clinical Psychology: Science and Practice*, 10:144–156.

Kaiser Greenland, S. (2010). *The mindful child*. New York, NY: Free Press.

Karlsson, H. (2011). How psychotherapy changes the brain. *Psychiatric Times*. http://www.psychiatrictimes.com/psychotherapy/how-psychotherapy-changes-brain#sthash.7pJMzei9.dpuf

Katz, D., Cushman, D., Reynolds, J., Njike, V., Treu, J., Walker, J., et al. (2010). Putting physical activity where it fits in the school day: Preliminary results of the ABC (activity bursts in the classroom) for fitness program. *Preventing Chronic Disease, 7*(4): A82 Retrieved from: http://www.cdc.gov/pcd/issues/2010/jul/09_0176.htm 02-17-15.

Kessler RC, Adler L, Barkley R, et al. (2006). The prevalence and correlates of adult ADHD in the United States: Results from the national comorbidity survey replication. *American Journal of Psychiatry, 163*, 716-723.

Khilnani, S., Field, T., Hernandez-Reif, M., & Schanberg, S. (2003). Massage therapy improves mood and behavior of students with attention-deficit/hyperactivity disorder. *Adolescence, 38*, 623-638.

Konofal, E., Lecendreux, M., Arnulf, I., Mouren, M. (2004). Iron deficiency in children with attention–deficit/hyperactivity disorder. *Archives of Pediatric and Adolescent Medicine, 158*(12), 1113-1115.

Konofal, E., Lecendreux, M., Deron, J., Marchand, M., Cortese, S., Saim, M., et al. (2008). Effects of iron supplementation of attention deficit hyperactivity disorder in children. *Pediatric Neurology, 38*(1), 20-26.

Lane, S., Reynolds, S., and Thacker, L. (2010). Sensory over-responsivity and ADHD: Differentiating using electrodermal responses, cortisol, and anxiety, *Frontiers in Integrative Neuroscience, 4:8.*

Larsen, S. (2012). *The neurofeedback solution: How to treat autism, ADHD, anxiety, brain injury, stroke, PTSD, and more*. Rochester, VT.: Healing Arts Press.

Levesque, J., Beauregard, M., & Mensour, B. (2006). Effect of neurofeedback training on the neural substrates of selective attention in children with attention deficit/hyperactivity disorder: A functional magnetic resonance imaging study. *Neuroscience Letters, 394*, 216–221.

Maddigan, B, Hodgson, P, Heath, S. Dick, B, St. John, K, McWilliam-Burton, et al. (2003). The effects of massage therapy and exercise therapy on children/adolescents with attention deficit hyperactivity disorder, *Canadian Journal of Child and Adolescent Psychiatry Review, 12*(2), 40–43.

Mangeot, S, Miller, L., et al. (2001). Sensory modulation dysfunction in ADHD. *Developmental Medicine and Child Neurology, 43*, 399-406.

Miller, L., Nielsen, D., Schoen, S. (2012). Attention deficit hyperactivity disorders and sensory modulation disorders: A comparison of behavior and physiology. *Research in Developmental Disabilities, 7*, 862.

Mize, W. (2004). Hemoencephalography; A new therapy for attention deficit hyperactivity disorder (ADHD) case report. *Journal of Neurotherapy, 8*(3), 77–97.

Monastra, V, Lubar, J, Linden, M, VanDeusen, P, Green, G, Wing, W et al. (1999). Assessing attention deficit hyperactivity disorder via quantitative electroencephalography: An initial validation study, *Neuropsychology*, 13(3), 424-433.

Monastra, Vincent. (2005). *Parenting children with ADHD, 10 lessons that medicine cannot teach.* Washington, DC: APA LifeTools.

National Sleep Foundation. Retrieved Feb. 18, 2015 from: http://sleepfoundation.org/sleep-topics/children-and-sleep and http://sleepfoundation.org/sleep-topics/teens-and-sleep

National Association of School Psychologists. (2002) Social Skills: Promoting Positive Behavior, Academic Success, and School Safety. Retrieved Feb. 6, 2015 from: http://www.nasponline.org/resources/factsheets/socialskills_fs.aspx

Nigg, J., Nikolas, M., Knottnerus, G.M., Cavanagh, K., & Friderici, K. (2010). Confirmation and extension of association of blood lead with attention-deficit/hyperactivity disorder (ADHD) and ADHD symptom domains at population-typical exposure levels. *Journal of Child Psychology and Psychiatry, 51*(1),58-65.

Nymark, T-B., Hovland, A., Bjørnstad, H., Nielsen, EW. (2008). A young man with acute dilated cardiomyopathy associated with methylphenidate. *Vascular Health and Risk Management, 4*(2),477-479.

Omizo, M. M., & Michael, W. B. (1982). Biofeedback-induced relaxation training and impulsivity, attention to task, and locus of control among hyperactive boys. *Journal of Learning Disabilities, 15*, 414–416.

Ottenbacher, K. (1982). Sensory Integration Therapy: Affect or Effect, *American Journal of Occupational Therapy, 36*, 571-578.

Pert, C. (2006). *Everything You Need to Know to Feel Go(o)d.* Carlsbad, CA.: Hay House.

Parush S., Sohmer H., Steinberg A., & Kaitz M., (2007). Somatosensory function in boys with ADHD and tactile defensiveness. *Physiology and Behavior, 90*(4),553-8.

Preston, S. DTLA-4: Detroit Test of Learning Aptitude - Fourth Edition. Available at: http://www.slosson.com/onlinecatalogstore_i1003126.html?catId=51515

Qiu, A., Crocetti, D., Adler, M., Mahone, M., Denckla, M., Miller, M., Mostofsky, S. (2009). Basal ganglia volume and shape in children with attention deficit hyperactivity disorder. *The American Journal Of Psychiatry, 166* (1), 74-82.

Ramsey, J.R. (2010). Nonmedication treatments for adult ADHD: Evaluating impact on daily functioning and well-being. Washington DC: American Psychological Association.

Ratey, J. (2008). Exercise: An Alternative ADHD Treatment, *Attitude.* Spring. Retrieved online: http://www.additudemag.com/adhd/article/3280.html

Ratey, J. (2008) *Spark. The revolutionary new science of exercise and the brain.* New York: Little, Brown and Co.

Rietveld, M. J. H., Hudziak, J.J., Bartels, M., Beijsterveldt, C.E.M., & Boomsma, D.I. (2004). Heritability of attention problems in children: Longitudinal results from a study of twins, age 3 to 12. *Journal of Child Psychology and Psychiatry, 45*(3), 577–588.

Rideout, V., Foehr, U., Roberts, F. (2010). Generation $M^2$ media in the lives of 8-18-year- olds. *A Kaiser Family Foundation Study.* Menlo Park, CA.

Rivera, E., & Omizo, M. M. (1980). The effects of relaxation and biofeedback on attention to task and impulsivity among male hyperactive children. *The Exceptional Child, 27*, 41–51.

Robbins, J. (2008). A symphony in the brain: The evolution of the new brain wave biofeedback. New York, NY: Grove Press.

Saulny, S. (2000) Turning Fidgets Into Karate Kicks; Some Find That Martial Arts Ease Attention Disorders, New York Times. Retrieved from: http://www.nytimes.com/2000/12/02/nyregion/turning-fidgets-into-karate-kicks-some-find-that-martial-arts-ease-attention.html?pagewanted=all 02-17-15

Sagiv, S., Thurston, S., Bellinger, D., Tolbert, P., Altshul, L., & Korrick, S. (2010). Prenatal organochlorine exposure and behaviors associated with attention deficit hyperactivity disorder in school-aged children. *American Journal of Epidemiology, 171*(5), 593-601.

Schoenthaler, S., Bier, I. (1999). Vitamin-mineral intake and intelligence: A macrolevel analysis of randomized controlled trials. *Journal of Alternative and Complementary Medicine, 5*(2), 125-134.

Shaw, P., Eckstrand, K., Sharp, W., Blumenthal, J., Lerch, J., et al. (2007). Attention-deficit/hyperactivity disorder is characterized by a delay in cortical maturation. *Proceedings of the National Academy of Science USA. 104*(49), 19649–54.

Shaw, P., Malek, M., Watson, B., Sharp, W., Evans, A., Greenstein, D. (2012). Development of cortical surface area and gyrification in attention-deficit/hyperactivity disorder. *Biological Psychiatry, 1*(3), 191–7.

Semple, R.J., Lee, J., Rosa, D., Miller, L. (2010). A randomized trial of mindfulness-based cognitive therapy for children: Promoting mindful attention to enhance social-emotional resiliency in children. *Journal of Child and Family Studies,* 19, 218–229.

Shaffer, R., et al. (2001). Effect of interactive metronome training on children with ADHD. *American Journal of Occupational Therapy, 55*(2), 155-162.

Siegel, D, (2007). *The mindful brain: Reflection and attunement in the cultivation of wellbeing.* (p.291) New York, NY: W. W. Norton & Company.

Schachar, RJ., Tannock, R., Cunningham, C., Corkum, PVJ. (1997). Behavioral, situational, and temporal effects of treatment of ADHD with methylphenidate. *American Academy of Child and Adolescent Psychiatry, 36*(6), 754-63.

Sinn, N., and Bryan, J. (2007). Effect of supplementation with polyunsaturated fatty acids and micronutrients on learning and behavior problems associated with child ADHD. *Journal of Developmental and Behavioral Pediatrics, 28*, 82-91.

Shapiro, L. (2004). *101 Ways To Teach Children Social Skills A Ready-To-Use, Reproducible Activity Book*, The Bureau for At-Risk Youth. USA. Retrieved March 3, 2015 from: http://www.socialskillscentral.com/free/101_Ways_Teach_Children_Social_Skills.pdf

Sorgi, PJ, et al. (2007). Effects of an open-label pilot study with high-dose EPA/DHA concentrates on plasma phospholipids and behavior in children with attention deficit hyperactivity disorder. *Nutrition Journal, 6*, 16-23.

Starobrat-Hermelin, B., Kozielec, T., (1997). The effects of magnesium physiological supplementation on hyperactivity in children with attention deficit hyperactivity disorder (ADHD). Positive response to magnesium oral loading test. *Magnesium Resource, 10*(2), 149-156.

Sterman, M.B., & Wyrwicka, W. (1967). EEG correlates of sleep: Evidence for separate forebrain substrates. *Brain Research, 6*, 143-163.

Swingle, P. (2010). *Biofeedback for the brain: How neurotherapy effectively treats depression, ADHD, autism, and more.* Piscataway, NJ: Rutgers University Press.

Takeda, A. (2001). Zinc homeostasis and functions of zinc in the brain. *Biometals, 14*(3-4), 343-51.

Tansey, M. (1991), Wechsler (wisc-r) changes following treatment of learning disabilities via EEG biofeedback training in a private practice setting. *Australian Journal of Psychology, 43*, 147-153.

Thich Nhat Hanh. (2011). *Planting seeds, practicing mindfulness with children.* Berkeley, CA: Parallax Press.

Thompson, L, & Thompson, M. (2003). *The neurofeedback book,* Wheat Ridge, CO: The Association for Applied Psychophysiology and Biofeedback.

University of British Columbia (2011). Weiss Functional Impairment Scale. Canadian ADHD Resource Alliance. Retrieved April 6, 2015 from: http://www.caddra.ca/cms4/pdfs/caddraGuidelines2011WFIRS_S.pdf

U.S. Department of Education. Teaching Children With Attention Deficit Hyperactivity Disorder: Instructional Strategies and Practices. Retrieved Feb. 25, 2015 from: http://www2.ed.gov/rschstat/research/pubs/adhd/adhd-teaching_pg3.html

Vučković, M., Li, Q., Fisher, B., Nacca, A., Leahy, R., Walsh, J., et al. (2010). Exercise elevates dopamine D2 receptor in a mouse model of parkinson's disease: In vivo imaging with [18F] fallypride. *Movment Disorders, 25*(16), 2777–2784.

Walker, H. (1988) The Walker Social Skills Curriculum: The ACCESS Complete Program Retrieved March 3, 2015 from: http://www.proedinc.com/customer/productView.aspx?ID=615

Wallace, B.A. (2006). *The attention revolution: Unlocking the power of the ocused mind.* Boston: Wisdom Publications, 6.

Weaver, L., Mace, W., Akhtar, U.W., Rostain, A.L., & O'Reardon, J.P. *Safety and efficacy of rTMS in the treatment of ADHD in adolescents and young adults.* Poster session presented at the annual meeting of the Association of Convulsive Therapy, Washington DC., May, 2008.

Weaver L., Rostain AL., Mace W., Akhtar U., Moss E., O'Reardon JP., Transcranial magnetic stimulation (TMS) in the treatment of attention-deficit/hyperactivity disorder in adolescents and young adults: a pilot study. The Journal of ECT, *28*(2), 98-103.

Wechsler, D. (2014). The Wechsler intelligence scale for children—fifth edition. London: Pearson Assessment.

Weiss B. (2008). Vulnerability of children and the developing brain to neurotoxic hazards. *Environmental Health Perspectives, 108* (suppl 3), 375–381.

Weiss, M., & Salpekar, J. (2010). Sleep problems in the child with attention-deficit hyperactivity disorder. Defining aetiology and appropriate treatments. *CNS Drugs, 24*(10), 311-828.

Weiss, Margaret D. et al. (2011). The screens culture: Impact on ADHD. *Attention Deficit and Hyperactivity Disorders, 3.4, 327–334.*

Wheeler, J. & Carlson, C.L. (1994). The social functioning of children with ADD with hyperactivity and ADD without hyperactivity: A comparison of their peer relations and social deficits. *Journal of Emotional and Behavioral Disorders, 2*, 2–12.

Wolraich, M.L., Lindgren, S.D., Stumbo, P.J., Stegink, L.D., Appelbaum, M.I., & Kiritsy, M.C. (1994). Effects of diets high in sucrose or aspartame on the behavior and cognitive performance of children. *New England Journal of Medicine, 330*(5), 301–7.

Wolraich, M. (2006). Attention-deficit/hyperactivity disorder can it be recognized and treated in children younger than 5 years? *Infants and Young Children, 19*(2), 86–93.

Woodcock-Johnson IV Achievement. (2014) Riverside Publishing. Retrieved 4/6/3025 http://www.riversidepublishing.com/products/wj-iv/pricing.html

Zimmerman, F., & Christakis, D. (2007). Associations between content types of early media exposure and subsequent attention problems. *Pediatrics, 120*(5), 986-992.

Zylowska, L., Ackerman, D., Yang, M., Futrell, J., Horton, N., Hale, T., et al. (2008). Mindfulness meditation training in adults and adolescents with ADHD: A feasibility study. Journal of Attention Disorders, 11(6), 737-746